THE TEACHER'S ESSENTIAL GUIDE TO THE BRAIN

THE TEACHER'S ESSENTIAL GUIDE TO THE BRAIN

Karen Ferry & Matthew Dahlitz

DAHLITZ MEDIA ☰

Dahlitz Media
Brisbane, Australia

Note to Readers: This book is intended as general information for mental health professionals and is not an appropriate substitute for training or clinical supervision. Neuroscience is a rapidly advancing field and neither the publisher nor the author can guarantee the complete accuracy or currency of the information herein. Clinical application of any information or techniques, including the contents of this book, should be undertaken only after certified training and appropriate supervision.

Chapters in this edition have previously been published in *The Neuropsychotherapist*.

For information about content reproduction write to: Permissions, *The Neuropsychotherapist*, PO Box 1030, Park Ridge, QLD, 4125, Australia.
Alternatively email cotact@neuropsychotherapist.com

Authors: Karen Ferry & Matthew Dahlitz

Cover image: dolgachov/bigstock.com

Title: The Teacher's Essential Guide To The Brain.

ISBN-13: 978-0-9944080-3-7 (paperback)

1. Education. 2. Brain. 3. Neuroscience. 4. Psychology. 5. Teaching.

Dahlitz Media
PO Box 1030
Park Ridge,
Queensland, 4125
AUSTRALIA

Printed in the United States of America

To the teacher who believes what a child can be.

Mr David Potter

- thank you for seeing beyond

Karen Ferry is a Counsellor and a Clinical Neuropsychotherapy Practitioner. Her experience in working with children and teenagers has been wide and extensive. Karen is also an educator and has worked in private and public school systems, as a classroom teacher, administrator, in curriculum development and has given specialist educational care for children in home education environments.

Karen has written a number of articles for *The Neuropsychotherapist*. Her book and program manual, Benson the Boxer: A Story of Loss and Life is a unique resource for clinicians, parents and caregivers to help children deal with loss, grief and trauma.

Matthew Dahlitz is a neuropsychotherapist, consultant, author and publisher. He is both university trained and an autodidactic who's knowledge spans across the arts, technology, psychology, neuroscience, emergency medicine, and business.

Matthew is the Editor-in-Chief of *The Neuropsychotherapist*, author of *The Psychotherapist's Essential Guide to the Brain*. He runs a consultancy business for entrepreneurs and business executives using the principles of neuropsychotherapy and neuroscience.

CONTENTS

PREFACE

A productive classroom seems to hit you with a buzz of energy as soon as you open the door! Students are interested; enthusiasm is running high; behavioural issues are minimal to non-existent, and everyone is involved in the learning process. The environment is exploding with discussion and new ideas. It is obvious the students want to be there, and the teacher's job, while busy and demanding, is satisfying, rewarding and fulfilling.

For many teachers, a classroom such as this is only a dream! But it doesn't have to be so. Recent neuroscience findings have significant implications both for the future of classroom teaching and school management as a whole. There is now available a wealth of information to explain student motivation and behavioural issues, the keys to successful learning, and effective teaching strategies. Neuroscience has given us a greater understanding of brain development and provides us with insights into the formation of neural pathways and the brain's ability to change (neuroplasticity), and form new connections. Knowing that behaviour development and motivational schemas are shaped by early life experiences gives teachers a real understanding of the importance of providing learning environments of acceptance, inclusion and security. When children feel safe, motivational schemas of approach strengthen curiosity and learning. A teacher can intentionally aim to reduce a student's inclination towards avoidance behaviours and promote a positive approach towards learning, peer interactions and life in general.

Individuals take up the profession of teaching for many reasons. It is a career that provides a range of experiences, including the challenge of a classroom environment. There is generally a love of working with children, and for most it satisfies a desire to positively influence the lives of others. Teachers often retell moments of delight when students work cooperatively, demonstrate an eagerness to learn, and enjoy the challenges a teacher brings to class each day. For many, the teaching profession is rightly termed a "most rewarding occupation". However, it can also be one of great stress. Students can stir teachers to various levels of frustration and disappointment. The challenges seem never-ending, and some situations can leave teachers confused and in doubt about how to manage them.

A typical example involved a wide-eyed little girl called Georgia (not her real name). Georgia was having many sick days away from school, and when she was present, she would sit on her own and find every excuse not to have to do her work. Georgia had shown no prior indication of learning difficulties, in fact was considered bright and inquisitive by her teachers; but lately, she just wasn't working to her potential and it appeared she was regressing. The teacher noticed subtle changes in Georgia's manner: if it was group work, Georgia had a stomach ache; if it was reading time, she refused to participate. In Maths, Georgia stayed as long as possible at the bin to sharpen her pencils. She dawdled to class and scuffed her shoes, was sensitive to others brushing past her, and would often get angry when she thought someone was not doing the right thing.

What does a teacher do in this situation? In desperation, a well-meaning teacher will often resort to punishment. There may be strong insistence to complete work and stay on task. Teachers may use threats to try to push a child into work or certain acceptable behaviours. Georgia was told if she didn't cooperate and do her work during the set class time she would have to come in at lunch time. This common classroom situation was met with a common teacher disciplinary response.

After time spent with the school counsellor, it was revealed that Georgia's home life was anything but favourable. Evaluating Georgia's behaviour from a neuroscience perspective provided insights into behavioural motivations and the effects of stress on her overall well-being. Georgia was unable to learn effectively and had become anxious, hypervigilant and over-sensitive; at the same time, she was unable to modulate the limbic system's response to the situation as the activation of the hypothalamic–pituitary–adrenal (HPA) axis was disrupting any ability to think clearly. Consequently, in order to feel safe, Georgia adopted protective behaviours of avoidance and withdrawal, preferring to stay inside to finish off schoolwork during lunch time rather than join her peers and hear their talk about fun things they were doing with their families each weekend.

The Teacher's Essential Guide to the Brain has been written from a neuroscientific perspective for teachers and school support staff to assist them with the challenges of the classroom and school environment. The authors acknowledge that neuroscience can be complicated, the terminologies difficult to understand, and the concepts possibly too broad or detailed for many teachers to even want to grasp. *The Teacher's Essential Guide to the Brain* was written with this in mind. The authors bring to this book a considerate and empathetic understanding of a teacher's busy work schedule and the myriad of things that need to be juggled, fixed, written up, managed and addressed—every day! This book offers a bridge between the complexities of neuroscience and many of the queries surrounding student behaviours, in language that is accessible, concise and succinct.

By applying neuroscience and the principles of neuropsychotherapy to education, this book answers many of the questions that teachers ponder at one time or another during their career. Questions such as: Why do some students ease into school life and spontaneously build friendships the moment they walk through the school gates, while others are timid and anxious, preferring to slink off somewhere and withdraw? Why do some students retaliate and routinely become angry and aggressive when challenged, while others accept responsibility and move on to the next task? Why do some students always seem to get bullied, while others move through the school system encircled by friends, sleepovers and birthday parties? Why is it that some kids seem to always be in trouble and have a "permanent spot" in the time-out area, while others seem to have a natural tendency to study, apply themselves, cooperate and learn? Why did a particular behaviour management strategy work with one child but not with another one?

As teachers, we have usually known *what* works! We have seen children who are keen and excited, enthusiastic and exuberant about coming to school—and not just because they are going on school camp! We have also been keenly aware and sometimes embarrassed about what did not work so well, but many of us have never really known *why*. It is our hope that this book will provide teachers and anyone involved in the field of education with insights into student motivations and behaviours. May this book be used as a tool when considering student management or behaviour policies within the school system; and also when considering and evaluating staff well-being, leadership issues and parent difficulties.

As you read and absorb this important information you will be given insights into the *why*! Understanding the *why* is the key to the success or otherwise of our teaching endeavours, the key to effective or problematic behavioural management strategies, and the key to teacher and student well-being! And it is understanding the *why* that gives compassion and empathy when dealing with difficult parents or the difficult situations that families may be going through. Not only will you become a more effective teacher, or administrator, but the experience of teaching will be far more rewarding—and who knows, you may even change a child's life!

INTRODUCTION

The Teacher's Essential Guide to the Brain provides an overview of the essential parts and functions of the brain that every modern-day teacher should be familiar with. Written in accessible language and consolidating a large body of neuroscientific knowledge, this handy "beginner's guide" forms a practical and accessible introduction to brain science for educators. The current chapter lays the groundwork for a big-picture view of how the brain functions, providing essential reference points from which the reader may go on to develop an understanding of what is happening in the brains of clients, as well as in his or her own.

The contemporary teacher has access to a more sophisticated model of education than ever before, through understandings of the neural functions that underpin behaviour, relationships, personality, and a sense of self and the surrounding world. This guide aims to bridge the gap between the often esoteric realm of neuroscience research and the pragmatic realities of working in a classroom. The teacher with a practical grasp of the concepts, regions and functions of the nervous system will be rewarded with improved teaching outcomes that reflect a more holistic and integrated understanding of their students.

Since Freud, the brain has been variously conceived in terms of an electrical system, a chemical system, and, more recently, a highly interconnected electrochemical network. In terms of convention, we are only now emerging from an outdated medical model that conceptualized the brain primarily as a chemical system that could be "fixed" by means of drug intervention, and coming to the realization that the brain is a malleable communication network where the patterns of connections within and between brain regions are as important as the chemicals that serve the impulses travelling these routes.

Understanding this communication network, which happens to be the most complex system we know, can enhance our teaching and classroom practice. As a stand-out example, understanding the basic concept of a fast-reacting limbic system versus a slower prefrontal cortex can shed light on why a student cannot think effectively, problem solve, or understand consequences of behaviours when the fast activating limbic system is activated. Our teaching and learning strategies, classroom control, student/teacher relationships take on a new and deeper meaning when we understand that memory is everything when it comes to brain function, and that memories can change, our neural networks can be altered, and even genetic expressions that support those neural networks can change.

And so, with a debt to modern neuroscience, we embark on this modest overview of the brain, trusting it will serve you well in your conceptualizations of your students and arouse your curiosity for further learning.

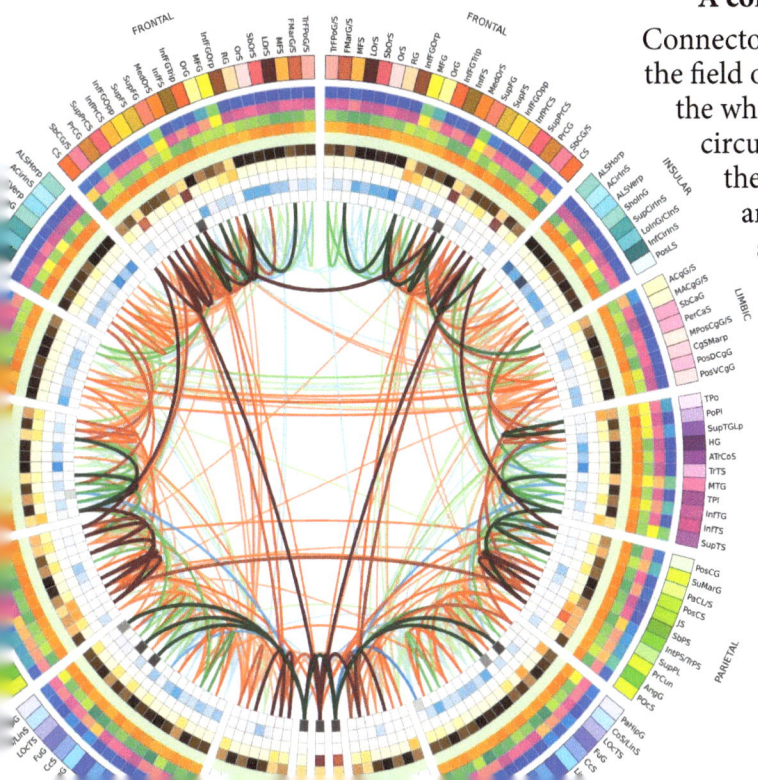

A connectogram of a healthy control subject.

Connectograms are graphical representations of connectomics, the field of study dedicated to mapping and interpreting all of the white-matter fibre connections in the human brain. These circular graphs based on diffusion MRI data utilize graph theory to demonstrate the white-matter connections and cortical characteristics for single structures, single subjects, or populations.

In this image: From outside to inside, the rings represent the cortical region, grey matter volume, surface area, cortical thickness, curvature, degree of connectivity, node strength, betweenness centrality, eccentricity, nodal efficiency, and eigenvector centrality. Between degree of connectivity and node strength, a blank ring has been added as a placeholder. This connectogram includes five additional nodal measures not included in the standard connectogram. Image: Wikipedia.

THE DIVIDED BRAIN

Iain McGilchrist, in his noteworthy book *The Master and His Emissary: The Divided Brain and the Making of the Western World* (2009), describes the asymmetry of the brain and the very different natures of the left and right hemispheres. This horizontal understanding of the mental system, as opposed to the vertical triune perspective, gives us insight into the distinctly different yet complementary functions of the two hemispheres. In short, the right hemisphere handles broad attention (what we attend to comes first to us through the right hemisphere); is good at making connections so that we can appreciate the wholeness of dynamic structures and relationships that change over time; is attuned to emotion; and is empathic, intuitive, and moral. In contrast, the left hemisphere has narrow attention; is good at deconstructing things into parts; and has an appreciation for static, decontextualized, inanimate structures and abstractions. McGilchrist (2009) summarizes the "two worlds" of the hemispheres in this way:

The brain has to attend to the world in two completely different ways, and in so doing to bring two different worlds into being. In the one [that of the right hemisphere], we experience—the live, complex, embodied world of individual, always unique beings, forever in flux, a net of interdependencies, forming and reforming wholes, a world with which we are deeply connected. In the other [that of the left hemisphere] we "experience" our experience in a special way: a "re-presented" version of it, containing now static, separable, bounded, but essentially fragmented entities, grouped into classes, on which predictions can be based. This kind of attention isolates, fixes and makes each thing explicit by bringing it under the spotlight of attention. In doing so it renders things inert, mechanical, lifeless. But it also enables us for the first time to know, and consequently to learn and to make things. This gives us power. (p. 31)

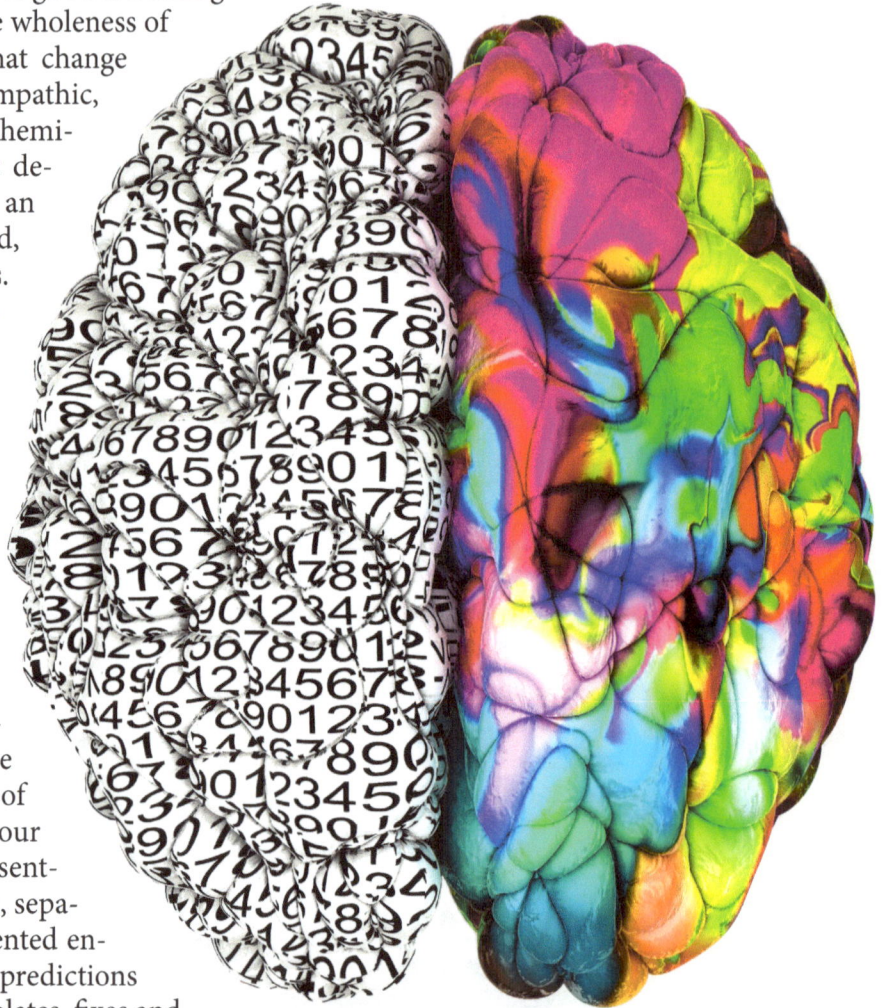

Allan Schore (2012) explains that the early-maturing right hemisphere is the locus of attachment formation and essentially the gateway to affect regulation later in life. Young children are more right hemisphere dominant, which is why we see a child dissolve into an emotional flood when life becomes unpredictable, sad or scary. When feelings are ignored or denied, the left-brain of logic and literal thinking dominates and children lack a sense of perspective and are unable to understand contextual meaning (Siegel & Payne Bryson, 2011). Daniel Siegel (2011) states that it is most crucial that our two hemispheres work together, as a team. Teachers and parents are most instrumental in integrating a child's brain hemispheres. Listening, comforting and supporting connects an adults right-brain to the child's right-brain. This right-brain connection calms and supports a child, encouraging the child to express the pain he is feeling. Once the child has calmed, cognitive processing can begin and behaviours can be redirected.

Left Hemisphere

- Less white matter—prioritizing local information transfer within regions, reflected in an increased ability to localize attention and enhancing its self-referring nature.
- More reliant on dopamine.
- Superior in the expression of anger.
- Highly focused attention to detail; local, narrowly focused attention—sees "parts".
- Attends narrowly to the right field of view, the right side of the body, the right side of objects (demonstrated in what is known as "hemi-neglect" following a right-hemisphere stroke).
- More engaged with the known, the learned, the expected; prefers what it knows—"grasps" what is in focus and has been prioritized.
- Efficient when routine is predictable.
- Finds solutions perceived to fit best with current knowledge or schemas
- Processes information in an increasingly focal way that suppresses information not immediately relevant.
- Suppresses the right-hemisphere ability to make distant associations among words or objects (and the broader scope of attention in general).
- Takes a local, short-term view.
- Identifies things by labels rather than context; does not deduce from context like the right hemisphere—in conversation takes things more literally and has difficulty understanding implied meaning. Things are decontextualized and interpreted by an internal logic.
- Proficient at abstraction—storing and manipulating information in abstracted types, classes, categories, and representations that are impersonal, fixed, and equivalent. Recognizes objects in a category in a generic, non-specific way, but not the uniqueness of individuals.
- Codes non-living things and has an affinity for the mechanical.
- Better at identifying simple shapes that are easily categorized.
- Interested in the utility of things—machines, tools, man-made things.
- Sees one's own body as an assemblage of parts from which it maintains a level of detachment.
- More sophisticated in language and symbol manipulation, with greater vocabulary and more subtle and complex syntax than the right hemisphere.

Right Hemisphere

- More white matter—facilitating faster transfer of information across regions, reflected in an increased ability to hold global attention.
- More sensitive to testosterone.
- More reliant on noradrenaline.
- More intimately connected with the limbic system—identifies emotions faster and more accurately than the left and is more involved in emotional expression (except anger).
- Open to broad awareness; on the lookout in a broad and flexible way with vigilance and global sustained attention—sees the "whole".
- Processes information in a non-focal manner.
- Attends to the peripheral field of vision and the entire left–right visual field.
- Alert and attentive to the new and the novel—awareness begins in the right hemisphere, grounding and integrating the experience, before being further processed in the left on a more detailed level.
- More engaged in the learning of new information—explores.
- Outperforms the left when prediction is difficult; more capable of shifting the frame of reference (important for problem solving).
- Can associate words or objects that are not closely related; can understand unfamiliar (non-clichéd) metaphor.
- Better able to integrate perceptual processes from different senses.
- Longer working memory.
- Recognizes broad or complex patterns.
- More involved in insight and deductive reasoning.
- Sees things in context and in terms of relationships; attentive to context in conversation—vital for a sense of humour.
- Can recognize the individual and uniqueness within a category, such as recognizing individual faces in the category of faces.
- Interested in the personal, the living, rather than the impersonal and non-living.
- Plays a primary role in empathy, the theory of "mind", identification with others, social interaction, and emotional understanding.
- Connected with the self as an embodied whole.
- Specializes in non-verbal communication, the implicit, subtle unconscious perceptions, emotional shifts, subtle clues and meanings.
- Gives an appreciation of depth in time and space.

THREE LAYERS

A well-known model of the human brain is that described by neuroscientist Paul MacLean as the triune brain (MacLean, 1990). This view of the brain describes three main regions in an evolutionary hierarchy: the primitive "reptilian" complex (the brainstem), the "palaeomammalian" complex (the limbic system), and the "neomammalian" complex (the cortex). The reptilian complex is fully developed at birth, while the palaeomammalian complex is partly developed and continues to develop during early childhood, and the neomammalian complex is mostly underdeveloped at birth and is the last part of the triune brain to develop (The Neuropsychotherapy Institute, 2014c). The implications of the model are that the survival instincts of the palaeomammalian complex (the limbic system) are significantly developed during the early years of life, distinct from the later-developing cognitive processes of the neomammalian complex (Rossouw, 2011). More sophisticated contemporary models of the brain and behaviour do not fully support MacLean's evolutionary model (the brain is much more integrated and seamless than MacLean's model might suggest); However, the "bottom-up" perspective of development remains relevant with instructive implications when considering teaching and learning in the classroom. A "bottom-up" approach, as distinct from a "top-down" approach looks to establish safety as the top priority in the classroom environment before any imparting of knowledge is attempted. A feeling of safety is established through the down regulation of sympathetic over-arousal and activation of a state of parasympathetic security. When a child feels safe, there is increased cortical blood flow to the left frontal cortex for effective activation of cognitive abilities and limiting 'looping' activity within the limbic system (Rossouw, 2011, p4) to allow for effective new learning.

The Primitive Brain (Reptilian Complex)

This system of the brain is responsible for the most basic survival functions, such as heart rate, breathing, body temperature, and orientation in space. Needless to say, functions like heart rate and breathing are of considerable importance, and the control mechanisms in this part of the brain are accordingly consistent.

It is important to recognize that the functions of the primitive brain will take precedence over other brain activity. For example, if you try to hold your breath (a prefrontal cortex-initiated activity), you will find that as carbon dioxide builds up in your bloodstream, this primitive part of your brain is going to want to take over and make you breathe again. Through training you may be able to increase your resistance to the basic urge to breathe, but inevitably you will eventually give in and take a breath.

Such threats to survival are first addressed by the primitive brain—as illustrated in "peripheral shutdown", where blood vessels on the periphery of the body are constricted in anticipation of physical trauma—and are prioritized over less vital functions.

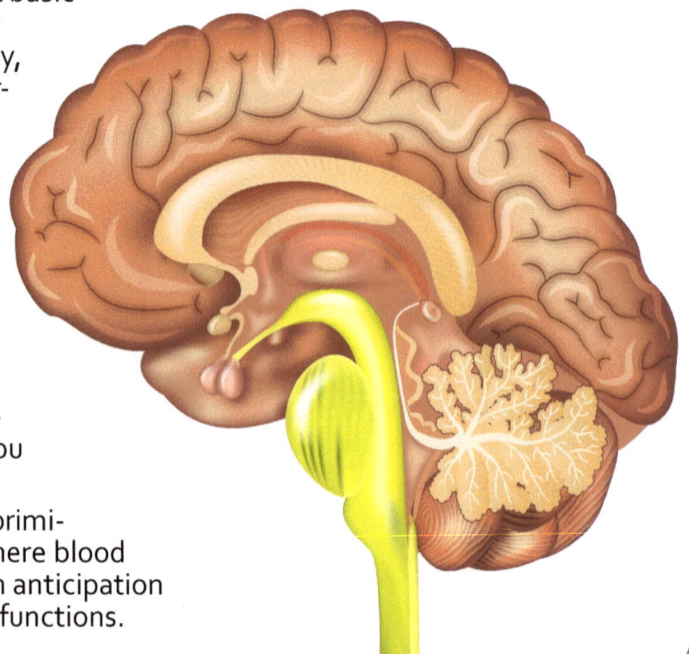

The Limbic System (Paleomammalian Complex)

Sometimes referred to as the "emotional brain", the limbic system is the reactive part of us that initiates the "fight or flight" response to danger. Key areas of interest to educators are the hippocampus, the amygdala, and the hypothalamus. These form a very fast subconscious evaluation and response system designed to keep us safe.

The amygdala is like an early-warning system, with the motto "safety first"—put that safety plan into effect before consulting the executive brain (the new cortex). Picture yourself jumping out of the way of a snake-like object before closer examination reveals it to be just a garden hose in the grass. This is a very important first response, because if it were left to the prefrontal cortex to initiate, for example, a leap out of the way of a bus you had inadvertently stepped in front of, then it might be too late: that evaluation system is too slow. The amygdala makes very fast, albeit not always accurate, evaluations and has a fast track from the thalamus (incoming information) through to the hypothalamus that can initiate a stress response to forestall impending doom. The hippocampus plays an equally important role by encoding events in time and space and consolidating them from short-term to long-term memory.

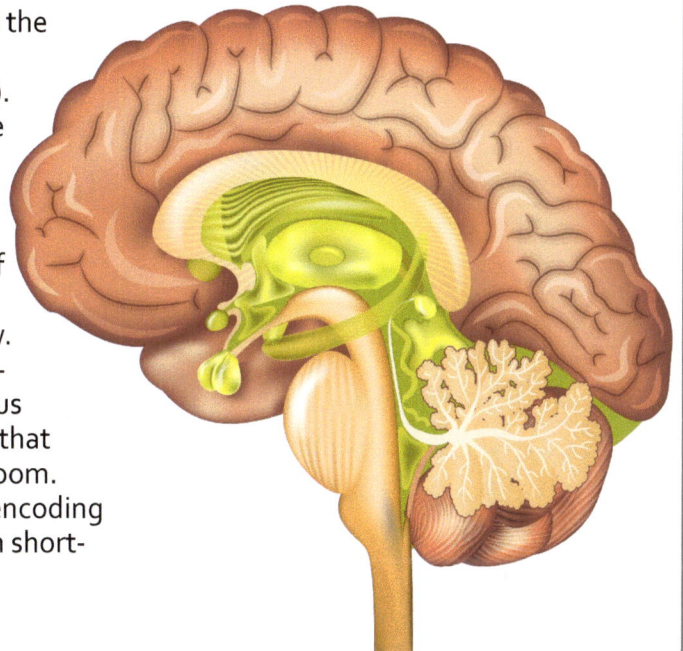

The New Cortex (Neomammalian Complex)

The new cortex is our "smart" brain, the executive part of our system that is responsible for all higher-order conscious activity such as language, abstract thought, imagination, and creativity, to name just a few. It also houses much of our memory—not just our biographical memory, but all of the automatic memories essential to talking, writing, walking, playing the piano, and countless other familiar activities (keep in mind, however, that the division of the brain into three large parts is a highly simplified conception: functionally the connectivity between all these regions greatly blurs the boundaries).

Of special interest to educators is the prefrontal cortex—the part of the brain right behind our forehead—which may be slower in responding to incoming information than the limbic system, but is much more sophisticated in its processing. Such "slow" thinking is the hallmark of our human intelligence. Complex and new thinking on technical, emotional, social, and logical planes takes place here. It is where we can be rational and logical, creative and inventive. But, significantly, the prefrontal cortex can be "hijacked" by the limbic system in the event of a perceived threat (whether imagined or real). Our prefrontal can "go offline" as blood flow is directed to the deeper limbic system, the first responder in a priority one mission to keep us safe.

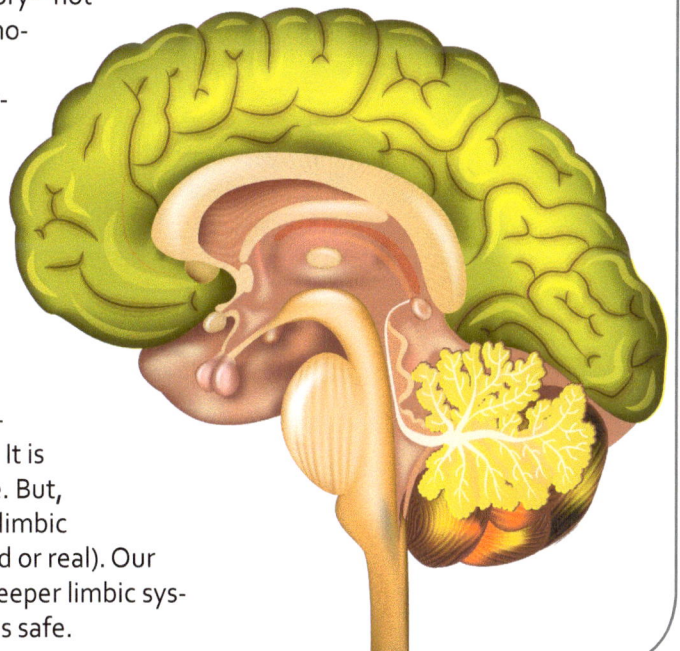

AMAZINGLY NETWORKED

The human brain has about 100,000 miles of white matter (bundles of myelinated axons) shooting electrochemical signals down 100 billion neurons through 100 trillion synaptic connections1—we are spectacularly connected!

The pattern of neural connectivity in our brains has long captured the attention of neuroanatomists. It can be described at several levels of scale: the individual synaptic connections that link individual neurons, networks connecting neuronal populations, and entire brain regions linked by white-matter highways. Mapping the large-scale connectivity within and between brain regions is what has captured the imagination of the National Institutes of Health in the US, which has funded the Human Connectome Project (HCP), a $40 million effort to map the human brain. Each of us has a unique neural map, rather like the uniqueness of our fingerprints, that has been shaped by our genetics, environment, and life experiences. It is this map, or "connectome", that researchers would like to recreate in a virtual space to model the highways and byways of neural connectivity.

The connectome is extremely complex and not yet well understood. It is the hope of the HCP that by mapping many individuals, they will establish a baseline of normal connectivity and reveal how connectivity differs across individuals.

In a recent study published in Nature Neuroscience (Smith et al., 2015), investigators found a significant relationship between the brain's default-mode network and personal traits such as IQ, language skills, and life satisfaction. The researchers examined 461 subjects, looking at the correlations between their resting-state functional connectivity and behavioural and demographic measures. They found that the subjects who returned high scores for cognition, memory, education, and income level—as opposed to more "negative" measures such as substance use and aggression—showed higher connectivity in components of their default network. Such connections included the medial frontal and parietal cortex, the temporo-parietal junction, the anterior insula, and the frontal operculum. This correlation between attributes of positive life functionality and underlying brain connectivity was interesting indeed—but did higher connectivity between components of the default network give rise to more "positive" life outcomes, or were there other developmental, relational, and en-

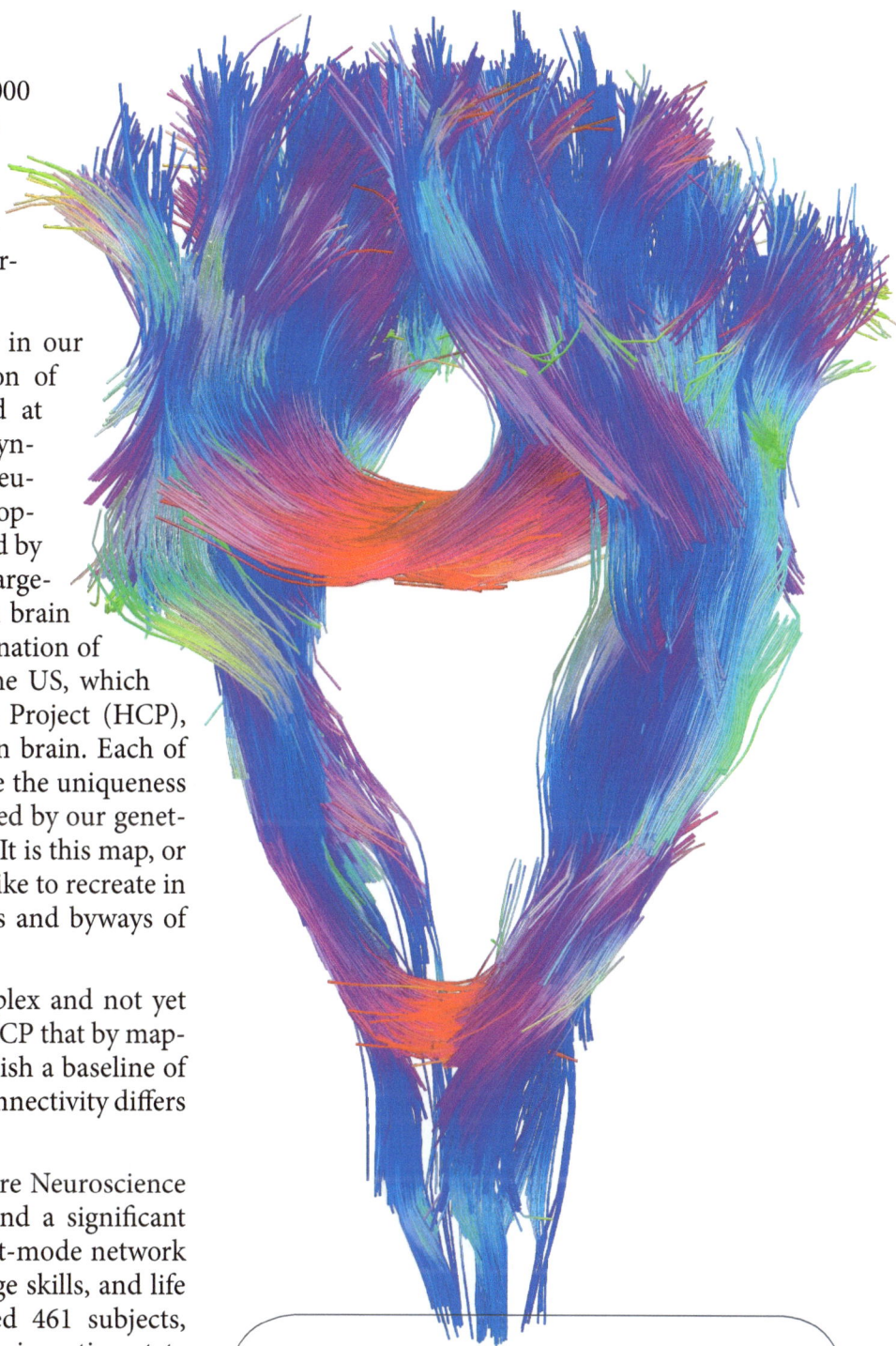

White matter fibre architecture from the Connectome Scanner dataset. The fibres are colour-coded by direction: red = left–right, green = anterior–posterior, blue = ascending–descending (RGB = XYZ).

Courtesy of the Laboratory of Neuro Imaging and the Athinoula A. Martinos Center for Biomedical Imaging, Consortium of the Human Connectome Project. www. humanconnectomeproject.org

vironmental factors at play? The researchers admit that it was impossible to tell from their study. However, as causal relationships are progressively better understood, it may become feasible to use this information to assist a transition in the brain toward the positive axis.

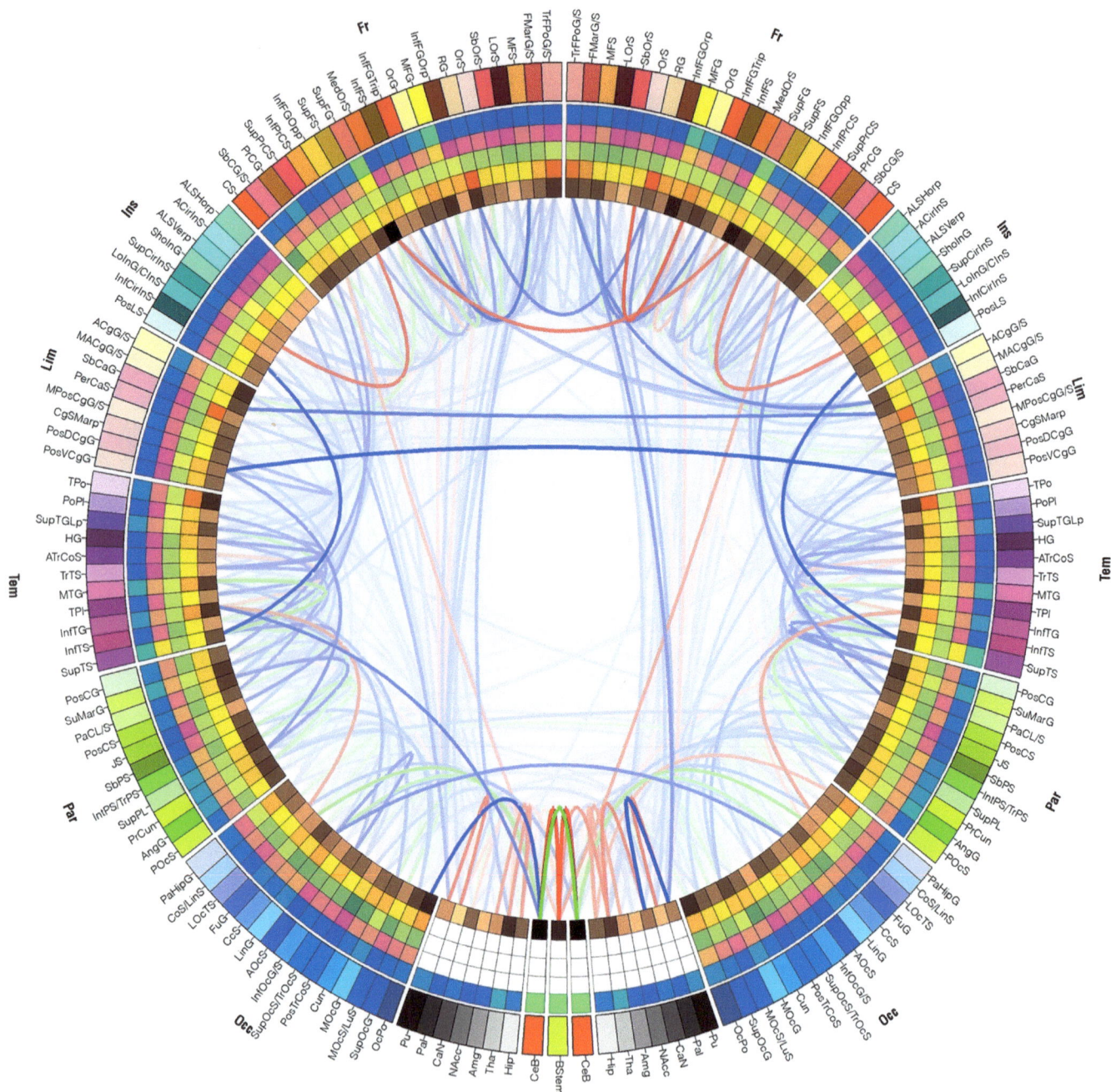

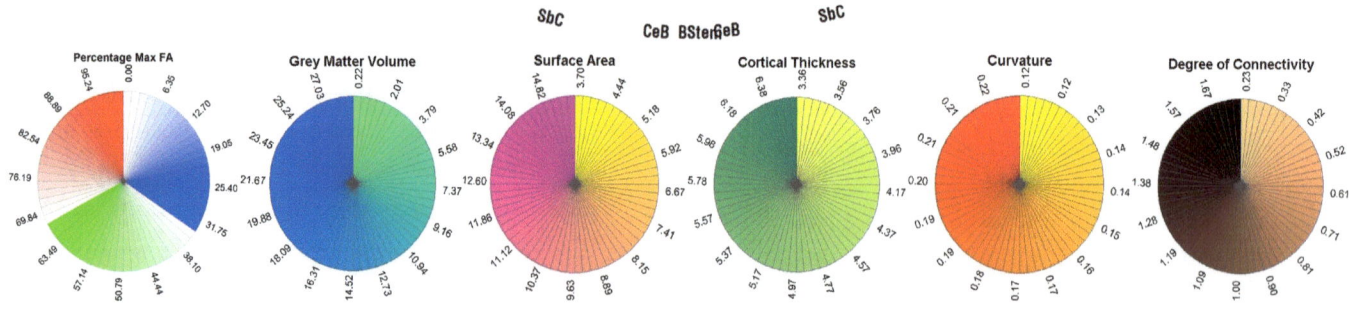

A connectogram showing the average connections and cortical measures of 110 normal, right-handed males, aged 25–36. Image by John Darrell Van Horn—PLoS One: http://journals.plos.org/plosone/article?id=10.1371/journal.pone.0037454

Van Horn, J. D., Irimia, A., Torgerson, C. M., Chambers, M. C., Kikinis, R., & Toga, A. W. (2012). Mapping connectivity damage in the case of Phineas Gage. PLoS ONE, 7(5):e37454. doi:10.1371/journal.pone.0037454

Interestingly, one of the factors that most impacted the brain toward the negative axis was marijuana use within the few weeks prior to the study. Such findings should raise a red flag and highlight the importance of more research to determine how marijuana affects the brain.

Massive change occurs in the developing brain of a child, and the challenge to map and understand it is substantial. One of the studies the dHCP is currently engaged in involves 8-year-old children, half of whom were born prematurely and half full-term, to see if there are any brain network differences between them. Premature babies are at greater risk of neuro-developmental problems, but little is known about how they develop such impairments. A huge amount of brain development in infants occurs just prior to full term, and for that development to take place outside the mother, in the case of pre-terms, may be significant for these children. For instance, the fibres forming connections to and from the thalamus, the central exchange centre of the brain, grow extensively during the time period in which dHCP teams monitor premature babies. A map of this area during these critical developmental stages could yield valuable insights.

One of the principal investigators, David Edwards, says that there are structures being developed in the last trimester that may underlie conditions like schizophrenia, autism, and depression, and it is his hope that the project can identify subtle differences in connectivity that may predispose some children to mental illness.

A recent study at the University of California, San Francisco (Chang et al., 2016) demonstrated measurable differences in the connective wiring of children with sensory processing disorder (SPD) compared to typically developing children. The study is the largest ever conducted with child SPD sufferers and the first to compare white-matter tracts in the brains of typically developing children against those with SPD.

The imaging done with these children detected abnormalities in the SPD subjects in the white-matter tracts that serve as connections for the auditory, visual, and somatosensory (tactile) systems involved in sensory processing, including in the connections between left and right hemispheres. The abnormal microstructure of sensory white matter tracts in children with SPD likely alters the timing of sensory transmission, so that the processing of sensory stimuli and the integration of information across multiple senses becomes difficult or impossible.

The imaging results showed a stronger correlation with the direct measurements of tactile and auditory processing taken during the neurological testing than with the parent report survey, which the researchers put down to the likelihood that the direct measurements were more objective.

Another impressive tool employed by researchers mapping the connectome is the connectogram, a two-dimensional graph used to study the arrangement of white-matter fibre in the brain. Based on diffusion MRI data, this circular graph highlights the strength of connections between different regions of the brain. The connectogram can display 83 cortical regions within each hemisphere, and unlike other representations of the connectome that require software to display the three dimensions, these representations can show connected regions in a flat, two-dimensional graph.

The left half of the connectogram depicts the left hemisphere, and the right half depicts the right hemisphere. The circular graph is further broken down into sections representing the frontal lobe, insular cortex, limbic lobe, temporal lobe, parietal lobe, occipital lobe, subcortical structures, and cerebellum. The brain stem is also represented, between the two hemispheres at the bottom of the graph. Each cortical area within the lobes is labelled and features a unique colour that can be used to designate the same cortical region in other figures, so that the reader can find the corresponding cortical area on a geometrically accurate surface and see exactly how disparate the connected regions may be. Inside the cortical surface ring are concentric circles representing different attributes of the corresponding cortical regions. In order from outermost to innermost, these metric rings represent the grey matter volume, surface area, cortical thickness, curvature, and degree of connectivity. The lines in the diagram on the facing page show the connections between regions. The opacity and colour of the lines represent the strength of the connection.

Our brains are wonderfully and complexly connected, and the cutting-edge research currently revealing the connectome is leading us to highly objective assessment using quantifiable biomarkers.

This may seem far too complex for the average teacher to even want to understand, however, it should be recognised that this information will not only yield a more refined and sophisticated definition of student pathologies, but will also lead to much more personalized treatments for students in days to come, which can only benefit their future learning and development.

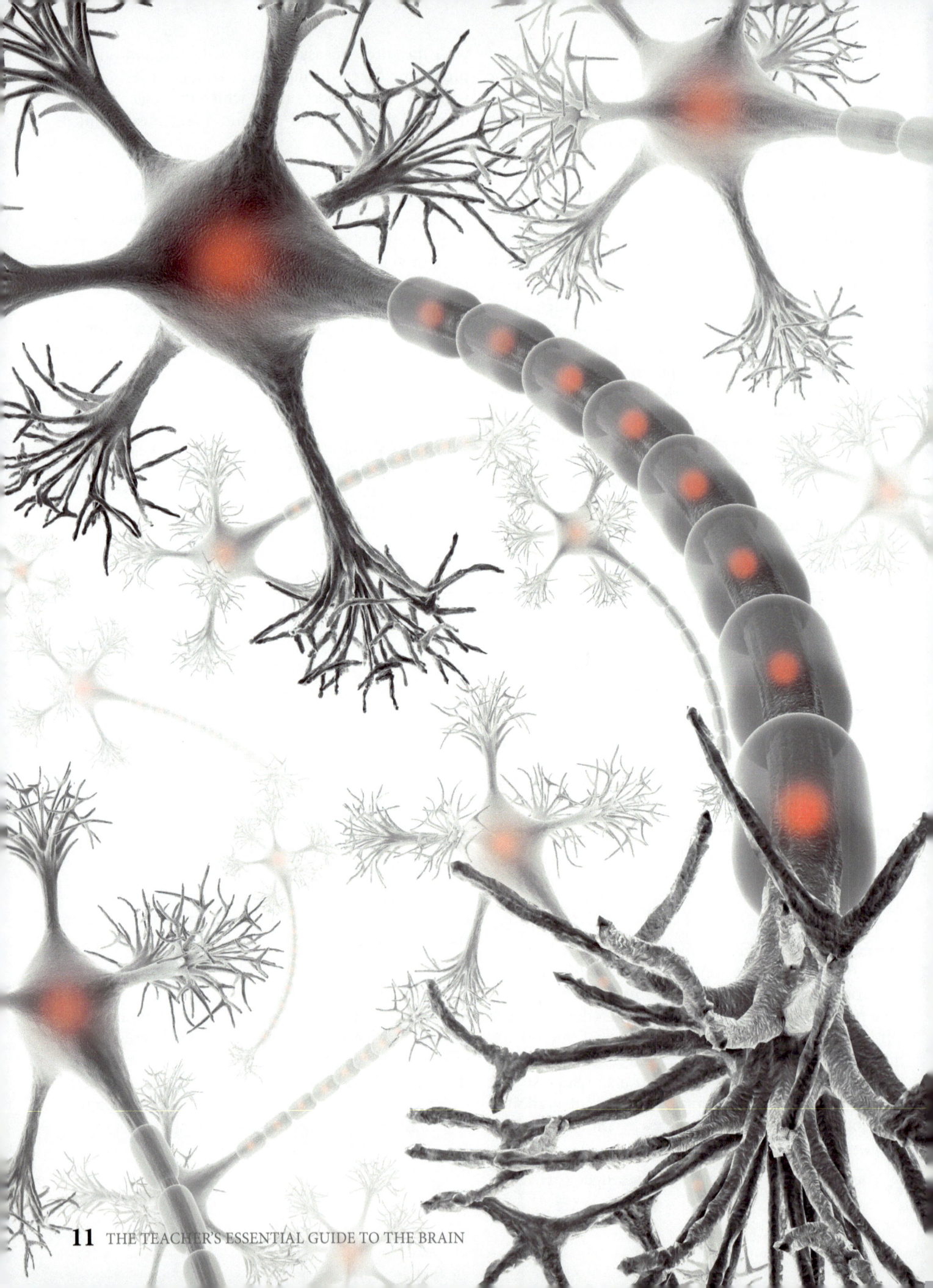

NEURONS

Our genes provide an organizational map for the development of our brains. While some designation of the place and function of neurons is fixed by coding genes, other functional aspects are subject to the influence of experience, in the form of noncoding genes that make up the so-called "nurture" part of our genetic expression (The Neuropsychotherapy Institute, 2014a). Our genetic blueprint, along with epigenetic (experience dependent) expression of genes and memory formation, creates a complex neural communication system throughout the nervous system, which is itself a complexity of synaptic/dendritic connections modulated by neurochemicals.

The nervous system has two main divisions of cells: nerve cells (neurons), and glial cells (glia). Glial cells have traditionally been recognized as a kind of support network for neurons, providing many essential functions to facilitate the neural network. However, they have more recently been acknowledged to form a communication network themselves, working in tandem with neurons (Keleman, 2013; Verkhratsky & Butt, 2007). The function of a neuron is determined by where it is in the brain, how it is connected with neighbouring cells, and its individual functional character. Take the analogy of a human individual: our function in society is determined by where we are, who we are connected to, and how we interact with others and our environment (Cozolino, 2014). The anatomist János Szentágothai estimated that our individual neurons are able to contact any other neuron via no more than six interneuronal connections (Drachman, 2005). This "six degrees of separation" has become a popular social idea—that people are connected six or fewer steps from each other in a "friend of a friend" relationship—popularized by the play and film Six Degrees of Separation by John Guare in the early 1990s and followed by numerous books, films, and TV shows based on the same idea.

While there are different types of nerve cells performing a variety of functions, it is helpful to consider a generic model that represents the fundamentals of all neurons. The figure to the left illustrates the main components of the neuron (see Chapter 2 of Kandel, Schwartz, Jessell, Siegelbaum, & Hudspeth, 2012, for a comprehensive description of neuron physiology).

Neurons communicate by means of two primary processes that have been comprehensively studied: an electrical signal within the neuron, and chemical signals between neurons. Using various chemicals known as neurotransmitters, neurons transmit signals across a very small gap between cells in an area known as the synaptic cleft. Most neurons can send and receive signals by different types of neurotransmitters, and different neurotransmitters work at different speeds (The Neuropsychotherapy Institute, 2014a).

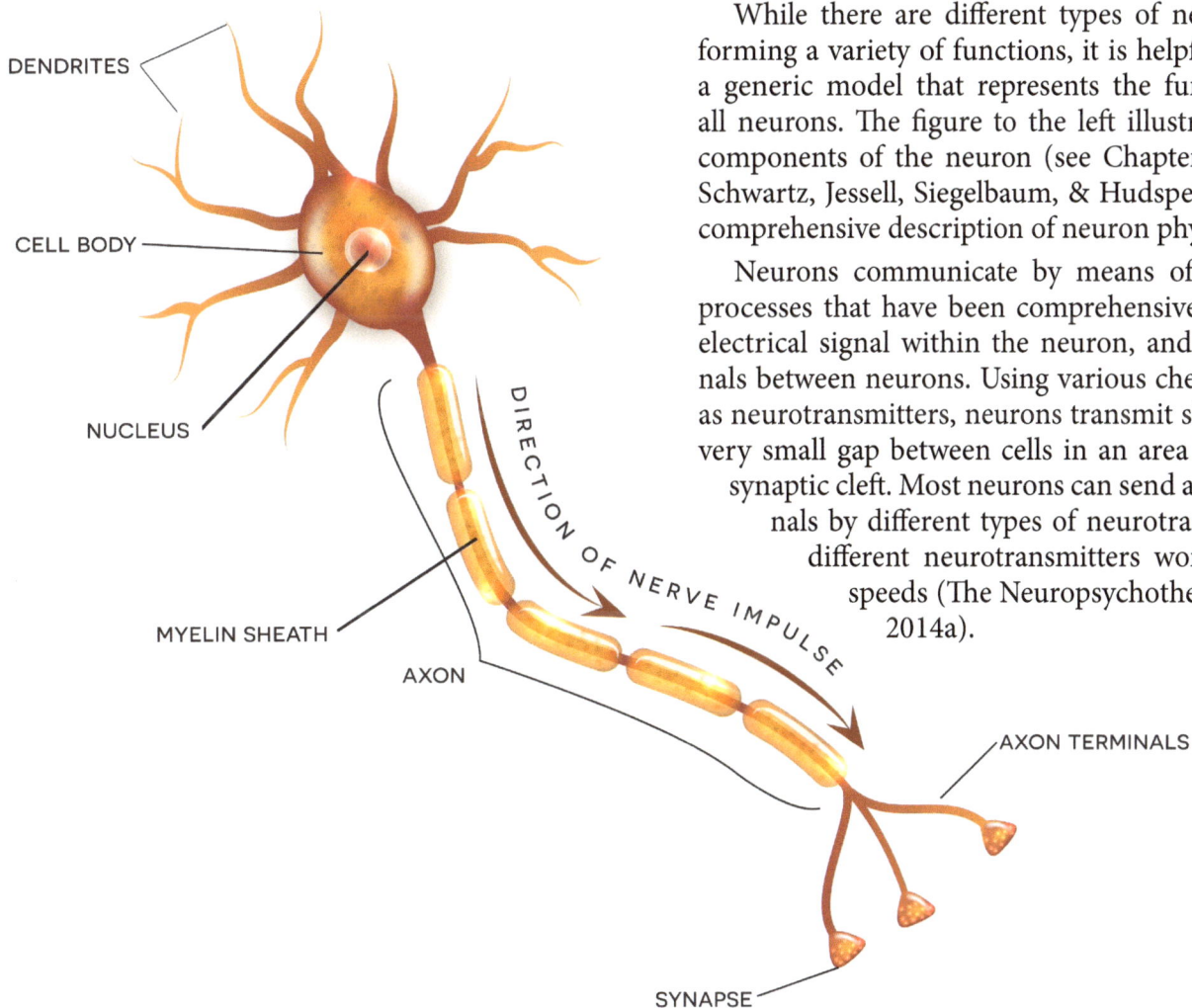

DENDRITES

CELL BODY

NUCLEUS

MYELIN SHEATH

AXON

DIRECTION OF NERVE IMPULSE

AXON TERMINALS

SYNAPSE

The figure below is a radically simplified representation of a synapse. The upper part represents the presynaptic terminal of one cell's axon, and the lower part the postsynaptic dendrite of another cell. Communication flows from the presynaptic terminal to the dendrites of a neighbouring cell. Dendrites are like the branches of a tree that spread out to reach other cells, and are the main areas for receiving incoming signals (Kandel et al., 2012).

Synaptic vesicles are packets of neurotransmitters that migrate to special release sites called active zones. These packets come to the surface of the presynaptic terminal and release their contents, by a process known as exocytosis, into the synaptic cleft. The released molecules diffuse across the gap, and some are received by receptors on the opposite-facing dendrite. The receptor sites on the dendrite bind to specific neurotransmitters, producing either an inhibiting or excitatory effect on the receiving cell. This occurs via an opening of ion channels in the membrane of the cell that essentially produces a membrane potential in the dendrite (a positive or negative charge within the cell). There can be many different types of ions in neurons, but the most common are sodium ions (Na+) and potassium ions (K+), and it is the balance of Na+ and K+ inside and outside the cell that determines the overall "charge" or potential of the cell. This balance is regulated by sodium–potassium pumps that continually exchange Na+ inside the cell for K+ outside the cell. The more positively charged a neuron becomes, the more likely it will pass a certain threshold of potential

Ionotropic receptors, such as AMPA, accept transmitters that directly alter the receiving cell's potential, and are thus fast-acting, whereas NMDA receptors require prior activation of the postsynaptic neuron through another channel before its ion channel can be opened (see Grawe, 2007, pp. 36–37). Some neurotransmitters will cause the receiving dendrite to become more positively charged, and others will cause the dendrite to become more negatively charged. The receiving dendrite "sums" the incoming chemical signals to arrive at a resultant synaptic potential which is then communicated to the main body of the cell. All of these signals are summed at the beginning of the axon, at the axon initial segment (Bender & Trussell, 2012). If the resulting charge rises above a resting potential, an electrical signal flows down the axon to the presynaptic terminals, causing the membrane of each terminal to open up channels allowing calcium into the cell. In turn, this causes the synaptic vesicles to release their chemicals into the synaptic cleft. This (albeit simplified) description of the process illustrates the binary nature of neurotransmitters in either initiating an action potential or not.

The figure below also shows some of the neurotransmitters being reabsorbed into the presynaptic terminal. Such uptake, via plasma membrane transporters, serves two purposes: recapturing the chemicals for reuse, and terminating the synaptic action of the cell (Kandel et al., 2012). Drugs used to inhibit the re-uptake of neurotransmitters will, in effect, keep the neurotransmitter in the vicinity of the postsynaptic dendrite, so that when recep-

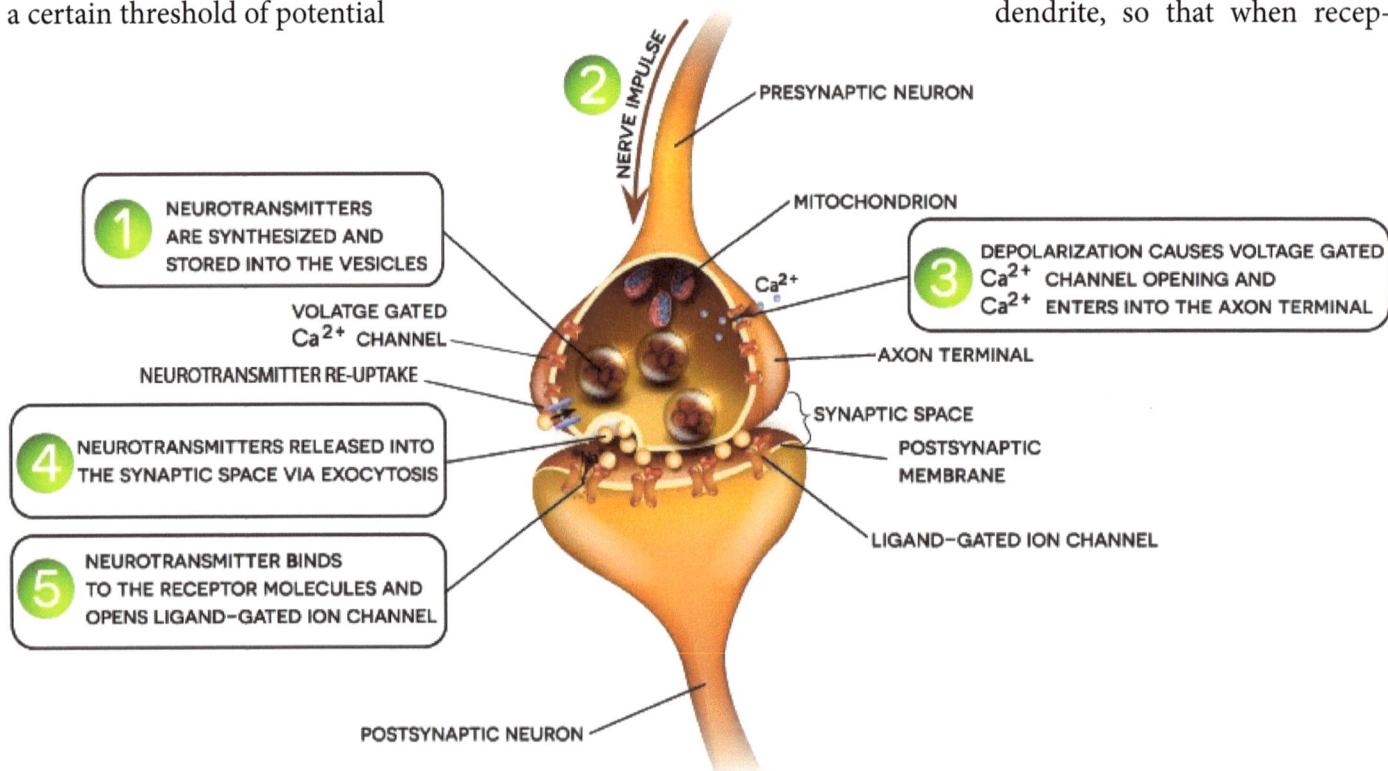

NERVE IMPULSE

2

PRESYNAPTIC NEURON

1 NEUROTRANSMITTERS ARE SYNTHESIZED AND STORED INTO THE VESICLES

MITOCHONDRION

Ca^{2+}

3 DEPOLARIZATION CAUSES VOLTAGE GATED Ca^{2+} CHANNEL OPENING AND Ca^{2+} ENTERS INTO THE AXON TERMINAL

VOLATGE GATED Ca^{2+} CHANNEL

NEUROTRANSMITTER RE-UPTAKE

AXON TERMINAL

SYNAPTIC SPACE

POSTSYNAPTIC MEMBRANE

4 NEUROTRANSMITTERS RELEASED INTO THE SYNAPTIC SPACE VIA EXOCYTOSIS

LIGAND–GATED ION CHANNEL

5 NEUROTRANSMITTER BINDS TO THE RECEPTOR MOLECULES AND OPENS LIGAND–GATED ION CHANNEL

POSTSYNAPTIC NEURON

tors are available for that particular chemical, they will bind with it. Thus, antidepressants are designed to inhibit serotonin re-uptake, keeping it in the synaptic cleft and prolonging postsynaptic activation (The Neuropsychotherapy Institute, 2014b). Another process whereby neurotransmitters are removed from the synaptic cleft is degradation, in which enzymes chemically break down the neurotransmitter and the resulting molecules are taken up by the presynaptic terminal. Within the presynaptic terminal, the neurotransmitter is then reassembled and repackaged for release once again. Finally, glial cells also remove neurotransmitters from the synaptic space to prevent further interaction with the postsynaptic cell.

Activation Patterns

A single neuron does not produce much information on its own through firing or not firing. Firing entails a certain rate, intensity, and resulting neurotransmitter output at the synapse. A single neuron simply responds to specific inputs from other neurons, or directly from the environment in the case of sensory cells. To make sense of the flow of information coming from our sensory organs, the neural system is organized into a hierarchy of increasingly complex networks. One hundred billion individual neurons, boasting and average of 7,000–10,000 synaptic connections each, together contribute to neural network profiles that represent an aspect of brain function (such as perceiving a particular sound), and these profiles integrate with many others to form various functions of our nervous system, some of which are concentrated in different areas of the brain (Siegel, 2012).

The hierarchy of neural networks is organized from sensory input to the perception of complex objects/understandings to even more complex cognitive and affective processes. For example, the "raw" visual data streamed from the sensory input of the retina is recognized by neurons in a fragmented fashion whereby individual parts of the scene are processed by neurons tuned to "recognize" small, specific elements. These fragments are then assembled by more complex neural networks involving higher-order cells that recognize the assembly of the parts. At the top of the hierarchy are cells and networks in the cortex that recognize the "whole picture". Once this broader perception is realized, further cognitive/affective processes can occur as a result of this input. The flow of information is not serial but a complexity of parallel processing that utilizes feedback from various brain regions. There is no neuron that can recognize the complexities of an object like a chair. Only through the summation of complex networks, and with experience, can we recognize a chair for what it is. Nor is there a single area of the brain that handles a specific mental function in isolation. Just as neurons do not perceive on their own, neural profiles activate and integrate with other regions across the nervous system (Siegel, 2012).

The brain is further organized into functional systems that to some extent can be identified by elements of the physical architecture of the central nervous system. From a single sensory input neuron, the scale of operations increases to complex hierarchies of neural networks that form maps representing input features in specific areas of the cortex. These complex signals are in turn processed within broad functional systems of organization according to the physical architecture of the brain. Such functional architecture is currently being mapped by the Human Connectome Project (http://www.humanconnectomeproject.org).

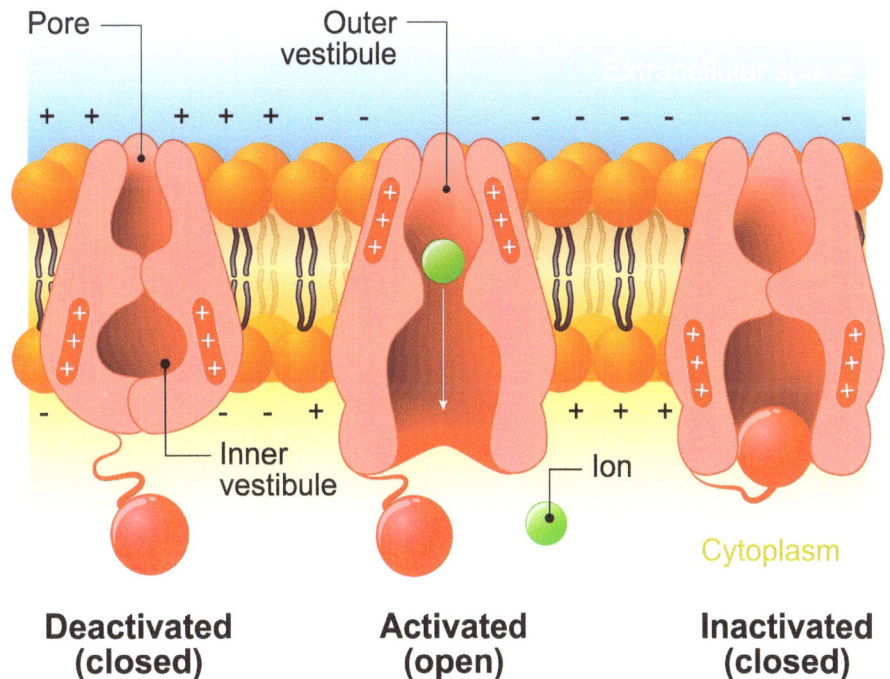

Above: Voltage-gated channels found along the axon and synapse of neurons propagate electrical signals down the neuron

GLIA THE OVERLOOKED CELLS

The brain contains two major classes of cells: neurons and glia. While both are neural cells, conventionally, the fundamental difference between the two classes has been understood to be that neurons are electrically excitable, whereas glia are non-excitable. Various types of glial cells make up about 90% of all cells in the human brain. In the central nervous system, they are referred to as macroglial or neuroglial cells, and can be categorized into three types: astrocytes, oligodendrocytes, and ependymal cells (Verkhratsky & Butt, 2007).

Glial cells have traditionally been regarded as passive supporting cells. The name *glia* is from Greek, literally meaning "glue". Rudolf Ludwig Karl Virchow (1821–1902), who coined the term for neuroscience, thought of glia as a sort of "nerve putty"—a connective tissue void of any cellular elements (Verkhratsky & Butt, 2007). However, today we have a very different understanding of the function of glia in the nervous system. Glia play a vital role in the growth and development of neurons as well as their maintenance and death. Atroglial cells provide the stem elements to birth neurons; they compartmentalize neurons, synapses, and capillaries into functional units and help modulate chemical signals between neurons. Oligodendroglia even myelinate the axons of neurons in the central nervous system (as Schwann cells do in the peripheral nervous system), creating faster communication pathways.

In 1984, researchers discovered that astrocytes and oligodendrocytes possessed GABA receptors. GABA (*Gamma-aminobutyric acid*) is an inhibitory neurotransmitter that plays a counterpart role to the glutamates, if glutamate is the accelerator of the brain, GABA is the brake. A few years later, others found that astroglial cells can communicate over long distances by propagating calcium waves. Since then it has been demonstrated that glial cells can express practically every type of neurotransmitter and can detect the activity of neighbouring neurons. In fact, far from being mere passive, non-excitable glue for neurons, glia form a whole other communication circuit in tandem with the neuronal circuit, the two systems communicating with each other via chemical and electrical signalling.

The communication network of glia is what Stanley Keleman (2013) has called the "slow brain"—a support system for a wide order of connections and cortical growth. This slower system is vitally connected to the voluntary muscular signalling from the body which has a bidirectional effect on the brain and body posture and responses.

Much is still being discovered about these cells that make up the greater part of our brain, but what is not in doubt is that there is much more to glia than we ever imagined.

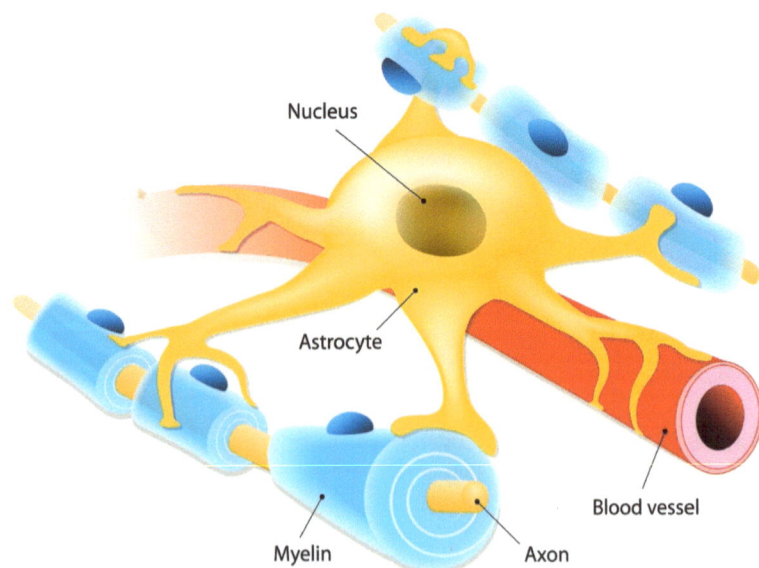

Astrocytes (meaning "star-like cells") are the most abundant cells in the central nervous system. This simplistic diagram shows an astrocyte forming the scaffolding for a number of neuron axons and a blood vessel. The blue myelin around the axons originates from oligodendrocytes (not shown here).

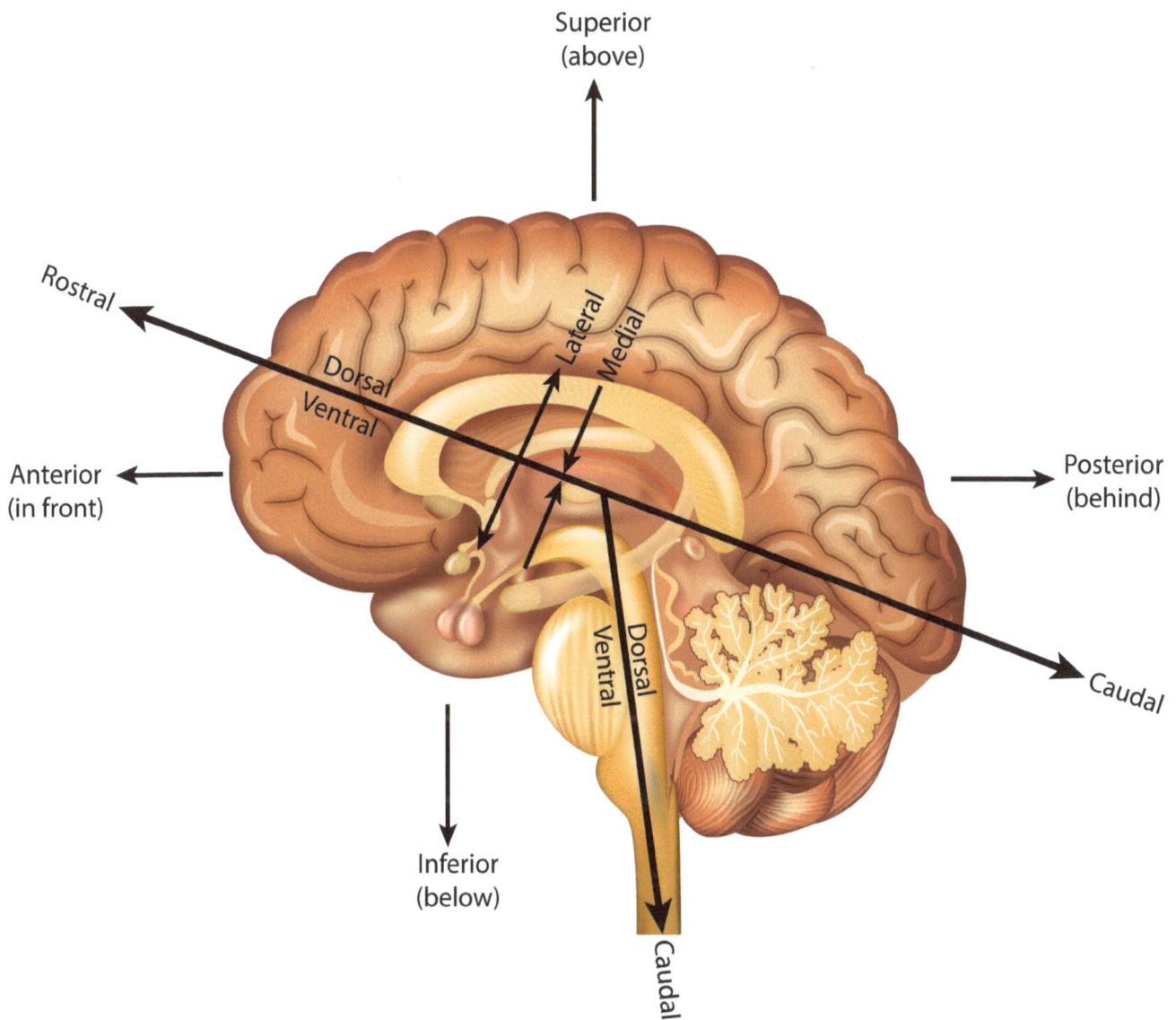

Superior (above)

Rostral

Dorsal
Ventral

Lateral Medial

Anterior (in front)

Posterior (behind)

Dorsal Ventral

Caudal

Inferior (below)

Caudal

Location Terminology	
Anterior	relating to the front or to the nose end
Dorsal	relating to the back or toward the surface of the back or top of the head
Lateral	relating to the sides or away from the midline
Ventral	relating to the underside or toward the surface of the chest or bottom of the head
Parietal	relating to the wall of the body or of a body cavity or hollow structure
Medial	relating to the middle or the midline
Basal	relating to the bottom layer or base

Planes	
Horizontal	Horizontal sections are the images of the brain you would see as if from directly above or from directly below (the dorsal or ventral perspective)
Sagittal	The sagittal sections are the side-on views, like the image above
Frontal	The frontal sections are views from the anterior or posterior perspective
Cross	The cross sections are views from a rostral/caudal perspective

DEEP SYSTEMS

THE LIMBIC SYSTEM

The limbic system (also known as the paleomammalian brain) is a collection of brain structures located in the middle of the brain. It was first defined by Paul Broca in the 19th century as the structures between the cerebral hemisphere and the brainstem (i.e., the limbus, or border of the brain). The limbic system is not a discrete system itself but rather a collection of structures—anatomically related but varying greatly in function. The term has been in use for about 70 years, despite the belief of some neuroscientists that it should be abandoned for implying that the various structures represent a functionally unified system. Irrespective of terminology, collectively we can think of the limbic system as the centre for emotional responsiveness, motivation, memory formation and integration, olfaction, and the mechanisms designed to keep us safe. These are broad strokes, certainly—not to suggest that the neocortex is not involved in these functions, but these are the focal activities of the limbic system. For the purposes of this overview we will be considering the amygdala, hippocampus, and hypothalamus as the main limbic structures of clinical relevance to the practising teacher. We will also touch on the thalamus, which feeds the limbic system with sensory input.

The basal ganglia, a set of subcortical structures located near the thalamus and hypothalamus, are also included in the limbic system and are involved in intentional movements. The limbic system is closely connected to the prefrontal cortex, and it is this prefrontal–limbic connection that is strengthened when practising mindfulness. The functional relevance of the limbic system to effective teaching and learning is obvious, as affect, memory, sensory processing, time perception, attention, consciousness, autonomic control, motor behaviour, and more are all mediated in and through this collection of structures.

THE THALAMUS

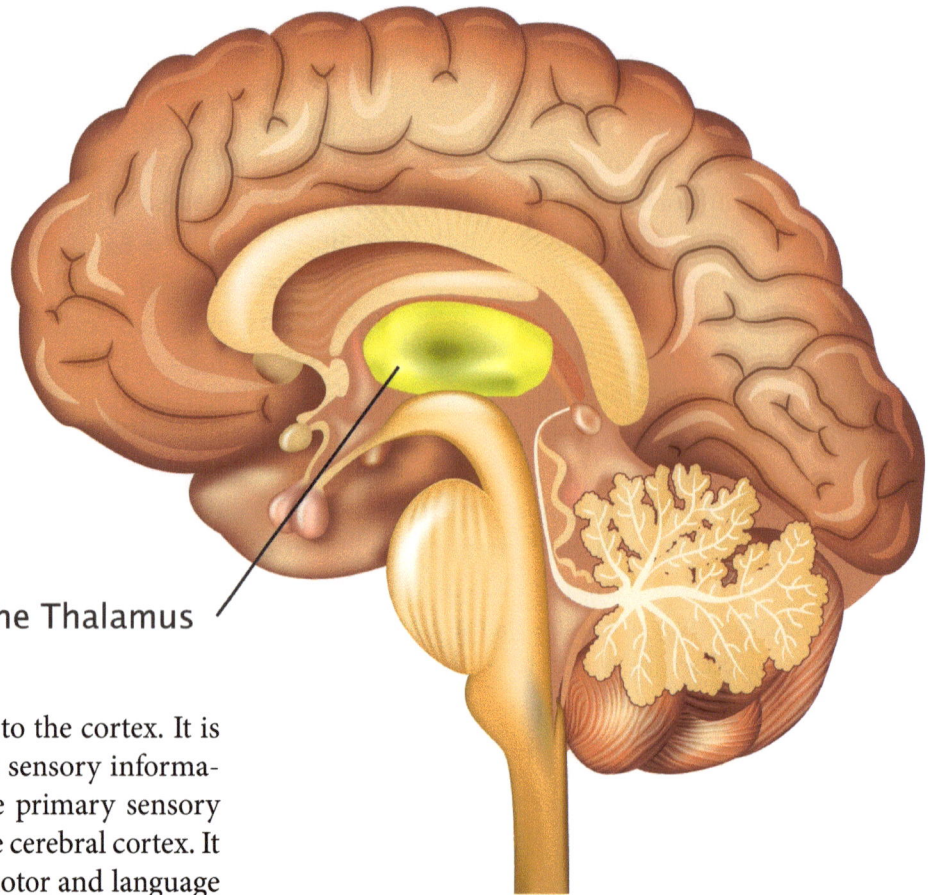

T he thalamus (from the Greek word meaning "chamber") is centrally located between the cerebral cortex and the midbrain and is known for its role in relaying sensory and motor signals to the cerebral cortex, and in the regulation of sleep, consciousness, and alertness—rather like a hub of information flow from the senses to the cortex. It is believed that the thalamus processes sensory information in addition to relaying it to the primary sensory areas and receiving feedback from the cerebral cortex. It plays major roles in the support of motor and language systems and (in connection with the hippocampus) the spatial memory that is critical for episodic memory.

The Thalamus

Interestingly, a common genetic variation in humans is that of the serotonin transporter 5-HTTLPR. People who inherit two short alleles (SERT-ss) also have more neurons and larger volume in parts of the thalamus. The SERT-ss inheritance is linked to a greater vulnerability to depression, PTSD, and suicide. The dorsal thalamus also plays a role in the inhibition of compulsive behaviour—we will examine this more closely later, when we consider the so-called OCD loop that involves the orbitofrontal cortex, striatum, and thalamus.

The thalamus is important for sleep regulation, in particular slow-wave sleep cycles, and coordinates parts of the cortex as sleep changes from state to state—the latter in orchestration with the activity of the hippocampus.

In sum, the thalamus appears to play a greater role than merely the relay of sensory information and is integral to brain function in a cortico–thalamo–cortical pathway of processing.

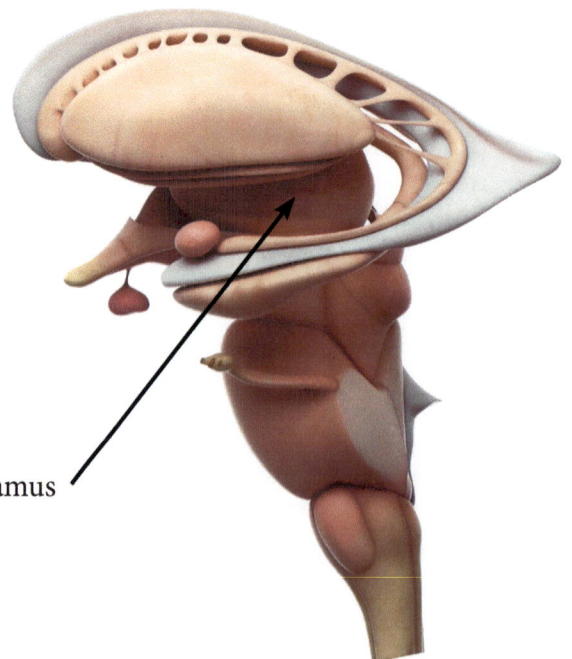

Thalamus

THE AMYGDALA

The amygdala is located in both hemispheres of the brain and is involved in a range of cognitive processes. The lateral amygdala receives input from visual, auditory, and somatosensory systems: the central nucleus is connected with the brainstem that controls innate behaviour and associated physiological responses, while the medial nucleus is connected with the olfactory system. Most of the pathways into the amygdala are excitatory, using glutamate as a transmitter. Information flow through the amygdala is modulated by a number of transmitters, including norepinephrine, serotonin, dopamine, and acetylcholine.

The amygdala forms part of the limbic system. It is most commonly recognized as the emotional processing centre that receives incoming sensory information and processes it for an emotional response. The response may be a defence to a perceived threat, a critical function of this "early-warning system". The amygdala learns how to respond to various stimuli based on its reference to implicit memory and makes decisions on how to initiate an emotional reaction to such stimuli. The emotional memory learned and utilized by the amygdala is episodic–autobiographical memory that can be notably implicit or unconscious, in contrast with explicit or declarative memory processed by the hippocampus.

The left and right amygdalae have separate memory systems, but they work together to evaluate incoming information and process an emotional response, encoding, storing and retrieving memories that are associated with certain cues in the environment. The right amygdala is more strongly associated with negative emotions such as fear and sadness, whereas the left amygdala has been associated with both positive and negative emotional responses.

The amygdala has an attentional role, focusing our attention on the most important stimuli in the environment. It helps us define a stimulus and primes our immediate response, for example in recognizing a dangerous stimulus and initiating a stress response. Pro-

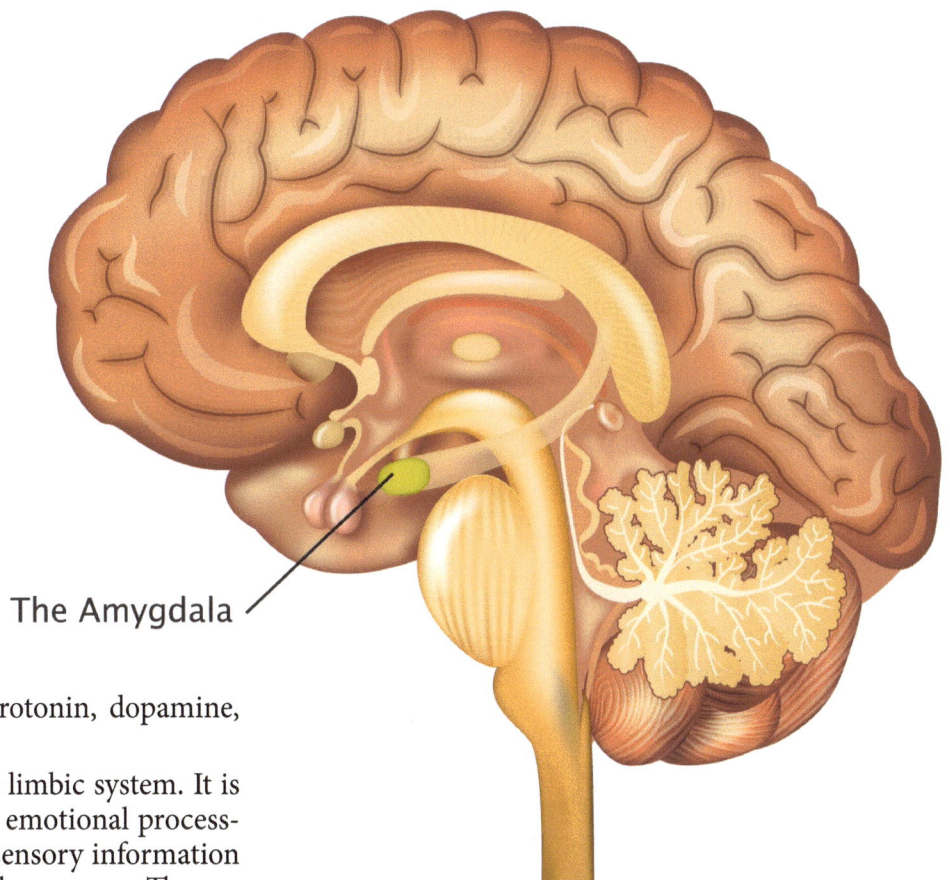

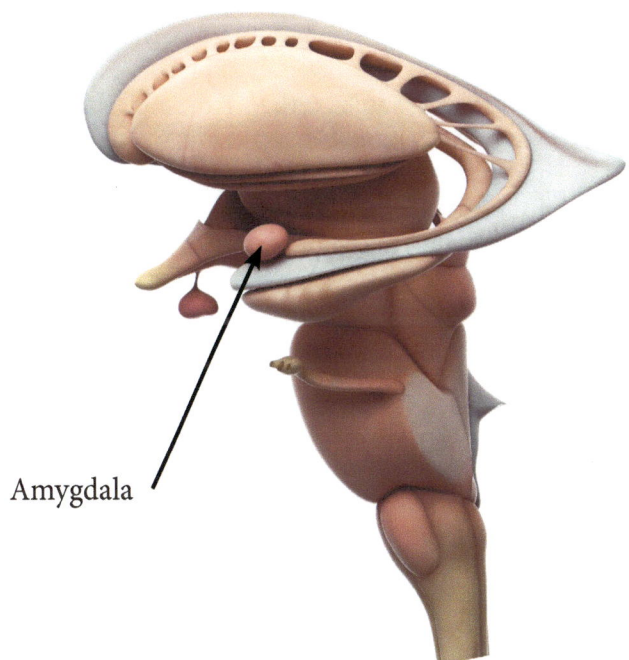

The Amygdala

Amygdala

cessing social cues (e.g., evaluating faces) is also part of what the amygdala does prior to these cues being processed in higher cortical areas like the medial prefrontal cortex. Evaluating faces (e.g., the trustworthiness of a face) is an important social processing skill that is carried out very quickly in the limbic system. The amygdala also plays a part in processing reward learning and the resulting motivation, and modulating emotional states such as aggression, maternal instincts, and sexual and digestion behaviours as well as attention, perception, and explicit memory—generally thought to be part of processing the emotional significance of what we are encountering. Such processing causes the amygdala to respond with the release of hormones, or neuromodulators, that can alter the cognitive processing in cortical areas as well as activate the body for an appropriate response via the hypothalamus.

In terms of information flow, sensory input goes to the thalamus and then directly to the amygdala (except olfaction, which goes directly to the amygdala), while it is sent also via a slower path to the neocortex. The amygdala is especially activated by surprising, ambiguous, and uncertain situations or stimuli. If the amygdala perceives a correspondence between the record of experiences in the hippocampus and incoming information, and judges that the stimulus warrants a fight, flight, or freeze response, then it will trigger the hypothalamic–pituitary–adrenal (HPA) axis and "hijack" the prefrontal cortex (PFC), partly in the form of blood flow being redirected from the PFC to the limbic system. This amygdala activity processes information milliseconds earlier than the neocortex, so in the case where implicit memory matches an incoming stimulus, the amygdala acts before any possible direction from the neocortex can be received. On the other hand, if the amygdala does not perceive a match to the incoming stimulus, it acts according to the directions received from the neocortex. This means that when the amygdala perceives a threat, it initiates a response to keep us safe from that threat, although this may not be the most adaptive response. We know a lot more about the fear response of the amygdala than its other functions, but there is likely much more going on in this structure than we yet realize.

In the case of depression, the amygdala is often found to be enlarged from continual hyperactivation, with studies showing that there is an increased metabolic activity in the amygdala of depressed subjects. There is a positive correlation between the degree of amygdala activation and the severity of the depression. The depressive symptoms do not seem to dampen the anxiety-readiness for negative events or the ability to recall negative memories to ruminate upon.

Hypersensitivity and overactivity of the amygdala are at the core of anxiety-based disorders such as generalized anxiety disorder, phobias, PTSD, and other limbic-driven states that inhibit positive, rational (cortical) responses to stressors. Down-regulating amygdala reactivity and the resulting HPA axis stress-response cascade is of primary importance in a school environment. Why? Because school can be challenging, especially to those children who experience social, emotional and behavioural difficulties (Cooper, 2011). Many students fear failure, they worry that they will look foolish in front of their peers, many experience anxiety about not keeping up with their studies, others stress when topics are difficult and the understanding of concepts hard. Most children worry about fitting in and being accepted by their peers (Geldard & Geldard, 2009; McWhirter, 2013). Add to these normal childhood stressors a family situation where parents are critical, maybe abusive, controlling and demanding, and a child can be in a continual state of angst.

The classroom environment should always employ a 'bottom-up' approach to learning. A bottom-up approach addresses the fact that students may be experiencing fear and anxiety during their day and creates an environment of safety and calm. Teachers who approach class with 'drill sergeant' tactics, sarcasm or put-downs further stimulate a child's fear-based brain, adding to a child's stress and essentially stopping any possibility of effective cognitive learning to take place (Schenck, 2011). Calming the amygdala is the first step in helping a child regulate any stress related reactivity and allows for learning readiness and classroom engagement. Allison and Rossouw (2013) describe the importance of a safe and controlled environment to effect change:

> Safety is essential for people in distress because it down-regulates the hypothalamus–pituitary adrenal system. When the fear response, which is triggered from the pons, amygdala, basal ganglia, hypothalamus, pituitary and adrenal glands, is activated, the distress activates the release of the corticotrophin releasing factor, adrenocorticotrophic hormone, adrenalin and cortisol. If these patterns are activated frequently, the patterns of firing will become well established, resulting in a default neural activation when a trigger is received. (p. 24)

A safe, nurturing and supportive teacher facilitates down-regulation of a child's stress response system and encourages the development of new patterns of neural activation through experiences of controlled incongruence.

THE HIPPOCAMPUS

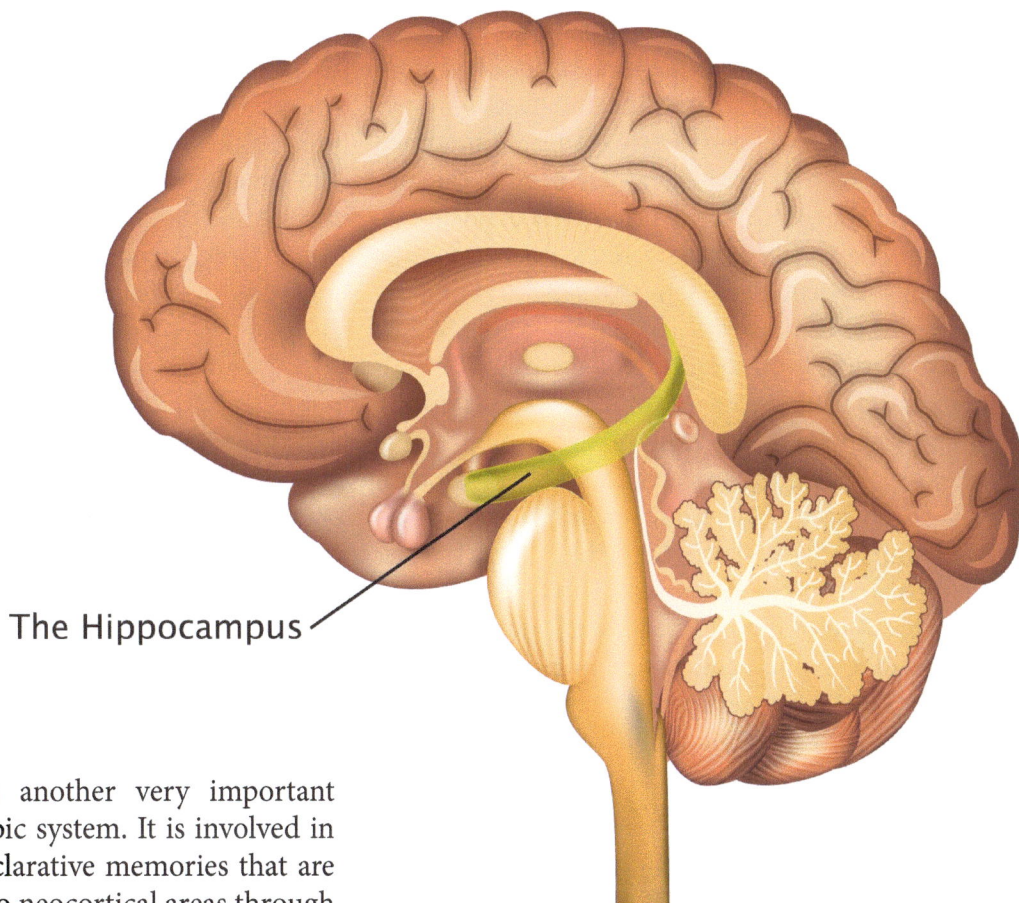

The Hippocampus

The hippocampus is another very important structure in the limbic system. It is involved in the formation of declarative memories that are processed and transferred to neocortical areas through the process of memory consolidation and, notably, in the contextual anchoring of experience in time and space. The process of how the hippocampus transfers information to the neocortex to consolidate memory may be explained by what is called the hippocampal–neocortical dialogue. Structured interactions between the hippocampus and neocortex happen during slow-wave sleep, when sharp wave patterns dominate the hippocampus and there are bursts of neuron activity in synchrony with state changes in the cortex. This may be part of the process of consolidating memory into long-term state while you sleep.

Some researchers conceptualize the hippocampus not as a storage location for memory, but as a control centre that connects areas of the neocortex to activate the effective recall of memory. From this perspective we might think of the hippocampus as the brain's Google search engine, allowing fast and efficient searching of established memories in the neocortex to help assess and plan. A well-known function of the hippocampus is the capacity to learn and retrieve spatial memory: the what, when, and where qualities of an experience.

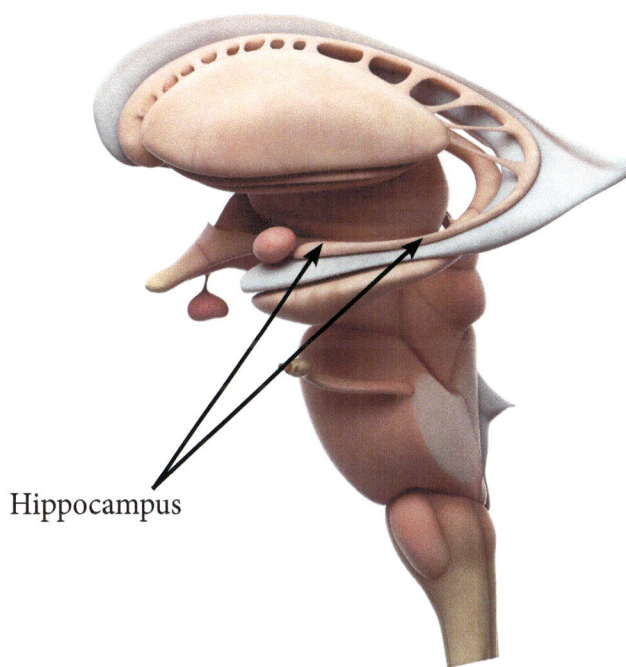

Hippocampus

Researchers have found that neurogenesis—the creation of new neurons—happens in the hippocampus with new learning. There is an upsurge of new neurons and associated circuits when a new task is learned, particularly in the case of physical tasks, and in enriched, stimulating environments. If the hippocampus is damaged, however, this can have significant effects on overall cognitive functioning, especially on spatial memory, and on explicit memory in general. Damage to the hippocampus can occur through prolonged exposure to stress hormones such as glucocorticoids (to which the hippocampus is particularly sensitive), highlighting the seriousness of chronic stress and its physiological impact. Basic feedback mechanisms in the hippocampus that help modulate the release of glucocorticoids during stress may be compromised, compounding the effects of chronic stress by leading to chronically elevated cortisol levels. It has been observed that some people suffering post-traumatic stress disorder (PTSD) have smaller hippocampal volume than the general population, and one study has found that this volume did not necessarily increase after therapy and symptom reduction (Lindauer et al., 2005). A compromised hippocampus may not anchor emotional reactions to a traumatic event to a specific time and space, and such reactions can reoccur inappropriately, as is typical in PTSD.

The hippocampus is also implicated in major depression, with findings of hippocampal volume being reduced as much as 8–19% in those with major depression, the reduction in volume being positively correlated with the duration of the depressive state. Similar correlations can be found with bipolar disorder and borderline personality disorder. It is possible that reduced hippocampal volume may be a risk factor rather than a consequence of chronic or excessive stress, so that individuals with a smaller hippocampus will be more prone to fear responses when exposed to traumatic events and less able to regulate that fear response (i.e., to keep the HPA axis stress-response cascade in check) and effectively integrate explicit and implicit memory of the trauma into long-term memory.

Much has been learned about the functions of the hippocampus through the study of a certain subject, Henry Gustav Molaison. Molaison, who in 1953 at the age of 27 had almost all of his hippocampus removed in an attempt to stop epileptic seizures, lost his ability to hold on to new semantic and episodic memories, being unable to consolidate them into long-term memory. He was able to remember what had happened a long time previously, and the older the memory the better he seemed to remember—just the opposite of what is normally observed. Molaison's general knowledge of the world (his semantic memory) was intact, but everything that happened after his surgery seemed new to him: he could only remember new experiences for a few seconds. Even the ability to recognize himself as he aged was lost, although he could recognize himself in old pictures. Interestingly, Henry was able to learn complex motor skills, and retain these skills (what we know as procedural or implicit memory), but was unable to remember learning them (declarative or explicit memory).

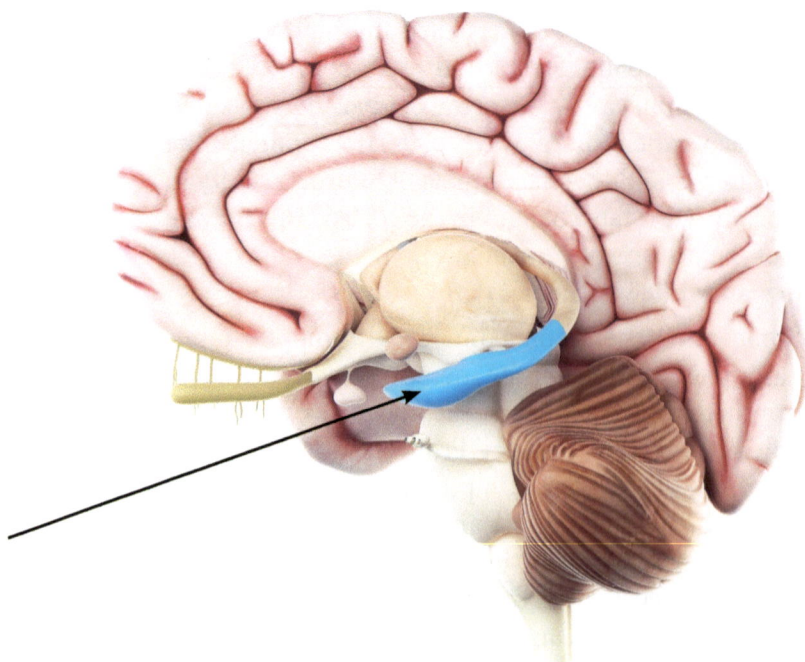

The left side hippocampus is represented here in blue. A compromised hippocampus may not anchor emotional reactions to a traumatic event to a specific time and space, and such reactions can reoccur inappropriately, as is typical in PTSD

THE HYPOTHALAMUS

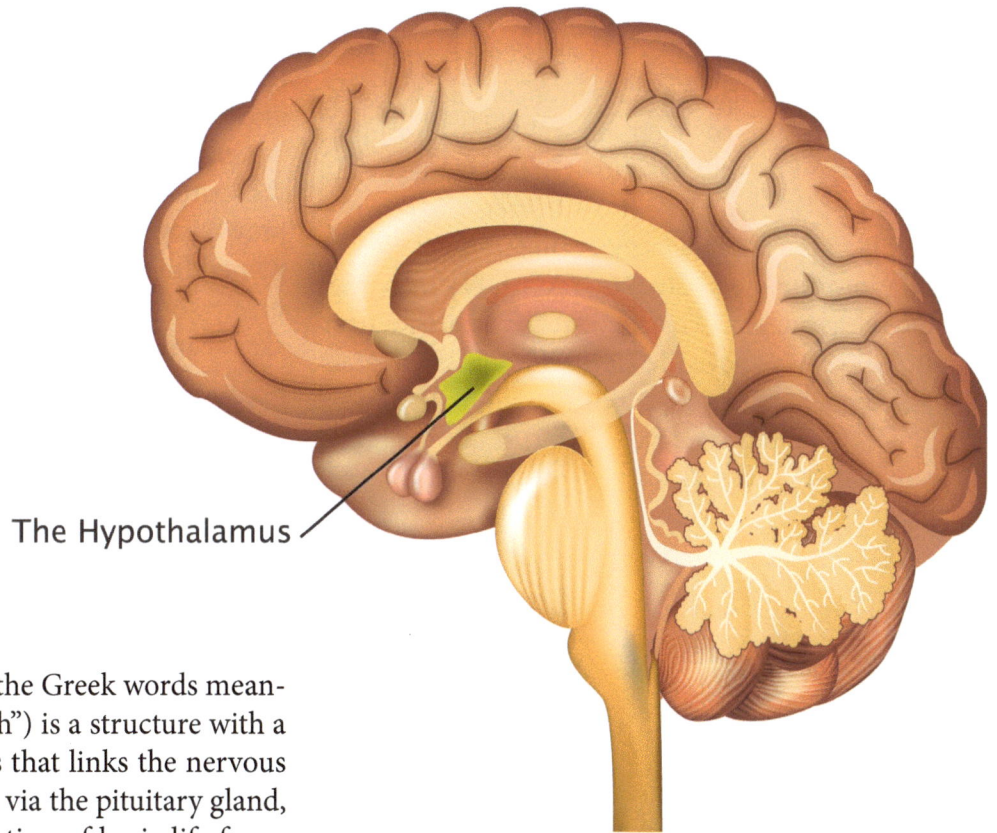

The Hypothalamus

The hypothalamus (from the Greek words meaning "chamber underneath") is a structure with a variety of vital functions that links the nervous system to the endocrine system via the pituitary gland, for the regulation and coordination of basic life functions. The hypothalamus, as the name would suggest, is located below the thalamus and above the brainstem. It receives sensory inputs that detect changes in both internal and external environments. It receives direct inputs from smell, taste, visual, and somatosensory systems and also senses blood temperature, blood sugar, mineral levels, and a variety of hormones. The hypothalamus is closely connected to other limbic structures such as the hippocampus, amygdala, and cingulate cortex, and thus forms part of the continuum of emotional responsiveness. The medial zone of the hypothalamus is involved in motivated behaviours such as defensive behaviours.

The hypothalamus acts as a control centre for certain metabolic processes and activations of the autonomic nervous system involved in fluid and electrolyte balance, energy metabolism, circadian rhythms, sleep, fatigue, thirst, body temperature, hunger, attachment behaviours (including sexual and reproductive behaviour), to name a few. It synthesizes and secretes certain neurohormones that stimulate or inhibit the secretion of pituitary hormones.

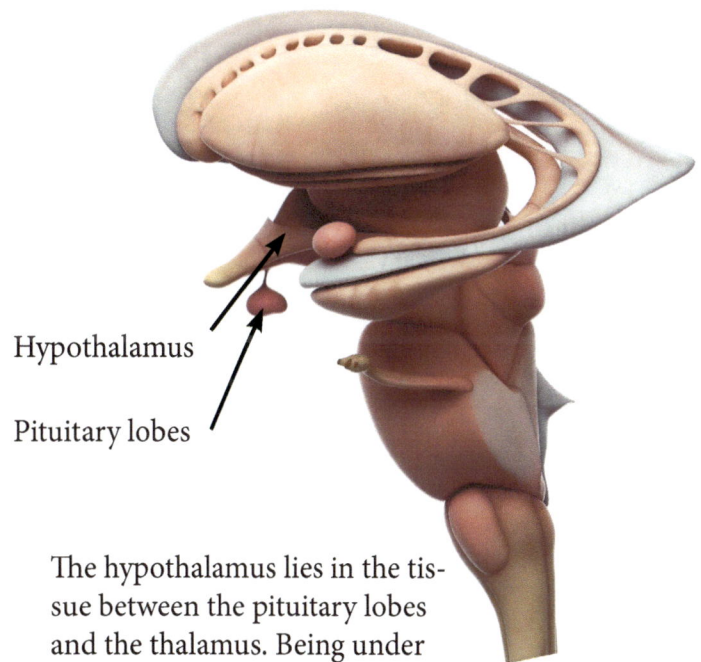

Hypothalamus

Pituitary lobes

The hypothalamus lies in the tissue between the pituitary lobes and the thalamus. Being under the thalamus it has been named the *hypo*thalamus.

The HPA Axis Response

The hypothalamic–pituitary–adrenal (HPA) axis response is the physiological mechanism that activates the body to respond to a threat. When a threat is detected by the amygdala, a physiological response is mediated through the hypothalamus–anterior pituitary gland. A neurohormone—corticotropin-releasing hormone (CRH) that has been manufactured in the paraventricular nucleus of the hypothalamus—triggers the anterior pituitary gland to release adrenocorticotropin hormone (ACTH) into the blood stream. The ACTH then triggers the release of glucocorticoids such as cortisol from the adrenal cortex above the kidneys. Feedback mechanisms in the hippocampus, hypothalamus and pituitary gland monitor the rising levels of cortisol in the blood and modulate the HPA axis stress-response cascade accordingly.

In the case where someone feels they are dealing with an extreme, uncontrollably stressful situation (such as the severe physical or sexual abuse of a child, or constant life-threatening situations as in war), the feedback mechanisms that dampen the HPA axis stress-response cascade can be damaged, and glucocorticoid levels continue to escalate. These excessive amounts of glucocorticoids can damage activated glutamate synapses and pyramidal cells in the hippocampus (where there are many glucocorticoid receptors), destabilizing previously formed neural connections and thus neural/mental function in the hippocampus. This may be positively correlated with the reduction in volume of the hippocampi of individuals who have suffered extreme stress and been diagnosed with PTSD.

The HPA Axis

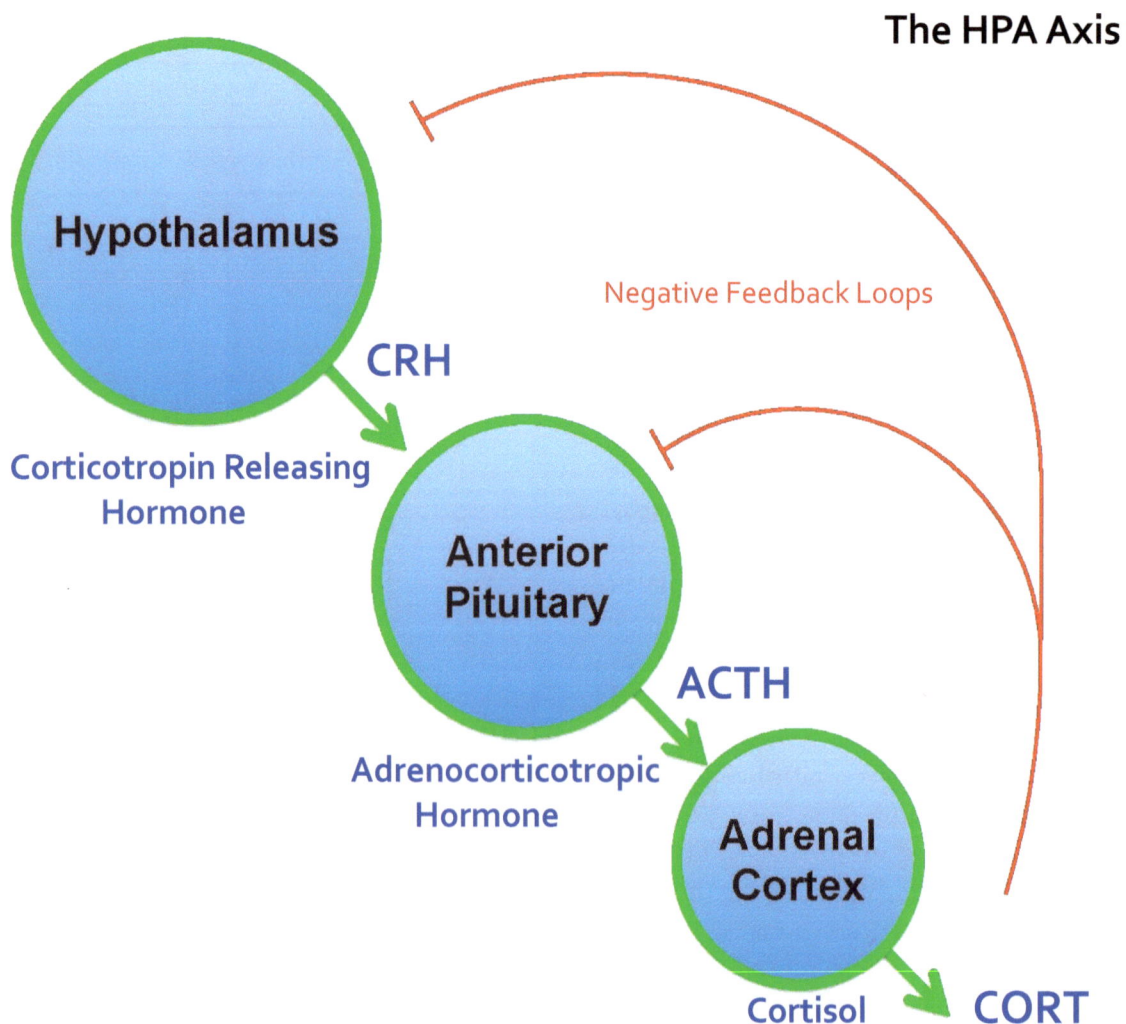

Hypothalamus

CRH
Corticotropin Releasing Hormone

Negative Feedback Loops

Anterior Pituitary

ACTH
Adrenocorticotropic Hormone

Adrenal Cortex

Cortisol → CORT

Brian M Sweis - Wikimedia Commons

HPA Axis Response Pathway

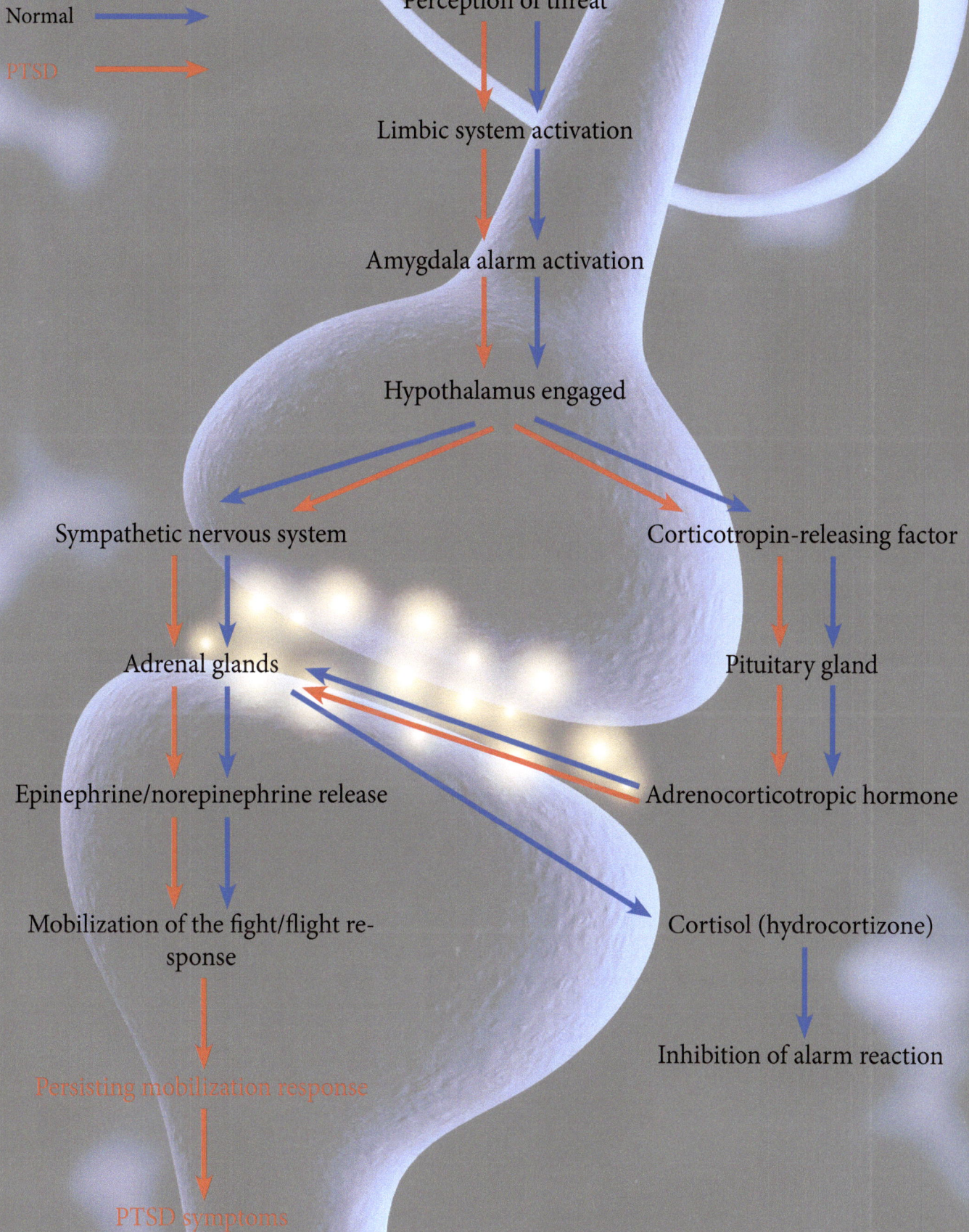

Normal →

PTSD →

Perception of threat

Limbic system activation

Amygdala alarm activation

Hypothalamus engaged

Sympathetic nervous system

Corticotropin-releasing factor

Adrenal glands

Pituitary gland

Epinephrine/norepinephrine release

Adrenocorticotropic hormone

Mobilization of the fight/flight re-sponse

Cortisol (hydrocortizone)

Persisting mobilization response

Inhibition of alarm reaction

PTSD symptoms

THE NEOCORTEX

The neocortex ("new bark") is composed of the topmost layers of the cerebral cortex, the part that is visible when looking at the external surface of the brain with all its folds and ridges. More than two thirds of the cerebral cortex is buried in grooves or fissures known as sulci: these folds give it a much greater surface area within the limited space of the skull. There are six layers to the neocortex, each layer about the thickness of a business card, and each functionally distinct. The layers consist of (and are linked by) vertical columns of neuronal clusters called "cortical columns". The communication between the columns and the layers allows for complex and sophisticated processing. It has been postulated that the top two layers provide an anticipatory function based on previous experience, and the bottom two layers attend to new information, while the middle two layers are devoted to forming a creative summation of the two (Hawkins & Blakeslee, 2004). It is also generally understood that the cortical columns in the left hemisphere are less cross-connected than those in the right; this correlates with the more connected and global view of the right hemisphere and the more linear and categorising view of the left. When we engage in the long-term practice of mindfulness—attending to sensations in the here and now—the bottom two layers of the neocortex are energized, adding thickness to the prefrontal cortex (PFC) and insula, at the same time shifting prefrontal activation toward the left side of the PFC, increasing the ability to be approach-oriented and reducing avoidance.

The Blue Brain Project (http://bluebrain.epfl.ch/) is an exciting multinational and multidisciplinary enterprise that is attempting to understand and model this complex system by building biologically detailed digital reconstructions and simulations of a rodent's brain– with the ultimate goal of doing the same for the human brain. The amount of computing power, together with the sheer size of the multidisciplinary team needed to grasp just a rudimentary understanding of these neural networks, attests to the sophistication and complexity of this system.

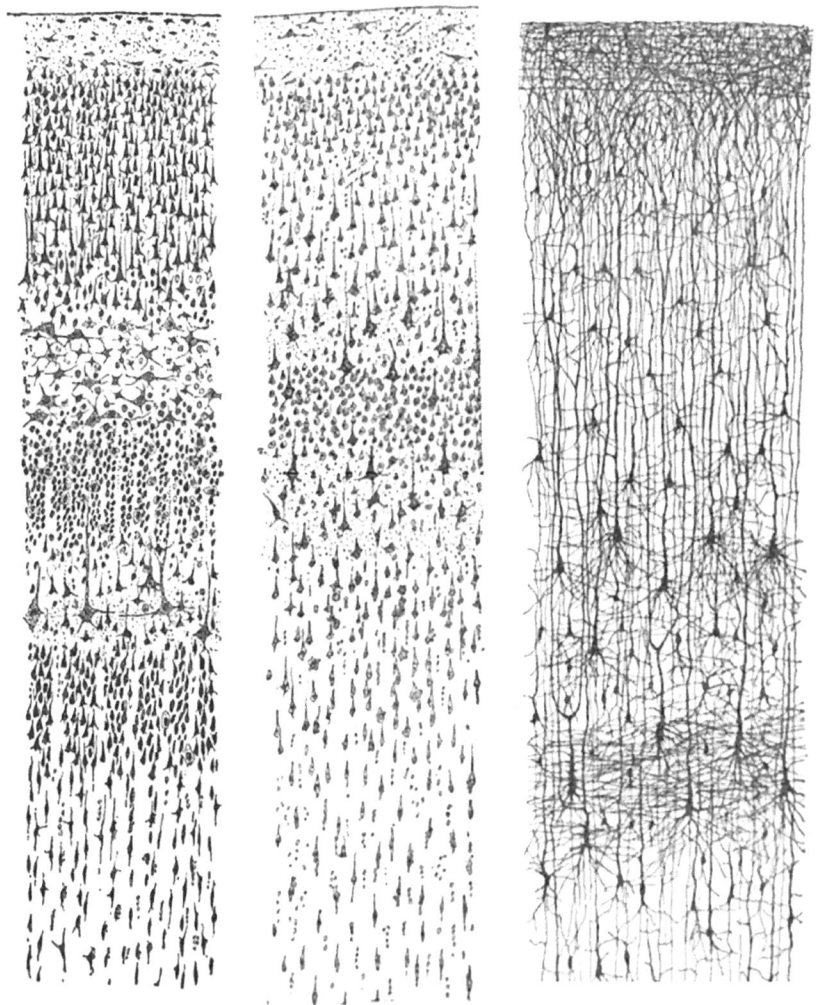

Above: Cortical lamination by Santiago Ramon y Cajal, each showing a vertical cross-section, with the surface of the cortex at the top. Left: Nissl-stained visual cortex of a human adult. Middle: Nissl-stained motor cortex of a human adult. Right: Golgi-stained cortex of a 1½-month-old infant. The Nissl stain shows the cell bodies of neurons; the Golgi stain shows the dendrites and axons of a random subset of neurons.

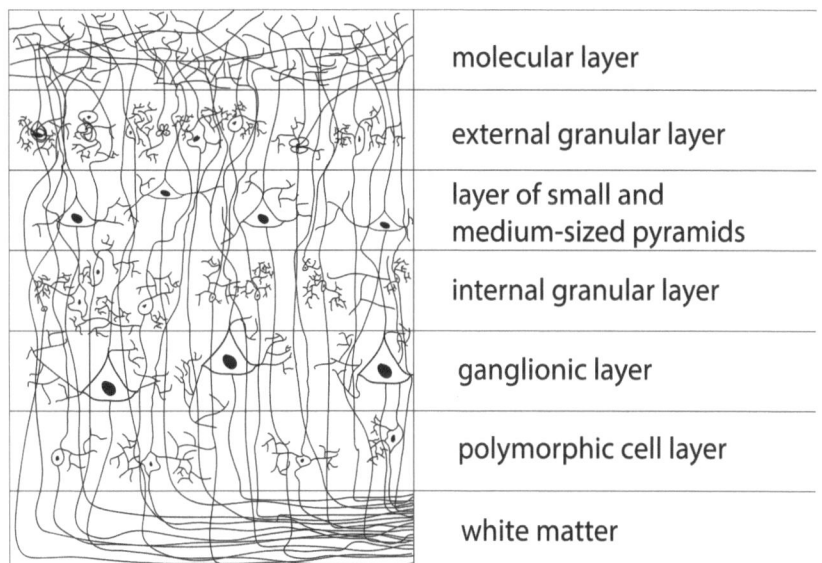

molecular layer

external granular layer

layer of small and medium-sized pyramids

internal granular layer

ganglionic layer

polymorphic cell layer

white matter

A representative column of the neocortex with layers labeled.

MAJOR DIVISIONS

The neocortex has traditionally been divided in different ways to highlight various functional and structural areas. Here we will cover the broad strokes of functional areas, namely the occipital lobe, parietal lobes, temporal lobes, and the frontal lobes. But in any survey of the cortex, it is important to first acknowledge a widely used cortical map deriving from the work of German anatomist Korbinian Brodmann. Brodmann based his division of the cortex on the cytoarchitectural organization of the neurons, or the observation of how layers of neutrons look under a microscope after staining. Different areas of the cortex show specific patterns of cytoarchitecture, and thus a discrimination is made between different areas. Brodmann divided the cortex into 51 different areas and numbered them. Areas 1, 2, and 3 represent the primary somatosensory cortex, for example, while Area 10 is the anterior prefrontal cortex. Many texts and studies have used Brodmann's numbers to identify different areas of the cortex under discussion.

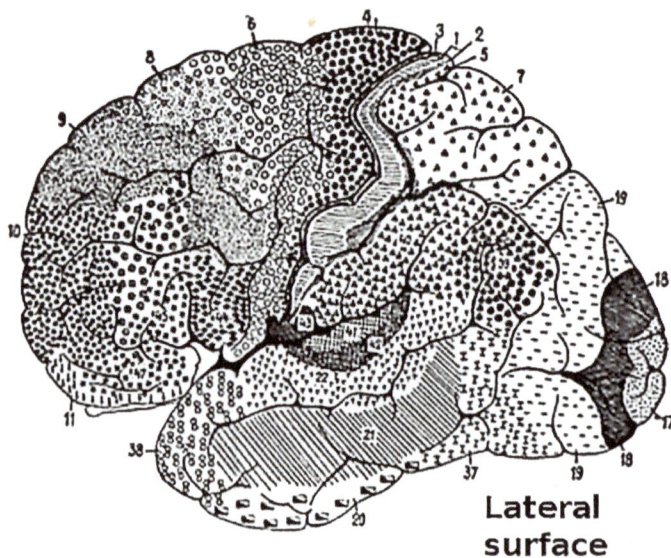

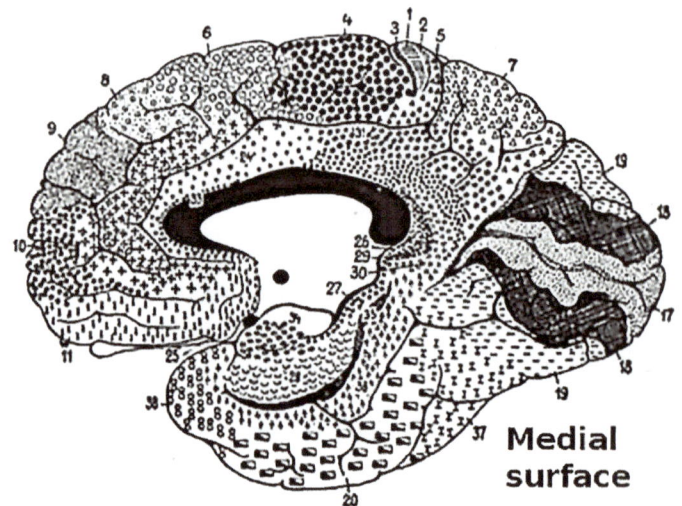

Lateral surface

Medial surface

Above: Regions of the human cerebral cortex delineated by Korvinian Brodman on the basis of cytoarchitecture. This image scanned and modified from the book *Anatomy of the Nervous System* by Stephen Walter Ranson & W. B. Saunders, 1920, p. 288.

Below: A 3D representation of Brodmann's areas by Mark Dow, research assistant at the Brain Development Lab at the University of Oregon.

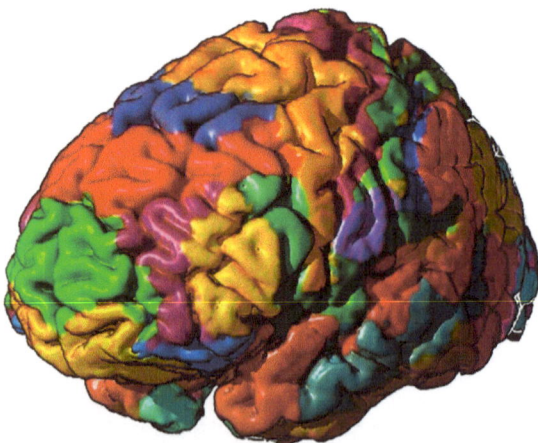

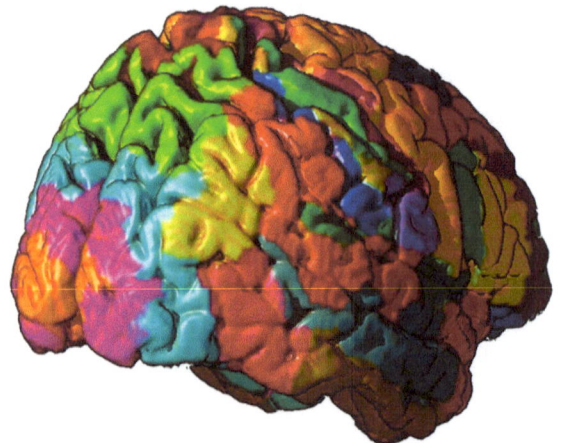

Occipital lobe

Across the back of the brain is an area of the cerebrum—the occipital lobe—that is dedicated to processing visual information into meaningful chunks of perceptional material. The region is divided into a number of subregions, known as the primary visual cortex, the ventral stream, and the dorsal stream. The primary visual cortex processes low-level descriptions of orientation, spatial frequency and colour properties, whereas the ventral stream, sometimes called the "what" pathway, provides important information for the identification of stimuli, and the dorsal stream, sometimes called the "where" or "how" pathway, helps guide movement in response to outside stimuli.

It is worth noting that in borderline personality disorder there may be a deficit in the operation of the occipital lobe, leading to difficulties evaluating emotional facial expressions as well as other difficulties in processing visual information, which could lead to body dysmorphic disorder.

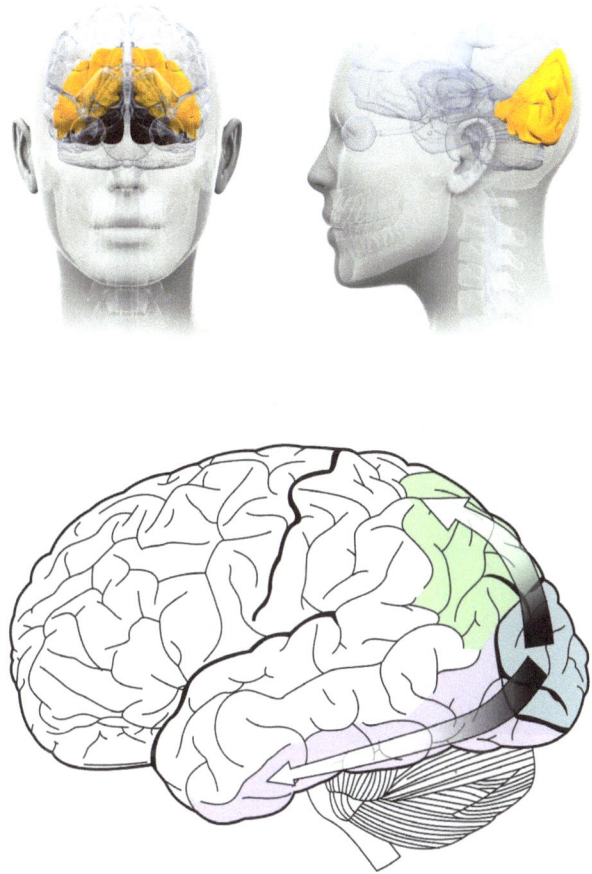

Image above showing dorsal stream (green) and ventral stream (purple) in the human brain visual system. (https://commons.wikimedia.org/wiki/File:Ventral-dorsal_streams.svg)

Parietal lobes

The parietal lobes play a major role in sensory processing and integrating information such as spatial/navigational sense, touch, and language, and the dorsal stream of the visual system. These lobes help us to become oriented and to establish an understanding of where we are in space. They also have a role in helping us understand speech and comprehending other sensory input.

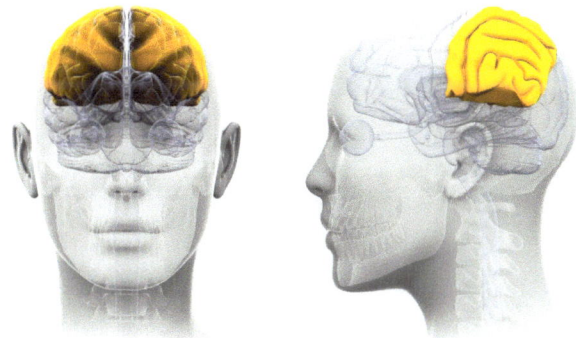

Temporal lobes

Processing and integrating information about smells and sounds (such as recognising the sounds of one's language), and how these relate to our memory and emotions, is the domain of the temporal lobes. Closely associated with the hippocampus, the temporal lobes play a part in the formation of explicit long-term memory. The primary auditory cortex is situated within the left temporal lobe and processes the semantics of speech and vision: speech comprehension, naming, and verbal memory.

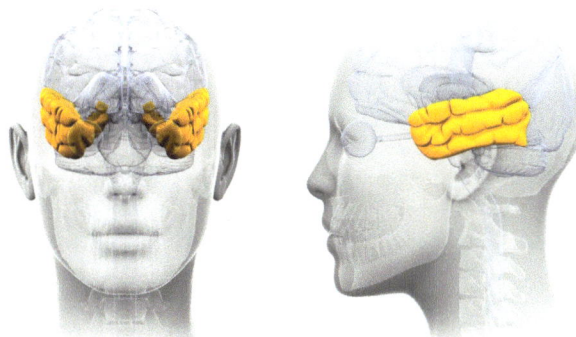

Frontal lobes

The frontal lobes are probably of most interest to teachers because they are home to the PFC, an area vitally involved in executive functions such as concentration, organization, judgement, reasoning, decision-making, creativity, emotional regulation, social–relational abilities, and abstract thinking—in other words, all the functionality we rely on for healthy relationships with ourselves and others. The frontal lobes in general regulate voluntary movement, the retention of non-task-based memories that are often associated with emotions, dopamine-driven attention, reward motivations, and planning, to name just a few.

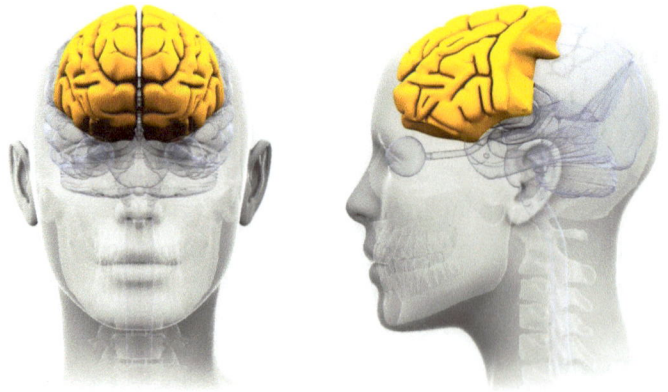

The Prefrontal Cortex

The PFC is the part of the cerebrum that lies directly behind the eyes and the forehead. More than any other part of the brain, this area dictates our personality, our goals, and our values. When we have a long-term goal, for example, which we are pursuing with value-congruent action, we maintain a neural representation of that goal so as to not be distracted or influenced by competing goals or alternate values (Grawe, 2007). If the PFC is damaged, it affects our personalities and the ability to orient our behaviour in line with our values and goals. The PFC is vital to the sense of self and others necessary for healthy interpersonal relationships and decision making.

As in the case of so many discoveries in neuroscience, we often learn what a brain area can do when it becomes damaged in some way. Phineas Gage was a young, reflective, determined, and goal-oriented man who, despite his youth, had been promoted to foreman on an American railroad construction project. But in an unfortunate accident on September 13, 1848, an explosion drove a tamping rod up through the left side of his face and out the top of his head. The rod passed through and destroyed much of his left PFC. Amazingly, Gage survived, and was even speaking within minutes of the accident. He was still conscious and talking to a physician about half an hour later, having introduced himself saying, "Doctor, here is business enough for you." Following his recovery, an early observation of a change in Gage's personality was noted by Dr. John Harlow:

The equilibrium or balance, so to speak, between his intellectual faculties and animal propensities, seems to have been destroyed. He is fitful, irreverent, indulging at times in the grossest profanity

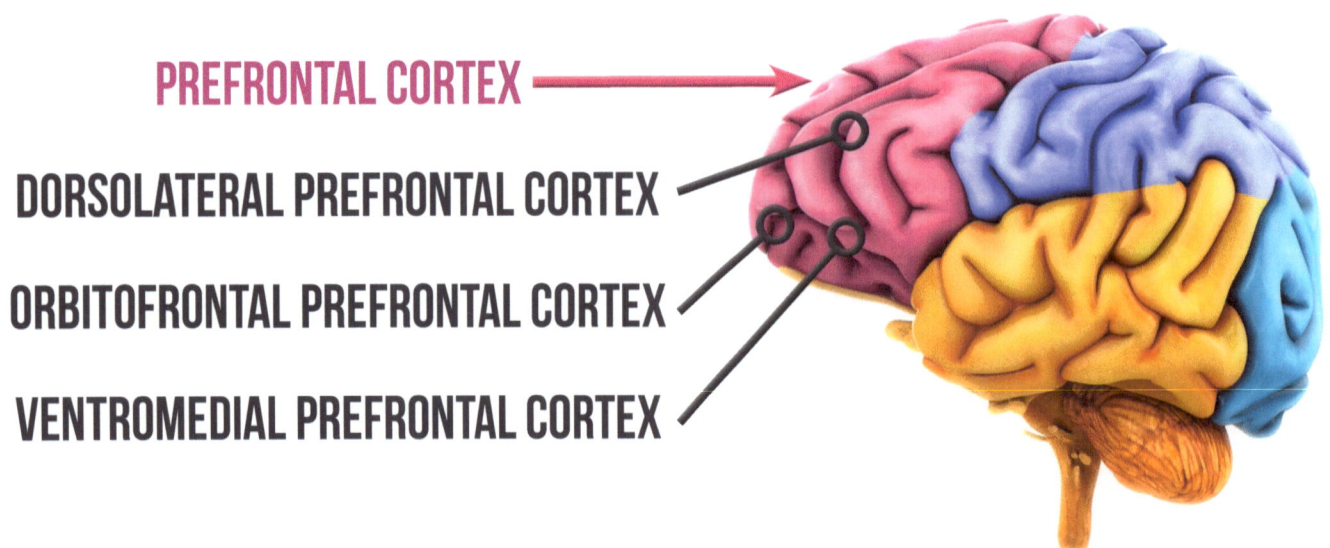

PREFRONTAL CORTEX →

DORSOLATERAL PREFRONTAL CORTEX

ORBITOFRONTAL PREFRONTAL CORTEX

VENTROMEDIAL PREFRONTAL CORTEX

(which was not previously his custom), manifesting but little deference for his fellows, impatient of restraint or advice when it conflicts with his desires, at times pertinaciously obstinate, yet capricious and vacillating, devising many plans of future operations, which are no sooner arranged than they are abandoned in turn for others appearing more feasible. A child in his intellectual capacity and manifestations, he has the animal passions of a strong man. Previous to his injury, although untrained in the schools, he possessed a well-balanced mind, and was looked upon by those who knew him as a shrewd, smart business man, very energetic and persistent in executing all his plans of operation. In this regard his mind was radically changed, so decidedly that his friends and acquaintances said he was "no longer Gage". (Harlow, 1869, pp. 13-14)

Clearly, some important functions of Gage's personality had been altered by his injuries, although he did become more functional and socially adaptable as the years went on. Given a structured environment in which clear sequencing of tasks was part of the rehabilitation, Gage managed to retrain his brain to regulate itself in reference to values and goals.

The left and right sides of the PFC have different biases, with the left side oriented more toward approach, positive goals, and emotions, and the right side specialized more in avoidance and negative emotions. It is also worth noting that the left side of the PFC hosts more dopamine receptors/activity (associated with motivation and reward), while the right has greater norepinephrine activity (associated with anxiety). Individuals who appear to have a bias toward positive emotions may have a more activated left PFC, whereas right PFC activation is correlated with more negative emotional experiences. Any suggestion of a clear binary division is an oversimplification, as the experience of positive or negative emotions does not hinge purely on left/right PFC activation, but there is nonetheless evidence of a strong correlation. In studies of the neural correlates of depression, it has been found that left PFC activity is underactive relative to right PFC activity. It seems that less access to the positive bias of the left PFC may make it more difficult for the depressed individual to engage in positive goal-oriented thought and behaviour. Similarly, the left PFC is more responsive to rewards than the right PFC, which is more responsive to punishment.

Studies have found that the depressed individual is generally more sensitive to what may be perceived as punishment and does not respond as well to rewards. Moreover, the relative underactivation of the whole PFC in depressed individuals could account for them having less motivation for planning, problem solving, creativity, and so forth. In depression, not only is there underactivation of the PFC, but its volume has been found to be reduced as well. A depressed person with an underactive PFC of reduced volume is not going to demonstrate the rational problem solving abilities of someone without such deficits—the neural integrity to support such resilience is simply not there. This is of particular relevance to teachers who find themselves frustrated at seemingly lazy, unmotivated and perhaps negative students who don't appear to have goals or are enthusiastic about learning. This frustration can frequently lead teachers to employ threat and punishment strategies, in an effort to motivate the negatively biased student, or to entice, and somehow 'push' the student to work harder. However, this approach merely arouses the limbic system of the child and increases anxiety and effectively inhibits any cognitive thinking.

It is in the awareness of the left and right PFC re-

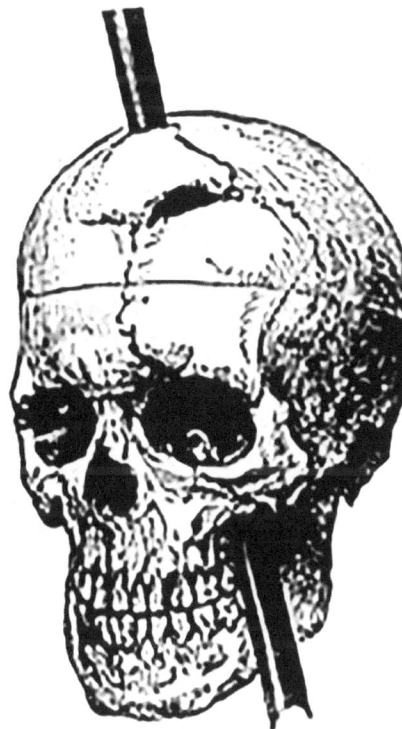

1868 diagram of Phineas Gage's skull and the damaged caused by the tamping rod – by John M. Harlow

ceptors and how they affect mood that a teacher can have empathetic understanding of the students who struggle with depressive tendencies and lack of motivation. Right-brain to right-brain engagement between a teacher and student promotes relationship and safe connection, which of itself, opens neural pathways of engagement and prompts students into thinking and learning.

Dorsolateral prefrontal cortex (DLPFC). The DLPFC is the topmost part of the PFC and is considered to have overall management of cognitive processes such as planning, cognitive flexibility, and working memory. This is an area specialising in problem solving and how to direct and maintain attention to a task. When we are focused on what is happening now, our working memory is engaged with the DLPFC and connecting with the hippocampus for the retrieval and consolidation of long-term explicit memories. A dysfunction in this area may lead to problems with working memory, processing in the hippocampus, and long-term memory, as well as the integration of verbal expression with emotions. Such memory deficits have been associated with PTSD due to an underactive left DLPFC.

Other DLPFC deficits can manifest as a lack of spontaneity and affect (flat rather than negative), and attention deficit—due to an inability to maintain sufficient attention to see a task through to completion. In obsessive–compulsive disorder (which we will consider separately in a later section the DLPFC plays an important role in strengthening attentional skills to momentarily break the compulsion circuit and give the orbitofrontal cortex a chance to inhibit the runaway activation of the amygdala. As with many brain regions, there are significant hemispherical differences within the dorsolateral prefrontal cortex, the left DLPFC being associated with approach behaviours and the right with more avoidant behaviours.

Orbitofrontal cortex (OFC). The OFC, like the DLPFC, is involved in the cognitive processing of decision making; however, because of its close connection with the limbic system, it is particularly associated with our ability to make decisions based on emotional information. The OFC also plays a major role in forming social attachments and regulating emotions. This region can be thought of as a convergence zone for sensory and emo-

Ventromedial prefrontal cortex

The ventromedial prefrontal cortex helps us make decisions based on the bigger picture gathered from connections to the amygdala, temporal lobe, ventral segmental area, olfactory system, and the thalamus.

tional information, effectively integrating external and internal worlds. Social information is processed and used to guide us in our perceptions and interactions, and the OFC plays an important role in the interpretation of these complex social interactions, including, for example, the ability to understand a joke. The OFC may help us predict the reactions of others and modulate our behaviour accordingly. When there is a dysfunction in the orbitofrontal cortex, the normal cortical–subcortical modulation is not optimal—as is likely the case in borderline personality disorder (Schore, 2012). As with other areas of the PFC, the OFC has hemispherical differences. The left OFC is associated with positive emotions, while the right OFC is associated with more negative emotions.

Ventromedial prefrontal cortex (vmPFC). This part of the PFC helps us make decisions based on the bigger picture gathered from connections to the amygdala, temporal lobe, ventral segmental area, olfactory system, and the thalamus. It is very well connected, receiving and sending a lot of information that influences many brain regions, including the amygdala. The vmPFC plays an important role with the OFC in regulating our emotions, especially in social situations. It is also vital for personal and social decision making and the ability to learn from our mistakes. Our capacity to make judgements and allow our emotions to assist in decision making is mediated by this region of the brain. Activation of the vmPFC is also associated with courage, suppression of negative emotions, compassion, shame, and guilt.

THE NEUROCHEMISTRY OF STRESS

In 1914, the physiologist Walter Cannon named the sympathetic response to a threat the "fight or flight" response. As we have observed, the chemical response to this fight-or-flight response is known as the hypothalamic–pituitary–adrenal (HPA) axis response.

When we perceive a threat, the corticotropin-releasing hormone (CRH) is released from the hypothalamus together with beta endorphins. CRH is produced in the paraventricular nucleus (PVN) of the hypothalamus, and this triggers the release of adrenocorticotropin hormone (ACTH) in the pituitary gland. Interestingly, CRH will also inhibit the secretion of reproductive hormones and subsequent reproductive functions. The beta-endorphin release from the hypothalamus plays a role in pain reduction and stimulates the release of epinephrine from the adrenal medulla. Vasopressin is also released from the PVN, and this plays a role in regulating blood pressure and facilitates the release of ACTH.

ACTH flows from the pituitary gland into the bloodstream and releases the hormone cortisol from the adrenal cortex. (The adrenal glands sit above each kidney.) Levels of glucocorticoids like cortisol are closely monitored at each step of the HPA axis as a feedback mechanism to regulate the stress response. Cortisol increases blood-sugar levels, suppresses the immune system, and increases metabolism. Because high levels of cortisol suppress the immune system—the assumption being that the suppression helps to protect against an overactivation of the immune system and minimize inflammatory tissue damage—it has been observed that high levels of cortisol will lengthen wound healing time. As in the monitoring of glucocorticoids to modulate the HPA-axis response, there is also a feedback loop involving the immune system in which certain cytokines can activate the HPA axis.

When the HPA axis is set in motion by a perceived threat, or an exaggerated fear of something that is not an actual, physical threat, the physiological response can be taxing and potentially damaging to the body. Chronically raised glucocorticoid levels not only increase blood-sugar levels and suppress the immune system but also inhibit learning, because new neural connections in the hippocampus are damaged, and even previously established memory retrieval is inhibited.

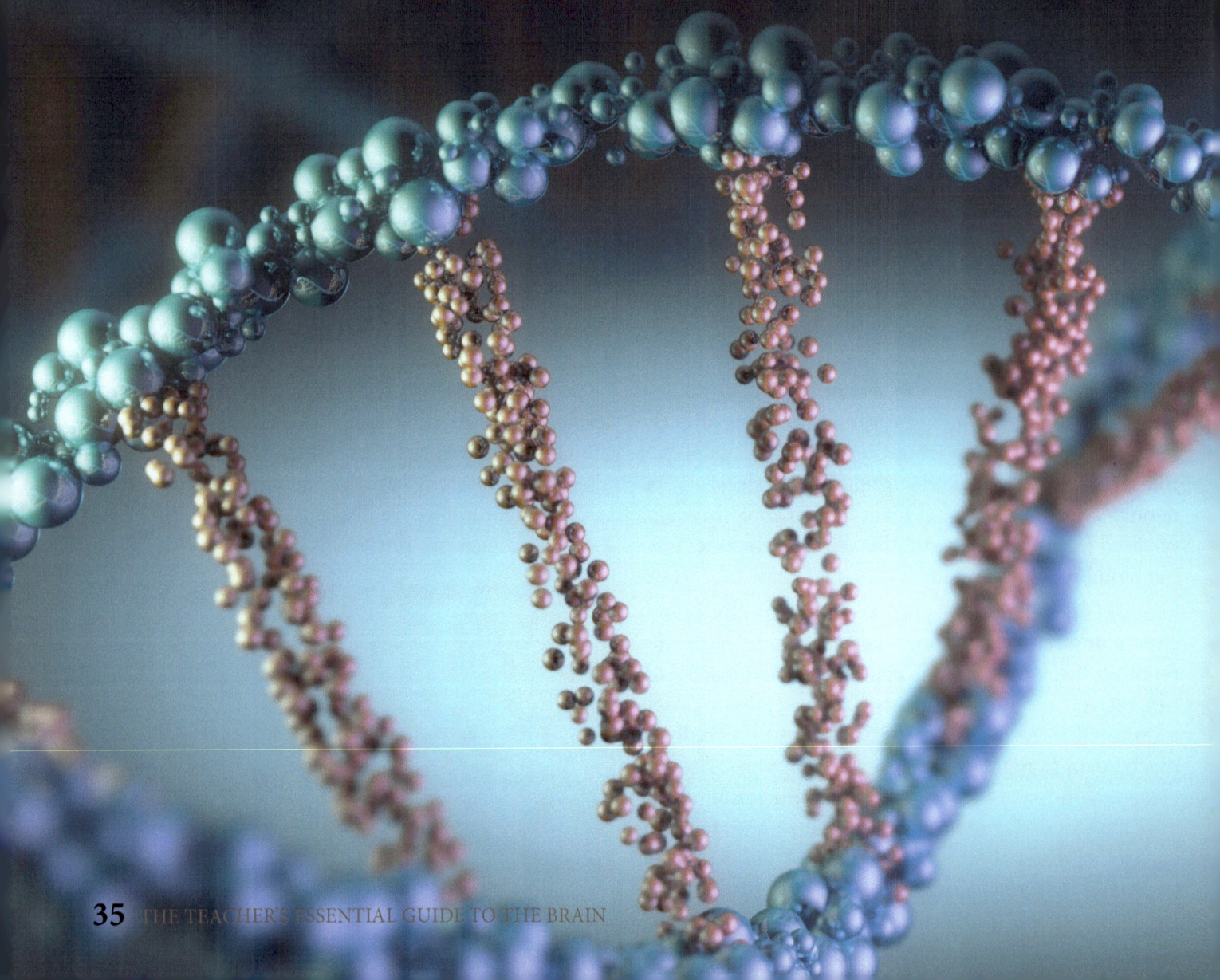

EPIGENETICS

The mature brain was once thought immutable, until evidence began to accumulate that it was, in fact, somewhat malleable. Now the remarkable plasticity of the brain is common knowledge. Similarly we have undergone a paradigm shift in our thinking about DNA. We now know that DNA is not fixed—in fact it is also quite malleable, and genes are as capable of modification as the brain. Both the brain and our genetic make-up have a level of plasticity that allows wiring pathways and gene expression to change with experience over time. This is illustrated by the case of genetically identical twins, who have obvious DNA-driven similarities, yet also differences that develop in response to personal experience (Kaminsky et al., 2009).

DNA, the molecule that acts as long-term storage for our genetic information, is also capable of regulating its own use. Most of our DNA is in fact not dedicated to the primary role of protein production. This non-protein-coding DNA was believed for years to be relatively useless, even acquiring the moniker "junk DNA". We are only now discovering that junk DNA performs a number of important functions, and that RNA strands (ribonucleic acid transcribed from certain non-coding DNA) act to regulate, stimulate, and disrupt the activity of protein production. Much of this is an epigenetic response: in other words, it is dependent on the nature of the individual's experience in the context of particular environmental conditions. This discovery represents an enormous breakthrough in our understanding of our malleable biology.

Epigenetics (literally "above the genes"), also known as behavioural epigenetics, is the study of how environmental factors influence gene expression both within and through heritable changes in DNA. The environment can "mark" genes, dramatically or subtly, changing levels of expression either transiently or for a lifetime—even to subsequent generations (Peckham, 2013). It is the mechanism by which genes adapt to the environment, shaping gene expression to best adapt to whatever circumstances confront us.

When the environment prompts heritable changes in gene expression, no changes are made to the underlying DNA sequence (Levenson & Sweatt, 2005). In any strand of DNA, only a well-defined portion of the genetic possibilities within the DNA are expressed, and the rest are permanently, semi-permanently, or temporarily turned off. To use the language of geneticists, the universal DNA genotype is epigenetically changed to a cell-specific phenotype. The detail of epigenetic ac-

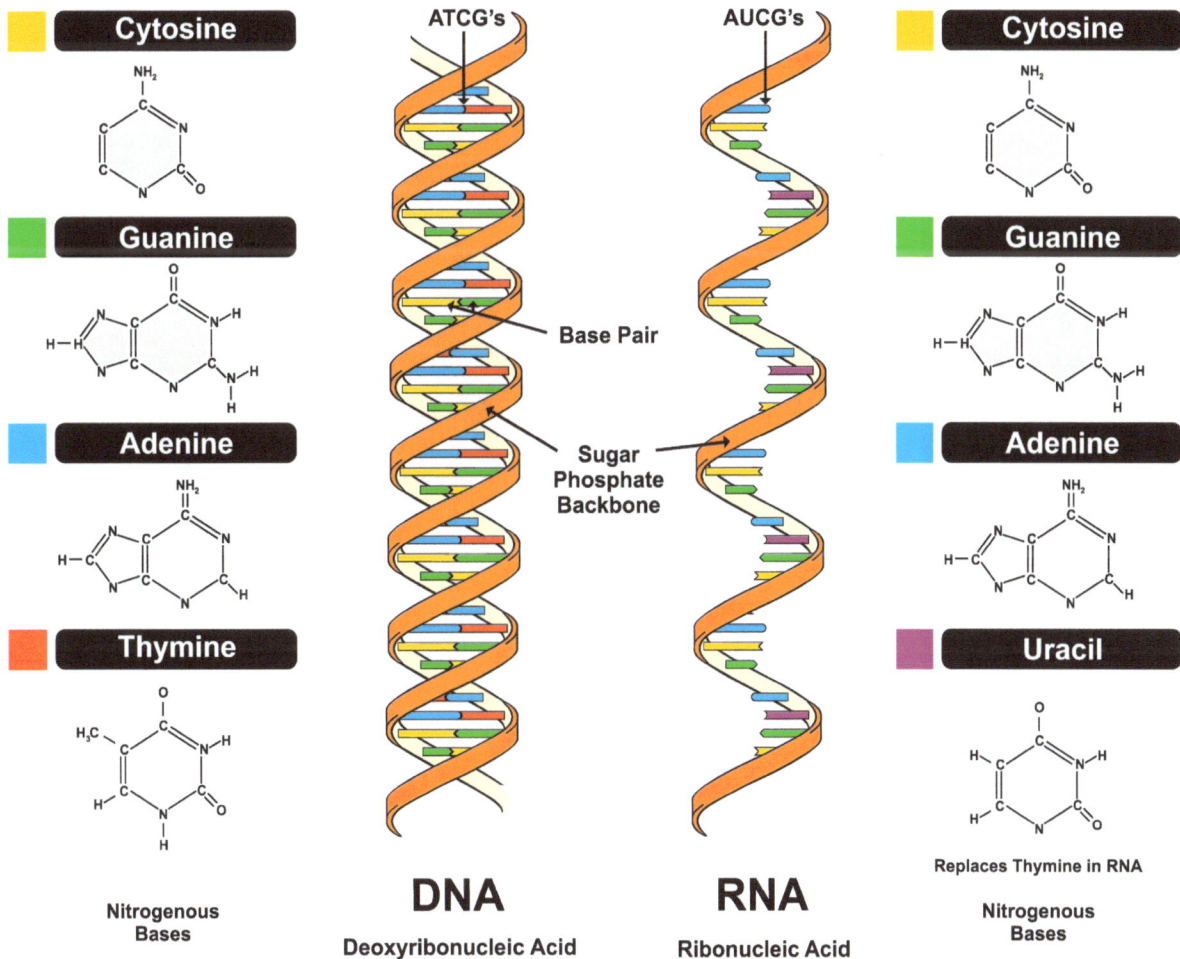

Cytosine

Guanine

Adenine

Thymine

Nitrogenous Bases

DNA
Deoxyribonucleic Acid

ATCG's

Base Pair

Sugar Phosphate Backbone

AUCG's

RNA
Ribonucleic Acid

Cytosine

Guanine

Adenine

Uracil

Replaces Thymine in RNA

Nitrogenous Bases

tion is complex, but the principle is quite straightforward. By adding or subtracting chemicals, it is possible to "silence" a gene and thus make it impossible for that gene to be expressed in that cell or in any of its daughter cells. This is not exactly the same process we refer to as "turning genes on and off", which is more about utilizing genes that are readily available in accordance with particular needs at the time. Genes that are epigenetically silenced are taken completely out of the picture (Hill, 2013).

One way that a gene is silenced is when chemical alterations are made to tiny chemical tails that emerge from each of the eight histones (proteins that act as spools around which DNA winds and becomes compact). Addition or subtraction of these chemicals allows or disallows transcription factors to attach to the promoter region (the part of the DNA that starts the transcription of a particular gene). The process that has received the most attention is acetylation: when a histone tail is acetylated, the difference in ionic (electrochemical) charge between the histone and the section of DNA wrapped around it is neutralized (the larger the difference in charge between objects, the stronger the electromagnetic attraction). The effect of acetylation in neutralizing this difference is that the DNA is looser and therefore accessible to transcription factors. When the histone tail is de-acetylated, the difference in charge increases, causing the DNA to wrap tightly around the histone so that it is impossible for transcription to occur (Grunstein, 1997; for a general discussion of DNA methylation and histone modification, see Peckham, 2013).

Another, entirely different silencing mechanism is a change added to the DNA code itself. In particular

positions, usually near the promoter region in the gene (at what is described as CpG nucleotides), the cytosine "letter" of the DNA code is methylated, which blocks the transcription factor from binding to the promoter region and, again, stops gene expression (Comb & Goodman, 1990). The crucial point here is that, through a series of intricate and elegant processes that evoke images of a symphony, the information in our genes is constantly being brought into activity or silenced.

Studies of rats and their maternal behaviour have demonstrated that the quality of maternal care of rat pups in the first weeks of life influences the patterns of gene expression that affect social engagement and self-defence (Kauffman & Meaney, 2007). The pups that received enriched stimulation from their mothers showed different patterns of gene expression in their hippocampus, prefrontal cortex, and amygdala from the pups who did not get as much maternal care. Subsequently, the well-cared-for rats demonstrated better social skills and were more approach-oriented in their environment and less fearful (Baylin, 2013). One of the most notable differences observed in the well-cared-for rat pups was the development of a robust stress-response system. The reason for this is that the hippocampus has corticosterone stress-hormone receptors that help turn off this system after a stressful experience. These receptors were more highly expressed in the well-cared-for rats, who were able to down-regulate the stress response faster than their not-so-well-cared-for peers. The nurturing contributed to less self-defensiveness in these individuals and more exploration and social connectedness.

The research with rats has since been extended to primates and humans, to investigate the extent of gene expression as a result of environmental factors, especial-

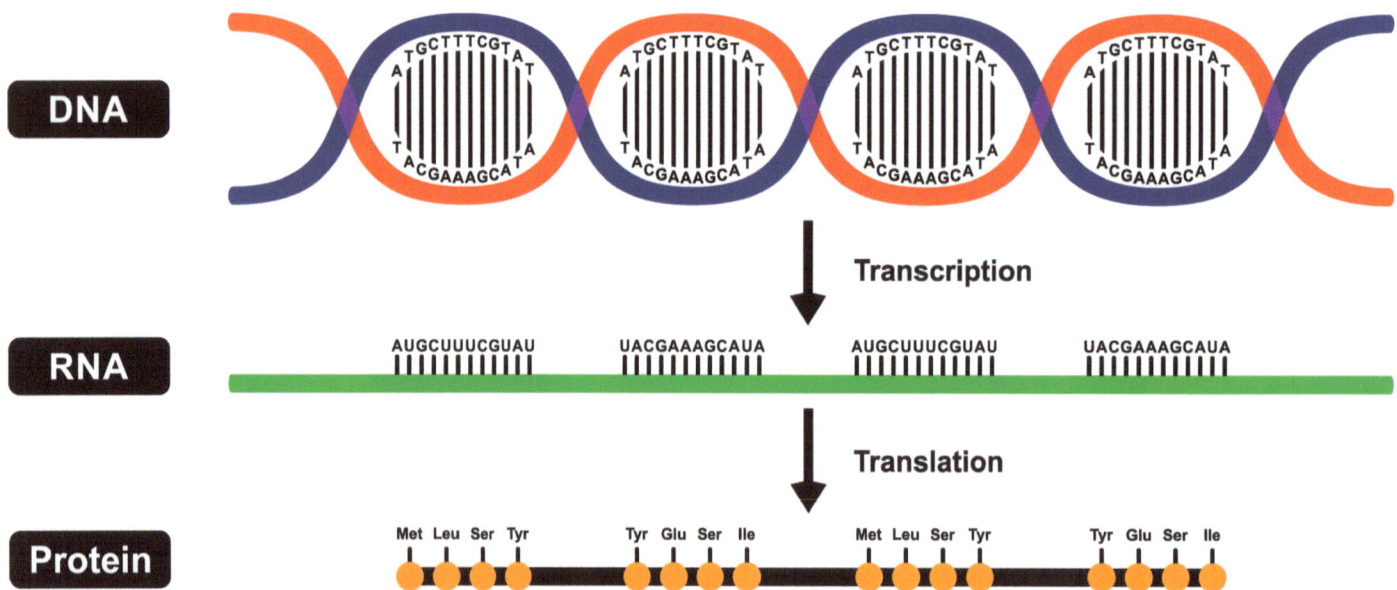

ly attachment factors. Interestingly, the human studies on levels of care and epigenetic effects show a striking parallel to the rodent studies, suggesting that all sorts of early childhood experiences (and even pre-birth and birth factors such as Caesarean section) heighten the DNA methylation that negatively affects neurons and brain plasticity. Peckham (2013) says of these studies:

> It is tempting to speculate that perhaps lower levels of care restrict the variety of genes that can be expressed, whereas higher levels of care are the epigenetic gateway to our available genome. We speak of wanting to give our children "every opportunity", but the reality of what epigenetic opportunities are available to our children could largely depend on the care we give them very early in life. Access to the widest potential of their genome could be profoundly influenced by their experience of our care, and if the genes that are accessed by enhanced care perform plasticity-related functions, the effect of that care is compounded for good or ill. Poor care may mean that fewer plasticity-related genes are expressed, thus restricting a child's (and the adult's) potential to learn, remember, or adapt within their environment, manifesting in less flexibility and perhaps more stereotyped or rigid responses. (p. 15)

Research suggests that early life experiences with attachment figures activate different patterns of gene expression—but that experience-dependent gene expression is not limited to these early experiences and continues throughout life (Baylin, 2013). These findings have significant implications for teachers. The adaptive role of epigenetic mechanisms is to ensure the young are well equipped to survive in the particular environments in which they find themselves. A safe and enriched environment, therefore, will help shape a healthy nervous system that connects with people, is approach-orientated, and is able to down-regulate fear responses quickly. In contrast, an unsafe and harsh environment will produce a nervous system that is epigenetically geared toward self-defence, avoidance, and an easily activated and prolonged stress response. The unfortunate outcome of this programming is a compromised system of self-regulation (in terms of the control mechanisms from the prefrontal cortex to the limbic system and a stress-response feedback mechanism to down-regulate an overly sensitive amygdala, to name just two), which can lead to a life of low self-esteem, avoidance, anxiety, and depression.

But are we to remain victims of our early childhood experiences forever, genetically speaking? Fortunately the answer is no. Just as we are learning that early experience shapes the development of neural networks, we are now learning that the early years are the most critical for the epigenetic shaping of our brains; but similarly, just as the plasticity of neural networks opens them to transformation via new experiences and memory reconsolidation, so we are discovering that our genetic expressions are open to change in response to perceived changes in our environment. Furthermore, not only are epigenetic processes associated with social and emotional factors, they are also associated with exercise, sleep/wake cycles, mindfulness practices, and diet. The enriched environment of safety, social connectedness, and sensory/motor/cognitive stimulation can have a mitigating effect on the negative epigenetic processes of the early years.

> Environmental enrichment is a powerful tool to effect epigenomic changes, which subsequently affect the levels of BDNF and modulate HPA axis activity, which, in turn, builds resilience to, or delays the onset of, various psychiatric or neurodegenerative disorders. (Peckham 2013, p. 17)

This has huge implications for educators. A teacher who develops positive, safe and caring relationships with their students, and provides a classroom environment of enrichment and nurture has the ability to mitigate negative epigenetic processes a child may have encountered in their early childhood years. Trajectories can be redirected and protective factors put in place to build resilience against possible psychiatric or neurodegenerative disorders. As the saying goes, "Every kid is one caring adult away from being a success story." (Shipp, 2018)

Brain plasticity has revolutionized our thinking about the capacity to make positive changes in our lives. Epigenetics is one way the body "writes down" and memorizes ongoing life experience in a way that helps us adapt to our experiences. Ultimately, what we do, when we do it, and how we feel about it while we are doing it all contribute to the way experience assembles and shapes the building materials in our DNA to construct the person that we see both in the bathroom mirror and in the mirror of our friends and loved ones. But what in childhood served as adaptive programming may no longer be appropriate to our needs and environment in adulthood, and so we can and should change. It is exciting to know that we have the capacity to change our neural networks, our emotional memory, and our mental schemas. And with a little help, we can even change the expression of our genes to better adapt to our current circumstances.

MOTIVATION

In 1988, French neurologist Michel Habib and colleague Michel Poncet became intrigued by stories of people who would, all of a sudden, lose their motivation and interest in life. For example, a 64-year-old retired police officer had suddenly become apathetic, inactive and prostrate. He was admitted to the neurology ward a few weeks after the onset of behavioural changes and was assessed as having some muscle rigidity with decreased spontaneous movements, facial amimia, and a Parkinson's-like gait. His CT scan seemed normal for a patient of his age, but he displayed a dramatic decrease in spontaneous activity: he was unable to make plans and seemed to have no will or identifiable desires—not even a desire to eat or a preference for any particular foods. Moreover, when asked what was going on in his mind, there appeared to be no spontaneous mental activity, yet he was fully conscious and orientated. When questioned about his mood, he said he wasn't sad, depressed, or anxious.

Another very similar case involved a 60-year-old university professor, highly respected in his field, who also displayed a dramatic decrease in activity and motivation, according to family and peers. His neurological exam identified a moderate slowing of movements and poor spontaneous verbal expression. For someone who had been a highly active professional, he was surprisingly unconcerned by his sudden loss of motivation. His relatives described him as having been energetic, motivated, and highly invested in both his work and leisure activities, such as gardening, reading, and fine cuisine. Something dramatic had happened to this man. The radical change in his motivation and demeanour persisted and was observed again at a 7-year follow-up. He described his condition in these words:

I just lack spirit, energy . . . I have no go. I must force myself to get up in the morning; I do things just because I ought to, without any liking or enthusiasm. I have no appetite or need for eating; I only eat by principle.

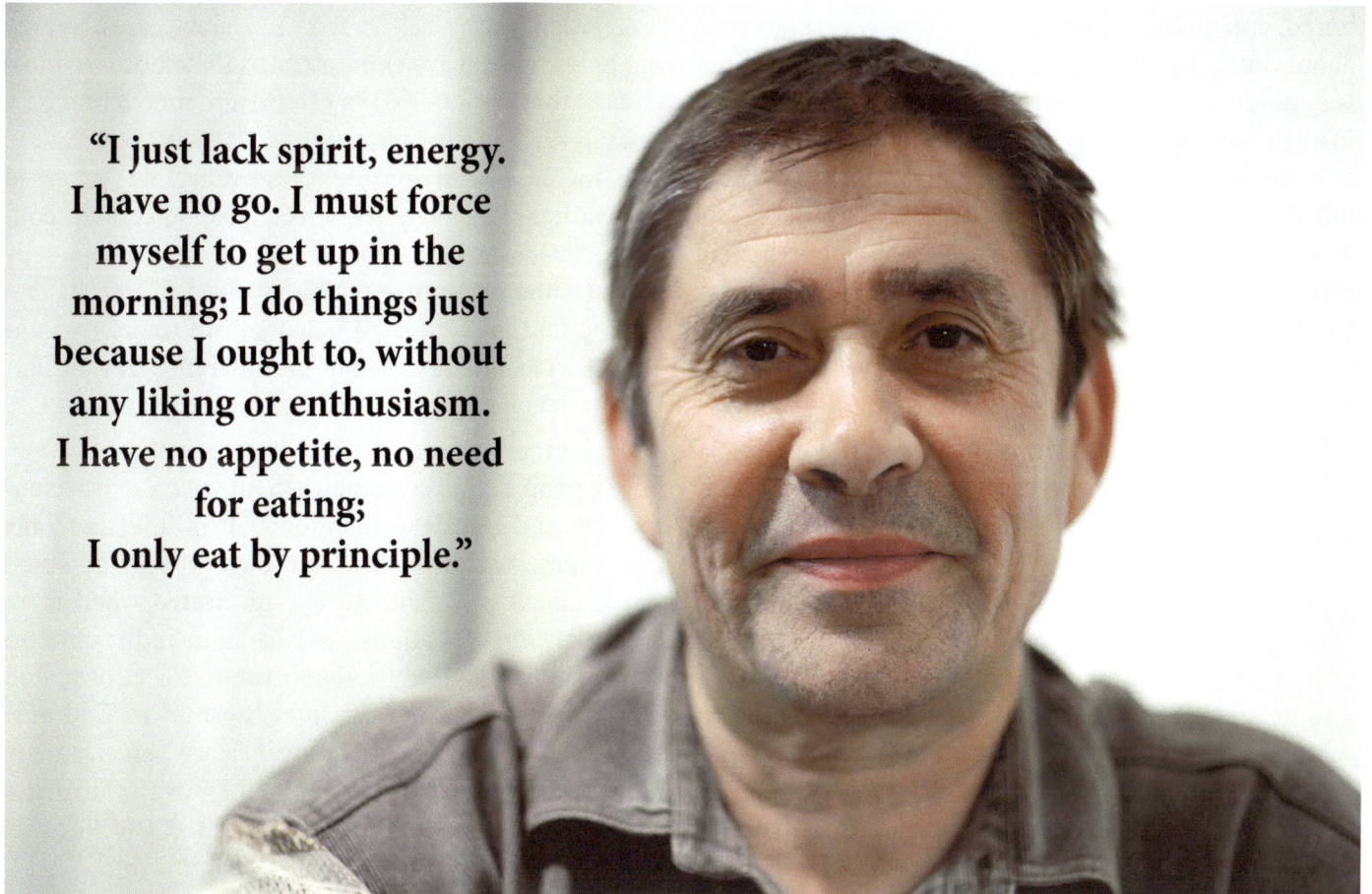

"I just lack spirit, energy. I have no go. I must force myself to get up in the morning; I do things just because I ought to, without any liking or enthusiasm. I have no appetite, no need for eating; I only eat by principle."

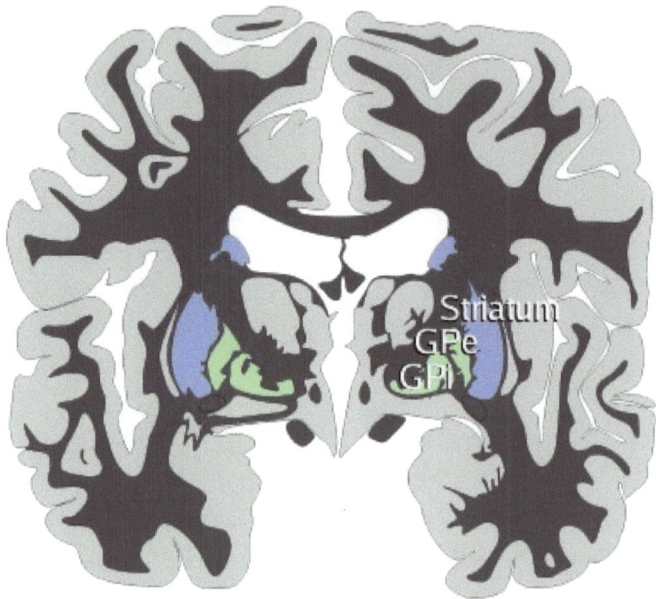

Coronal slices of human brain showing the striatum, and globus pallidus (GPe and GPi). White matter is shown in dark grey, grey matter is shown in light grey. Image Andrew Gillies, Wikimedia Commons

He could carry out some professional tasks, but as a routine only, not because he had any motivation to do them. He would not initiate conversations; he was never bored, anxious, or depressed; and he never complained about anything. He still attended board meetings but was never the first to speak. He seemed to be shut up inside a profound passivity, unaware and unconcerned. When asked a question he would answer appropriately, but when asked about what he was thinking or if he had anything to say, he would typically respond with, "I'm just thinking of nothing . . . no idea, no question, no thought at all."

These and other similar cases, Habib would find, had in common injuries to regions of the basal ganglia: damage to either the striatum, by way of tiny pinpricks of burst vessels restricted to the caudate nuclei, or the globus pallidus. After consideration of these cases and the neurological evidence, Habib went on to formulate a model of a cortical–subcortical loop involved in converting motivational processes into behaviour (Habib, 2004). He showed how the limbic (or ventral) striato-pallidal circuit he described received emotional information from the amygdala and hippocampus and projected that information to the rest of the basal ganglia involved in initiating and organizing motor acts (Habib, 2004).

Researcher Mauricio Delgado, who has studied the neural substrates recruited during decision-making, found that activity in the caudate nucleus increases when we have a choice. And having a choice, as Klaus Grawe identified in his consistency model (Grawe, 2007), equates to a sense of greater control. We could say that choice is the vehicle for exercising control (Leotti, Iyengar, Ochsner, 2010). Having a choice, then, is fundamentally motivating. In one study, Delgado and co-author Lauren Leotti stated that even "the anticipation of choice itself was associated with increased activity in corticostriatal regions, particularly the ventral striatum, involved in affective and motivational processes" (Leotti & Delgado, 2011, p. 1310). Having a choice is preferable even if making a certain choice makes no real difference to the outcome—we simply prefer to have a sense of control. In an earlier study conducted with residents of a nursing home, Langer and Rodin (1976) found that the opportunity to exercise choice influenced subsequent mood, quality of life, and longevity.

Our well-being depends on our belief that we have some control over our day-to-day environment. Indeed, Leotti and colleagues would argue that it is a biological imperative (Leotti, Iyengar, & Ochsner, 2010). The neural substrate for this need for control is the corticostriatal network—the same network that was implicated in motivation (or the lack thereof) in Habib's cases. Neuroimaging studies have demonstrated that choice recruits circuits that are involved in reward and motivation processing, which in turn increases activity in the striatum. This increased activity might also reflect an increased motivational incentive when there is choice. As Leotti and colleagues suggested, "If free choice preferentially activates the striatum, a region involved in reward processing and goal-directed behavior, we might hypothesize that choice itself may be inherently rewarding" (Leotti, Iyengar, & Ochsner, 2010, p. 460).

From these studies emerges a theory of motivation: giving people choices provides them with a sense of autonomy and self-determination that is fundamentally motivating. Each of us from our own experience would know that it is difficult to feel motivated when there seemingly are no options available to us in the circumstances. But increase the opportunity for choice, and our corticostriatal network lights up, and we find ourselves a little more motivated. When we perceive there are choices we are capable of making, we start to sense an internal locus of control—that rewarding feeling that tells us we have a degree of self-determination.

The practical implications of this research is relevant for teachers and school administrators. A school environment is often a place where student choice is limited, due to establishment regulations, safety policies, curriculum guidelines and testing requisites. While it is recognised that some things are out of a student's locus of control, educators are encouraged to continually look for ways to encourage more corticostriatal network activity by introducing choices, even small ones, in the school environment. Helping students believe they have options available to them, through choice and preferences, guides and often motivates a student to take responsibility and interest in their own learning (Scheck, 2011, p164).

A classroom teacher, aware of the necessity of student choice, provides and encourages student experimentation and error, backing innovations and new ideas with support and affirmation, and handling mistakes with sensitivity and encouragement. Curiosity, experimentation and an interest for learning is usually found in classrooms that are active, social, collaborative and authentic, with teachers showing supportive understanding, positive relationships and rapport, along with good classroom management (Tokuhama-Espinosa, 2014, p244). While some may view managing the classroom as meaning restricting and controlling students, this is far from the case. It is when students belong to a classroom that is managed well, with fairness, inclusivity, equal opportunities and consistent boundaries that students feel safe, knowing that when mistakes are made support will be there, hence the opportunities for choice are widened and learning is extended.

Our well-being depends on our belief that we have some control over our day-to-day environment. Indeed, Leotti and colleagues would argue that it is a biological imperative

MIRROR NEURONS

Italian neuroscientists in the mid-1990s were studying the premotor areas of the frontal lobes of monkeys when they discovered a remarkable connection between the firing of neurons in the motor cortex and visual perception (Gallese et al., 1996). While monitoring a neuron that had been activated when a monkey ate a peanut, researchers noticed that the same neuron was activated when the monkey simply saw the researcher eat a peanut. It was as if the motor neuron was "mirroring" what the monkey saw. Perception and action were seen to be linked in a way that had not previously been understood. As it turned out, some of these mirroring neurons where highly specific in their response to visual perception—such as only firing at the perception of picking up a banana with the right hand or peeling it with the thumb and forefinger (Rizzolatti & Arbib, 1998). Much research on mirror neurons has been conducted since this serendipitous finding, resulting in a deeper understanding of the social nature of our own minds.

Mirror neurons have both motor and perceptual function, and respond to acts that are perceived to carry purpose or intention. Mirror neurons will not "mirror" behaviour unless there is a predictable sequence based on intention—like the scientist bringing a peanut up to his mouth as opposed to randomly waving his hands around. The observing monkey knows from experience what bringing a peanut up to one's mouth is all about and can anticipate the ensuing sensation of putting the peanut into his mouth: the mirror system has learnt by experience.

Extending the study of mirror neurons from monkey to human, Marco Iacoboni and colleagues suggested that mirror neurons help us understand the intentional state of others (Carr, Iacoboni, Dubeau, Maziotta, & Lenzi, 2003). The basic premise is that our perception of another person's predictable movements helps us understand what is going on in their mind. Although single-cell recordings of mirror neurons in human subjects would be too invasive for research purposes, much can be surmised from the work with monkeys and less invasive scanning of human subjects (such as EEG, MEG, fMRI, and TMS; see Ramachandran, 2011, pp. 141–142). Iacoboni and colleagues found an integrated system that includes mirror neurons in the frontal and parietal cortex, which coordinated with the superior temporal region to form a neural image of the mental state of another—the foundation of empathic attunement. These areas are at the intersection of inner and outer experience, representing a convergence of visual, motor, and emotional processing (Iacoboni et al., 2001). Cozolino (2014) put it this way:

The frontal lobes, especially in the left hemisphere, ground us in time through action plans, means–goals relationships, and a memory for the future. The parietal lobes, especially in the right, construct three-dimensional space, the context within which our real and imagined actions take place. And since our actions contain both purpose and context, human experience emerges from within the interwoven matrix of "space–time" constructed by the synergy of these two executive networks. (p. 212)

It is thought that mirror neurons' capacity to internally simulate the perceived intentions of another is the basis of learning behaviours (Meltzoff et al., 2009) and our capacity to resonate with the internal state of another. However, this capacity to resonate is dependent on prior learning. As Daniel Siegel puts it:

If you are from New York City and I raise my hand in front of you, you may imagine that I am hailing a cab. If you are currently a student, you may imagine that I am intending to ask a question. If you have been abused, you may feel that I am going to hit you. Prior learning shapes the empathic interpretation and the internal simulation. (Siegel, 2012, p. 166)

This prior learning of the mirror-neuron system may have played a pivotal role "in our becoming the one and only species that veritably lives and breathes culture" (Ramachandran, 2011, p. 117)—a culture comprising an extraordinary complexity of knowledge, skills, and responses shared and passed down by way of language and imitation. Our unique ability to see the world from another's perspective and to construct mental models of another's thoughts and intentions (known as "theory of mind"), integral to the formation and transfer of culture, appears to rest—at least in part—on the capacity of our mirror-neuron system.

Looking at facial expressions is an activity that stimulates mirror neurons as we simulate the perceived expressions (Lundqvist & Dimberg, 1995), and this in turn activates the neural networks related to our own experience when we make those expressions. We see someone with a big, infectious smile, and we start to smile ourselves, even if it is very subtle. The inner experience we have lets us know what the smiling person must be experiencing.

If mirror neurons help us attune to others and develop empathy, then how should we understand the case of an autistic person, where there is a distinct lack of social intuition? It seems that the autistic have an impaired mirror-neuron system, leaving them with a limited capacity to learn through observation, emotionally attune, and behave empathically (Dapretto et al., 2006; Perkins, Stokes, McGillivray, & Bittar, 2010). While clearly there are additional factors involved in autism, this appears to be a crucial deficit. A series of studies by Ramachandran and colleagues used EEG to measure mirror-neuron activity via the suppression of mu-wave activity in autistic children. The subjects were found to produce mu-wave activity as normal children do, which was suppressed when they were asked to perform simple voluntary movements, as is healthy. However, when watching someone else perform an action that would normally suppress mu-wave activity (indicating mirror-neuron activity), the usual suppression did not occur (Ramachandran, 2011). Further independent studies have suggested that there is a reduced functional connection between the visual cortex and the prefrontal mirror-neuron system in autistic subjects.

Often autistic people will have difficulty with metaphorical language and take metaphors too literally. Ramachandran contends that this can be explained from the perspective of embodied cognition and a lack of mirror-neuron involvement in understanding metaphor. He and his colleagues noticed that patients with lesions in the left supramarginal gyrus who had apraxia also had difficulty with action-based metaphors like "Get a grip on yourself." The supramarginal gyrus contains mirror neurons, and the evidence suggests that a deficit of functional connectivity to this region can make it hard to interpret action-based metaphors.

Are these disconnects within the mirror-neuron system of autistics permanent? Keysers and colleagues performed experiments focusing on the facial expressions of higher-functioning autistic adults. They found that the activity in the mirror system of the youngest participants (aged around 18 years) was significantly low, as expected. But as age increased, the functionality of the insula and motor regions also steadily increased, until about the age of 30, when it was considered normal (Keysers, 2011). It seems the mirror system may not be broken, but delayed or hindered in making functional connections. This suggests that, at least in respect to the mirror system, the higher-functioning autistic brain does have mechanisms and a pathway to improved social integration and intuition.

Mirror neurons apparently play a role in our empathic attunement to others' experience of physical pain. The anterior cingulate is one area known to respond to physical pain, and it is this region that has been monitored during neurosurgery and in non-invasive neuroimaging studies. Monitoring sensory pain neurons that respond to pain receptors on the skin, researchers have found that these pain neurons also respond when the conscious patient sees another patient being poked, for example. Similar neurons for touch have been identified in the parietal lobe using brain-imaging techniques (Keysers, 2011).

The discovery of mirror neurons has enabled us to refine our model of the social brain. Although some researchers were guilty initially of overenthusiasm about mirror neurons and the role they might play in social perception, we have seen the pendulum swing back to a more sensible and integrative understanding of this system, as one of many that constitute our social brain. Mirror neurons are not the be-all and end-all of empathy and learning—they are but a part of a very complex interconnected whole. As with so many aspects of the brain, it is important to remember that it is not so much the individual functionality of mirror neurons that matters as the functional connectivity of the entire mirror-neuron system.

Some Key Areas of the
Empathic Brain
(Cozolino, 2014; Keysers, 2011; Ramachandran, 2011)

- **Anterior cingulate cortex:**
  Links emotions and actions.

- **Inferior frontal gyrus:**
  Programs complex actions and language.

- **Insula:**
  Senses the inner state of the body and controls visceral responses, emotions.

- **Primary motor cortex:**
  Controls muscles.

- **Medial prefrontal cortex**:
  Performs cognitive processing of the states of the self and of others.

- **Premotor cortex:**
  Plans actions.

- **Parietal lobe:**
  Integrates information from all senses and programs responsive actions. An important synergy exists between the mPFC and parietal lobes to integrate space–time context with action plans/goals/relationships. Includes the supramarginal gyrus.

- **Primary & secondary somatosensory cortex:**
  Senses touch and the position of own body (proprioception).

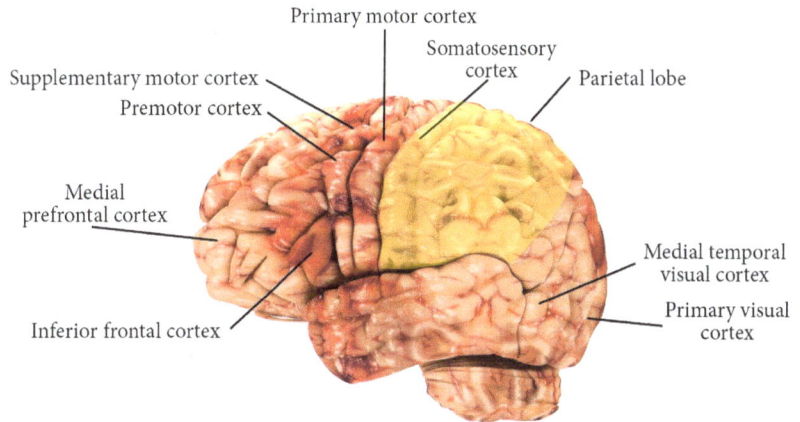

- **Supplementary motor area:**
  Plans and controls actions.

- **Primary visual cortex:**
  Detects simple features in the visual information from the retina.

- **Temporal visual cortex:**
  Combines simple visual features detected by the primary visual cortex and sometimes information from auditory cortices into neurons responding to the perception of socially relevant entities (faces, actions, etc.).

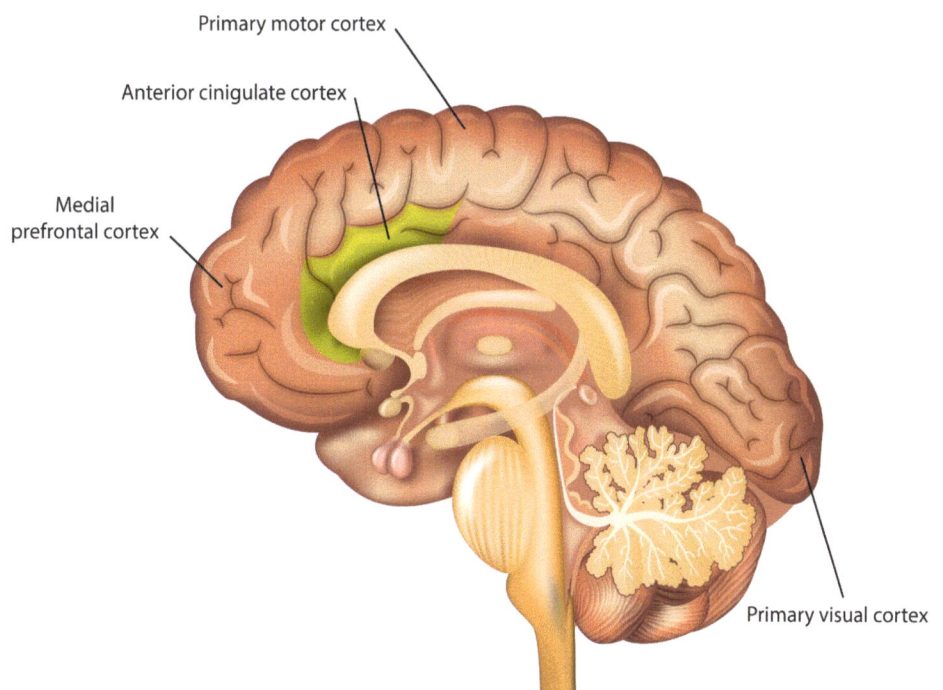

DEFAULT MODE

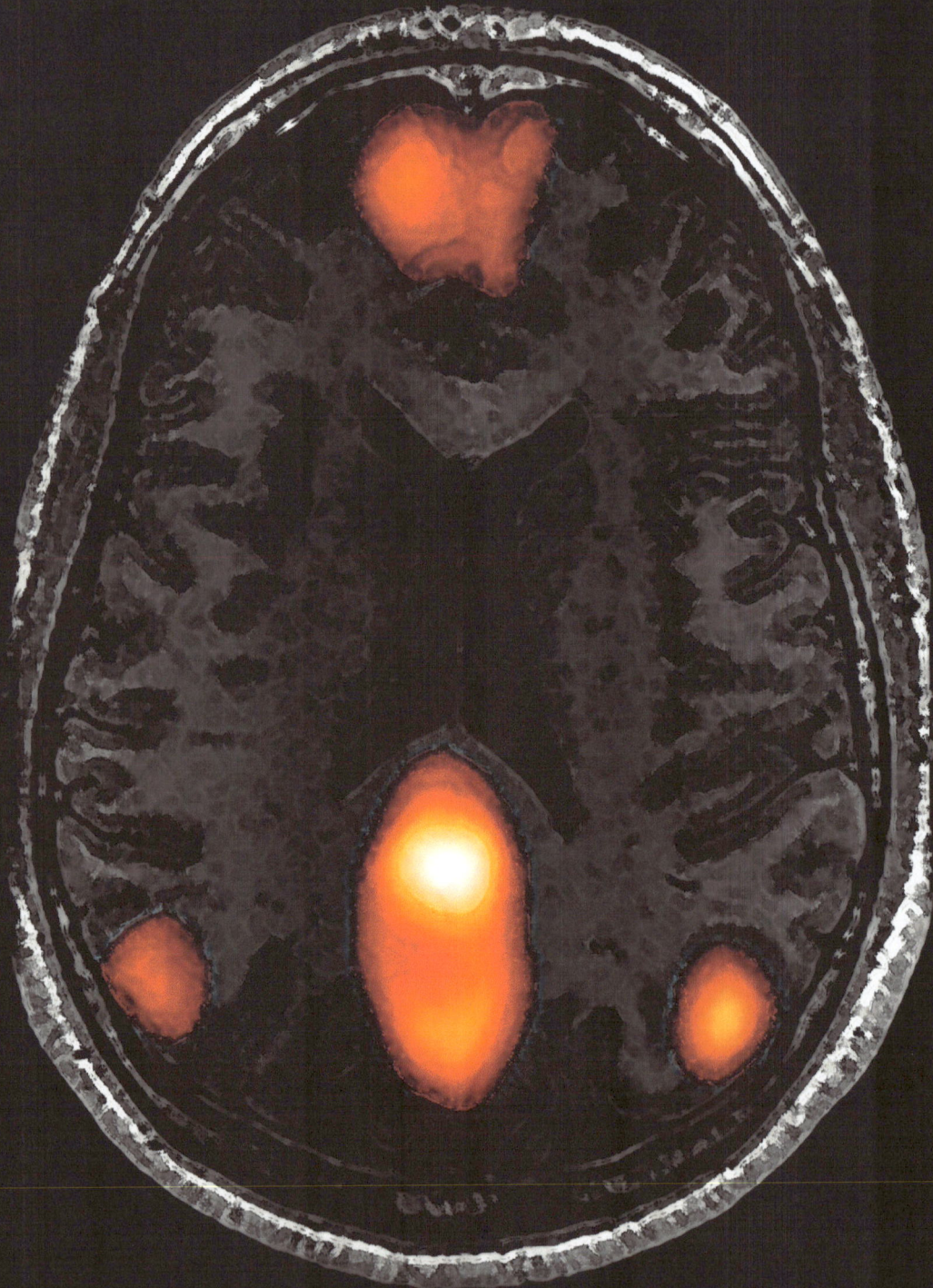

We are social beings with sophisticated and complex systems of relating to one another. The psychological needs of pain avoidance, orientation/control, and attachment are very often social in nature: the satisfaction, violation, or deprivation of these needs happens primarily in a social context, impacting our self-esteem and sense of well-being. We feel real pain when betrayed by a friend, disorientation when we get mixed messages about our role at work, a breach of attachment when our spouse fails to let us know they are going to be late home. All our fundamental psychological needs are most fully satisfied or most severely violated in the social context.

In 1997, Gordon Shulman and colleagues (Shulman et al., 1997; Shulman, Fiez, et al., 1997) reanalysed nine previous positron emission tomography (PET) studies on visual processing to find out which brain regions were commonly activated across a diverse number of cognitive tasks: the first paper looked at common activation of regions when doing a task, and the second paper focused on common activation of regions when not doing a task. They made the surprising discovery that a shared set of brain regions was activated whenever subjects were resting from a cognitive task. These regions were initially given the label "task-induced deactivation network", and later renamed the default mode, or default mode network (DMN; Lieberman, 2013). Since these early studies, investigations using similar imaging-based techniques have continued, as researchers try to understand what the default network is doing and why.

The activation patterns of the DMN revolve around episodic memory, self-projection, and self-referential processing, located in hubs in both the medial prefrontal cortex (mPFC) and the posterior cingulate cortex (PCC). In a nutshell, these activation patterns revolve around thoughts about ourselves and others and the relationships we have with others, remembering the past, and planning the future. Together they represent an automatic activation pattern that is always on when we are not focused on the external environment or on any particular cognitive task. We might be indulging in self-reflection, thinking about what others are thinking (theory of mind), re-evaluating a past conversation, or rehearsing a future one. The DMN network pattern that supports social thinking is deactivated when we engage in non-social thinking, and when we have finished with a non-social cognitive task the DMN immediately lights up again. This does not mean that the PFC does not light up with various individual nodes of the DMN during a non-social task, but rather that the broad DMN signature is not maintained during non-social cognition.

Higher-order thinking that involves imagining the future, taking the perspective of another person, or other complex introspection relies on representations (memory) not present in the immediate external environment, and thus the DMN comes into play.

Matthew Lieberman, a specialist in social cognitive neuroscience, introduced a number of interesting shifts in perspective concerning the DMN (Lieberman, 2013). One of the most interesting was that we are primed to be so social *because* of this default activity, rather than the reverse: that we are socially interested and therefore default to this network. When we are at rest from specific cognitive tasks, it seems the brain is engaged with thoughts about the very complex social world. Perhaps, as Lieberman suggests, this is an important priming of our thought processes that enables us to be more socially savvy when we engage with others.

If we are so socially focused, and our default state is to be thinking about self, others, and relationships, then the question arises: Do individuals with autism spectrum disorder (ASD) have the same default mode? Not surprisingly, there seems to be a deficit in the connectivity of the DMN in those with ASD—and the stronger the symptoms, the greater the disconnect. Specifically, there is a lack of connective strength between the mPFC and the PCC (known as the default mode midline core) in those with ASD compared to control subjects, and the deficit increases with the severity of the autism (Yerys et al., 2015). ASD is commonly understood to be characterized by a hypo-connectivity between remote cortical regions and a hyper-connectivity within certain cortical regions—fewer global connections but more local connections, in other words. Along these lines, studies have found that children with ASD show a reduced connectivity between the regions that make up the DMN, and increased local connectivity within these same regions (Washington et al., 2013). The long-distance connections between regions increase during childhood development, peaking at around 11–13 years, but children with ASD fail to undergo the typical strengthening of

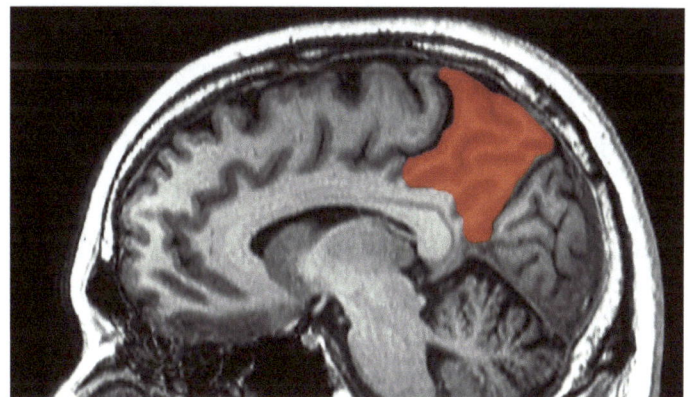

Sagittal MRI slice with the precuneus shown in red.
Image: Geoff B. Hall - Wikimedia Commons

connectivity within the DMN network in adolescence (Washington et al., 2013). Without normal DMN activation when at rest, the individual with ASD is not being primed—neither rehearsing nor evaluating their social situation, but rather defaulting to more specific processing within regions in a more neurally isolated way.

Increased functional connectivity within the DMN in conjunction with reduced connectivity between the DMN and the central executive network (CEN) has been correlated with major depressive disorder (MDD) (Ho et al., 2015; Posner et al., 2016)—a finding that makes intuitive sense given the depressed individual's immersive negative ruminations about self, others, past, future, and relationships. Depression may also involve a greater functional connectivity between the subgenual prefrontal cortex, which is associated with affect-heavy behavioural withdrawal, and the self-referential process of the DMN (Hamilton, Farmer, Fogelman, & Gotlib, 2015).

A recent study of interest suggests that the importance of religion or spirituality to a person can mitigate some of this increased DMN connectivity (Svob, Wang, Weissman, Wickramaratne, & Posner et al, 2016). The authors of this study found that individuals who were at high risk for MDD, and who also reported that religion/spirituality was very important to them, showed lower DMN connectivity than those high-risk participants who did not rate religion/spirituality as important. The importance of spirituality to an individual at risk of familial depression may support neural adaptation in the DMN in a protective manner. Unlike some previous research that found meditation-based activity reduced internal DMN connectivity and increased DMN-CEN connectivity, this study only found differences in the internal DMN connectivity, suggesting belief in religion/spirituality provides a different protective factor than that of the contemplative practices of mindfulness. Such a study does not determine whether the "chicken" came before the "egg", however: Does spirituality prevent the development of an overly connected DMN, or does the attenuation of such functional connectivity lend itself to spirituality?

There is evidence that exposure to trauma can disrupt the DMN in a somewhat different way to depression, although the exact relationship between trauma and the DMN remains unclear. Altogether this is fascinating work, revealing the nature of our brains' default activity and highlighting the importance of the social fabric we navigate daily. So next time you find yourself mentally wandering off into a world of relationships, past conversations, and ruminations about yourself, you know your DMN is fully engaged.

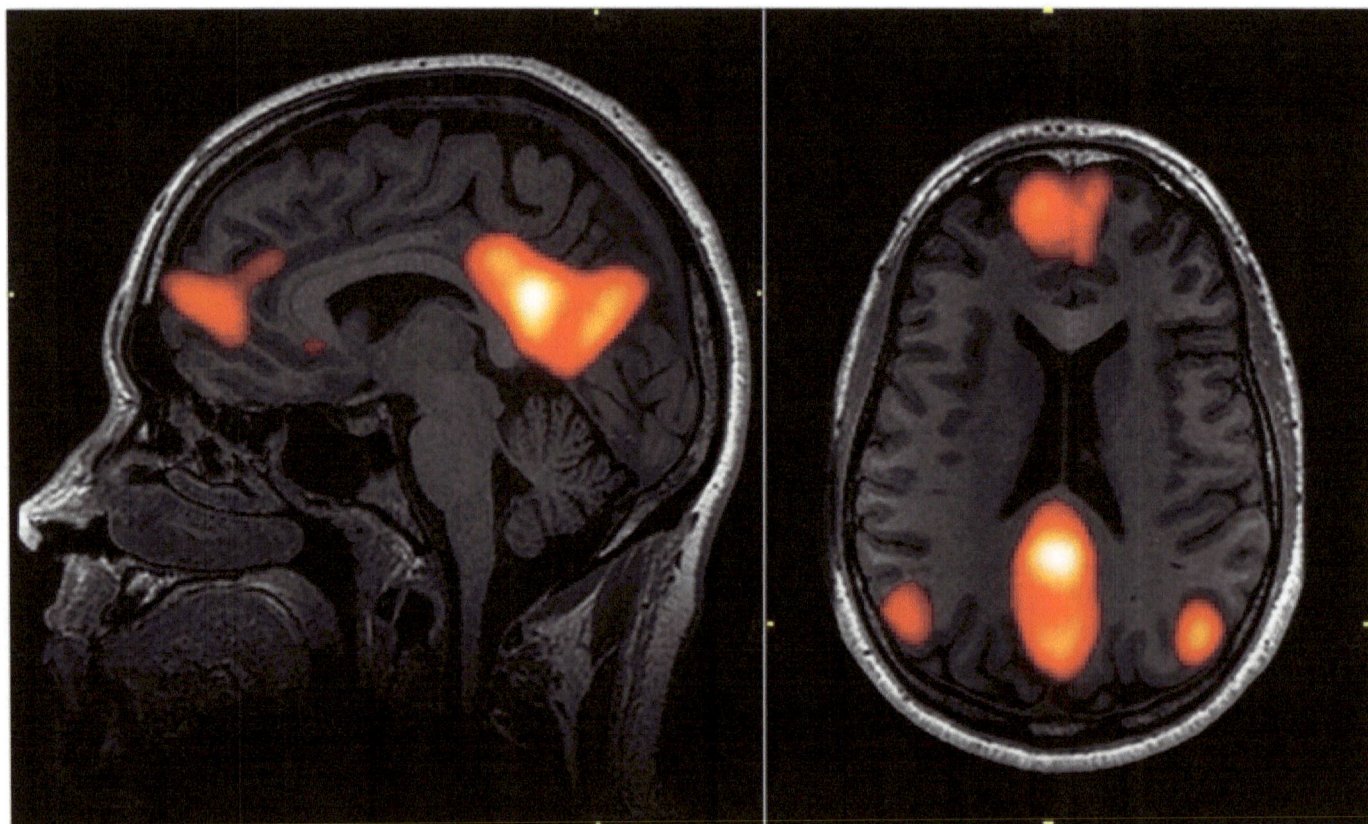

Magnetic resonance imaging of areas of the brain in the default mode network. Image: John Graner, Neuroimaging Department, National Intrepid Center of Excellence, Walter Reed National Military Medical Center, MD, USA. Wikimedia Commons

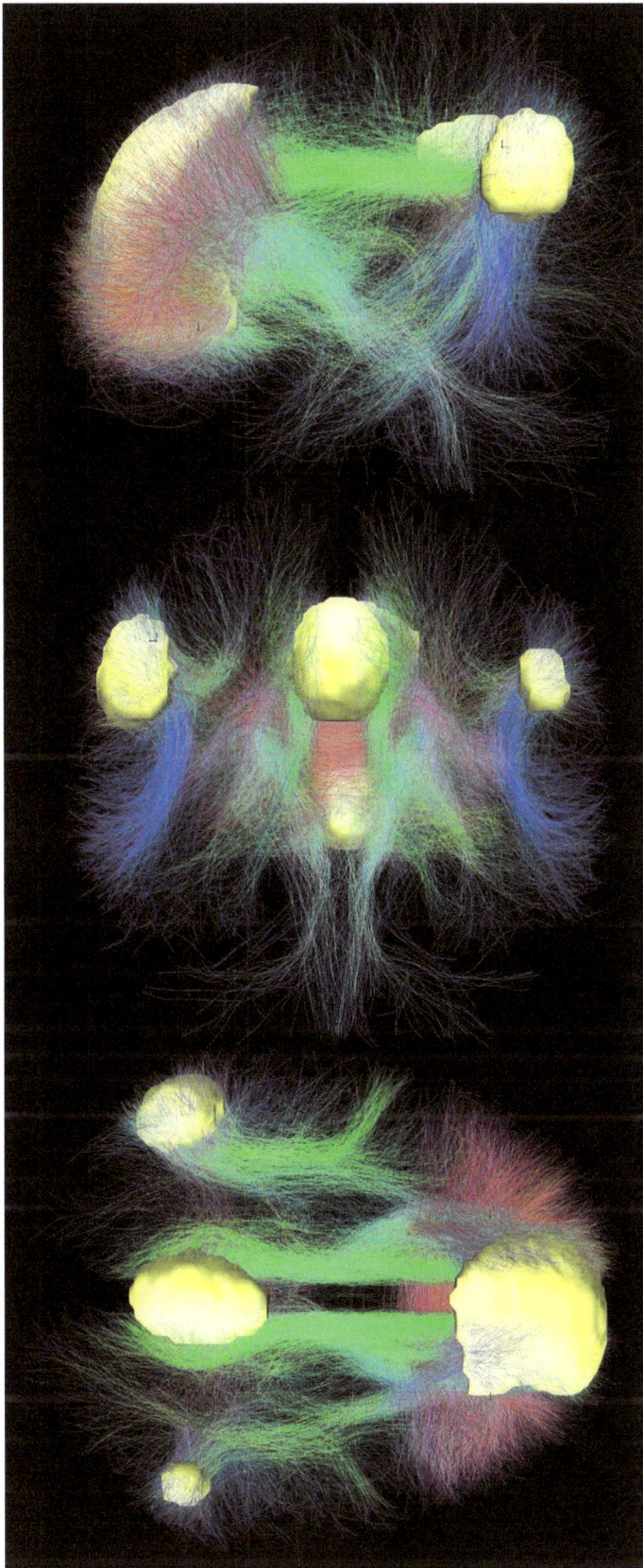

This image shows main regions of the default mode network (in yellow) and connectivity between the regions colour-coded by structural traversing direction (xyz -> rgb).
Image: Andreas Horn. Wikimedia Commons

OBSESSIVE-COMPULSIVE

Obsessive–compulsive disorder (OCD) is a common anxiety condition characterized by recurring upsetting thoughts (obsessions), typically along the lines of contamination, doubts, the need to order things, impending doom, or aggression—to name just a few. These obsessions are managed by ritualistic actions (compulsions) such as hand washing, checking, ordering, counting, praying, and other sequences of action or thought. People who suffer from OCD feel driven to outwork specific compulsions to mitigate the anxiety generated by the obsessive thoughts. One of the more common OCD experiences is that of feeling contaminated and being compelled to wash the hands or the entire body to be clean again. The feeling of being clean either never happens or is fleeting, despite excessive efforts to wash. Another typical example is persistent doubt upon leaving the house that the house is locked and windows closed or that the oven has been turned off, and such persistent thoughts lead to compulsive checking—a distressing state that intrudes on the harmonious flow of life and torments the sufferer when they are not in a position to do the checking.

Neural Underpinnings of OCD

What is known about the neurobiological underpinnings of OCD? As brain-imaging technology becomes more sophisticated, we are starting to identify specific brain structures implicated in OCD and some of the neurochemicals involved in modulating the OCD response.

At a Parisian hospital in 1967, psychiatrist and neurosurgeon Jean Talairach and his team were investigating the origins of seizures in epileptic patients when they discovered that the stimulation of the cingulum resulted in compulsive behaviours. The cingulum, located directly above the corpus callosum in the cingulate gyrus, is involved in complex repetitive movements and has been implicated in a bigger circuit involved in OCD.

This more elaborate neural circuit has become known as the OCD loop (Modell, Mountz, Curtis, & Greden, 1989) and includes the orbitofrontal cortex (OFC), striatum, and thalamus.

The OFC, covered in our earlier section on The Neocortex, is involved with the cognitive processing of decision making and expectation. It is an emotionally attuned part of the frontal cortex that is sensitive to threatening situations. Fed to the OFC is information from the striatum, a major part of the basal ganglia involved in reward and habit formation. It is the striatum that allows us to multitask by running automatic behaviour in the background, like the student who plays with her hair while listening to a challenging lecture. Part of the striatum, the caudate nucleus, working with the putamen, acts rather like an entrance or gate within the ba-

sal ganglia to activate or attenuate automatic responses. Part of what is believed to be happening in OCD is that when the striatum is not doing its gatekeeping job properly (i.e., the "entrance" is left open and unmanaged), obsessive thoughts and compulsions can flood the OFC uninhibited. There may be a "warning" from the amygdala about germs, for example, that prompts thoughts of washing hands. The OFC responds to such incoming information by reinforcing compulsive behaviours (such as hand washing) to "make things right". But a single action fails to satisfy the OFC, because there is an open loop in operation that recycles the "warning" signal (e.g., that there is still contamination) to the OFC. This hyperactivity of the OFC and the lack of inhibition by the dorsolateral prefrontal cortex (DLPFC) of the striatum could be one of the main causes of OCD.

The OFC receives messages from the amygdala that are sent back to the lateral amygdala. This fear circuit is mediated by the HPA axis (discussed in The Hypothalamus in our section on Deep Systems), and is further activated when sufferers of OCD do not engage in the compulsive behaviour—in other words, when they consciously stop the compulsive behaviour but the obsessive thoughts are still feeding back to the amygdala, letting the system know that "things are still not OK". With engagement in the compulsive behaviour there comes a temporary measure of relief, as the fear circuits are down-regulated. This management of fear and anxiety can lead to even more obsessive thinking and compulsive behaviours to avoid the uncomfortable consequences of an anxiety response.

Normally there is a balance between the OFC, the basal ganglia, and the thalamus that gives us flexibility as we activate or inhibit, in a situationally appropriate way, responses to thoughts and the environment. When the balance breaks down and there is less inhibition, as in the case of Tourette's syndrome, automatic behaviours become very difficult to inhibit.

Children with OCD are plagued by unwanted thoughts and images, making adjusting and fitting into a school environment very difficult. The obsessive desires to repeat rituals makes concentrating on learning and engaging with the class difficult. Teachers may feel confused and quite inadequate in knowing how to deal with impulse control or OCD behaviours. A teacher can lose patience, and become exasperated with the child who seems to 'waste time' ordering and arranging things, checking for mistakes, being a perfectionist when handwriting. A child may continually worry about things around the classroom or what others are doing. Excessive handwashing or checking for germs which may extend to not wanting to go to the toilet while at school, or eat their lunch with other children for fear of contamination. Some children with OCD check light switches, excessively worry that doors are not unlocked or continually want to rearrange and order library books. Teachers may also experience students that need excessive reassurance and continually ask "Is this OK Miss?" or "Am I doing it right?" The uniqueness of each child compels teachers to adopt strategies and provide support specific to each child's OCD tendencies. Telling a child to stop the rituals, allowing frustrations to show, sighing with exasperation, or disciplining OCD behaviours will only heighten the behaviours, as the child is already in severe discomfort and anxious. OCD has been described as "Having a bully stuck inside your head and no-one else can see it." (McDermot, 2015).

Anxiety disorders have a strong connection to environmental stressors (Jenson, 2015), therefore the support of a compassionate and understanding teacher, along with a positive school experience, can greatly reduce anxiety and help down-regulate the stress inflamed tendencies. For example; changes in the school timetable or altered routines can add to a child's anxiety, but this can be alleviated by the teacher taking time to carefully explain changes, draw diagrams, mark times on a clock, or in a diary, and work together on plans on how best to manage day to day school changes.

Unfortunately, other children can be insensitive to the needs of a child with OCD, therefore it is important to avoid drawing unnecessary attention to the child. Being singled out for oral reading, oral presentations or expecting a child will perform in a class role-play activity could be quite distressing for a child with OCD. Simple things such giving the child choice when to read or perform, or the option not to, can alleviate stress. Seating can be arranged to make sure the child feels protected from the glaring eyes of peers who often feel the behaviours of a child with OCD something to comment on or laugh at. Bullying or taunting of the child with OCD should never be allowed and a teacher should ac-

tively teach the class about acceptance, respect, inclusion and kindness.

Discussions with parents and encouraging them to seek professional help is important. There are many therapeutic interventions that can assist a child with OCD.

When the child's Orbitol Frontal Cortex (OFC) is flooded with input from the basal ganglia, it needs help in inhibiting the automatic behaviour that is trying to "make things right". This help can come from the DLPFC - the part of the frontal cortex involved in positive, goal-orientated, reflective, and rational behaviour—which can assist the more emotionally driven OFC in putting the brakes on the obsessive–compulsive loop. This is achieved by strengthening the control the OFC has over the amygdala to shut down the fear network. The DLPFC can strengthen attentional skills (such as focusing on the present moment, reframing, tolerance, and acceptance) and override the automatic and habitual flow from the OFC, in effect distracting the OFC from autopilot and training it to engage in something more beneficial than the habitual OCD response. As clients in therapy learn to ignore the compulsive urges and see the behaviour as non-functional, they can establish stronger connections from the OFC to the amygdala and regain control over what was an uninhibited autopilot of fear.

FEAR & ANXIETY

The emotional response of fear and anxiety is, of course, adaptive. It is a natural response designed to keep us safe from a perceived threat, be it physical or a more complex social/emotional threat. On one level we can appreciate that apprehension about failing an exam can motivate us to study a little harder, or that fear of losing our job spurs us to get to work on time. But when these adaptive and useful mechanisms become exaggerated and go into "overdrive", we have a problem: rather than achieving the goal of keeping us safe, fear cripples us, robbing us of a normal life. So what constitutes our fear mechanism, how does it become maladaptive, and what can we do about it?

The Rats of Fear

Joseph LeDoux has devoted his career to mapping out the fear network of the brain. By conditioning rats to elicit a fear response associated with a certain stimulus (a tone), LeDoux was able to trace the neural pathways of fear. His early experiments involved lesioning the auditory cortex to prevent the rats from "hearing" the feared stimuli, the assumption being that without auditory processing the rats would not respond with fear. Surprisingly, the rats continued to respond to the tone with fear after the lesion. How could the animals know to fear the tone without being able to process it in their auditory cortex? The fear network was unaffected, meaning that its mechanism must be operational before auditory information reaches the auditory cortex;

that is, there must be a pathway other than that of the thalamus–cortex. And it happens that there is. LeDoux developed the neuroscience of fear based on a non-cortical pathway he called the "low road"—a fast, direct pathway that requires no higher-order thought to activate a physiological response to a threat.

LeDoux's rats, which had learned to fear a specific tone, processed incoming auditory information from the thalamus directly to the amygdala—the small, almond-shaped fear-learning centre that was covered in our section on Deep Systems. LeDoux demonstrated the important role the amygdala plays in learning and memory. He showed that the auditory information entering the amygdala, specifically the basal and lateral aspects (known as the basolateral complex of the amyg-

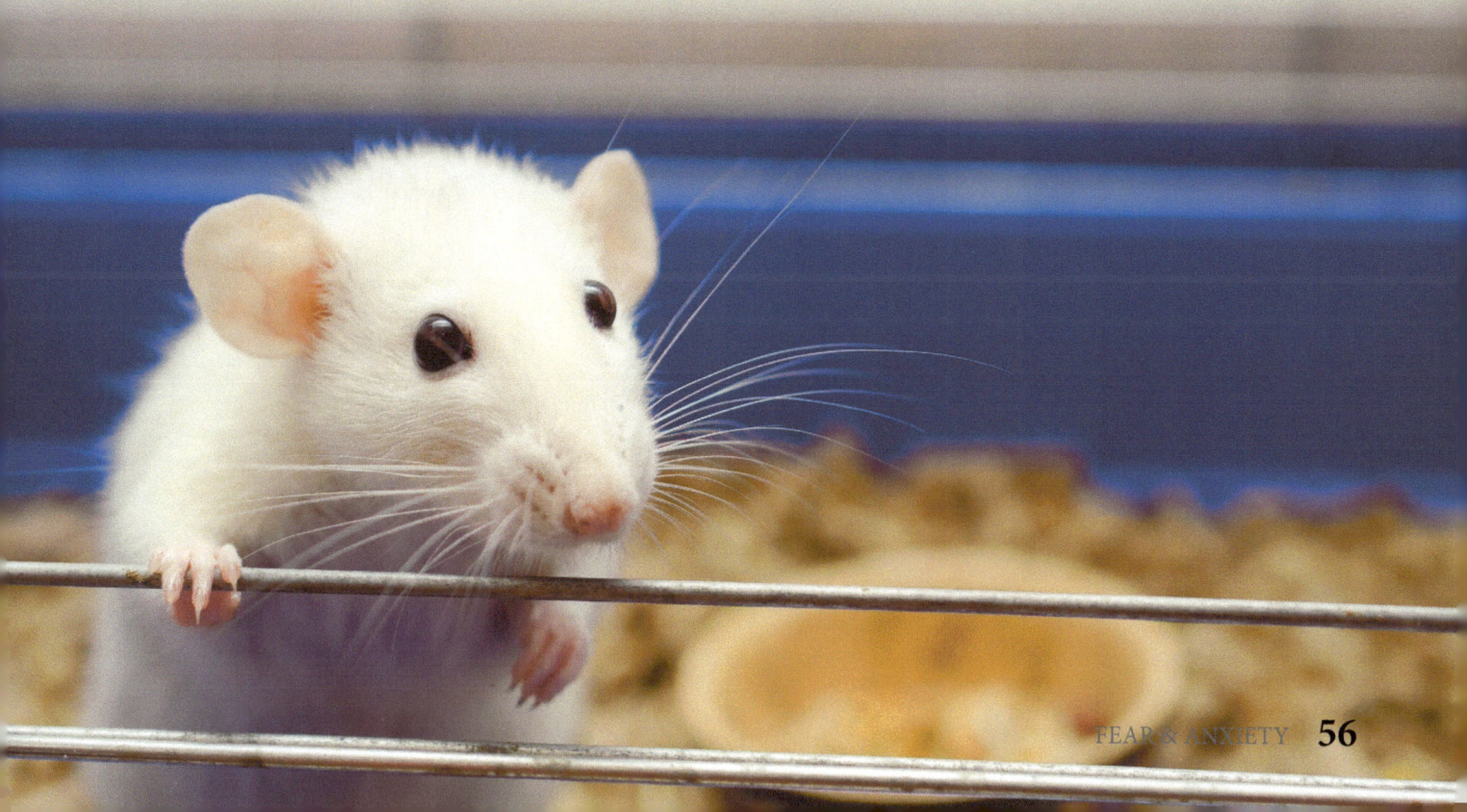

dala or BLA), has not been analysed by higher cortical processing, and that seemingly any tone that is similar to the conditioned tone will trigger a warning from the amygdala. In fact, all sensory information from the thalamus arrives first at the amygdala—the fast "low road" of information processing. The "high road" is a slower pathway that facilitates the passage of sensory information through the cortex before meeting the "low road" back at the amygdala. This slower pathway adds much more detail and character to the raw data as it is analysed in "smarter" parts of the brain. To illustrate, after an immediate and instinctive jump at a snake-like object on the ground, our "high road" processing recognizes the object as a hose rather than a snake, and this discrimination down-regulates the fear response. The output of the amygdala is connected to many neural structures that activate either the freeze response or the fight-or-flight response together with other systems to raise arousal levels and direct attention. It is the fast, unconscious "low road" of information processing that may be responsible for initiating panic attacks that appear to come out of nowhere. As an oversensitive amygdala springs into action, it instantly draws oxygen-rich blood flow from areas such as the right orbitofrontal cortex and anterior cingulate cortex (important for modulating the response of the amygdala), leaving the sufferer with that out-of-control feeling of dread and/or panic as a cascade of stress chemicals activates their body to deal with imminent danger.

The implicit emotional learning of the amygdala is unlike the explicit memory of places, events, and facts that is mediated by the hippocampus. The explicit learning of the contextual details of a fear-related incident is hippocampal-dependent. The memories of context by themselves are not emotional; emotional aspects of memory require amygdala activity and the pairing of contextual elements with the emotional representation of those elements. Unlike the rats in LeDoux's lab, we can make emotional associations just by recognizing a dangerous situation from context, with our amygdala coming into play to encode an emotional element to the learning—a helpful skill to have when the feared stimuli are oncoming trucks, exposed power lines, guns, or strange men offering a ride.

Fear vs. Anxiety

Fear is a response to a specific stimulus while that stimulus poses a threat. It is fear that motivates us to move out of the way of an oncoming vehicle, but once the vehicle has passed, it no longer poses a threat. Anxiety, however, is a different matter—it does not necessarily require a trigger, but is the anticipation of a threat. Anxiety is the continual vigilance for potential threats, an energy-consuming alertness for danger even if there is no immediate danger. In the consistency model of mental functioning described by Klaus Grawe, this state is characterized by an active avoidance network that is

always scanning for potential threats, never quite satisfied that all is safe (Grawe, 2007). It arises through a combination of an oversensitive amygdala and a reduction in the capacity of other brain regions to modulate the amygdala response. In some cases, the vigilance for threats can be generalized into what is known as generalized anxiety disorder (GAD), where the sufferer demonstrates a hypervigilance for threat and avoidance of anything that could be threatening but in a very diffuse, rather indiscriminate manner. For this individual, much of the environment—people, places, things—feels like a potential threat and either must be avoided or at best evokes a sense of unease.

Extinction

We have learned from LeDoux's work with rats that a fear memory can be created by pairing a shock with a tone, so that eventually the tone by itself will elicit fear. One of the key concepts that follows from this process of fear memory creation is that of "extinction": the unlearning of fear. If the tone that was previously associated with a shock is repeatedly sounded without any shock, a new learning is created, and the tone is eventually associated with no shock. Indeed, "extinction" may be a misnomer, as what is happening seems more like the creation of yet another neural network of association that competes with the previous learning. It has been observed that in different contexts or under stress the old learning (tone = shock) can rear its head again despite attempts at extinction.

Heart Rate Variability

A further aspect of fear and anxiety regulation involves the coordination between sympathetic and parasympathetic arousal measured by heart rate variability (HRV)—the subtle differences in timing between heart beats. A high HRV mediated through the vagus nerve and stellate ganglia indicates a healthy flexibility of attention to current situations, whereby healthy feedback mechanisms maintain an appropriate balance between the two branches of the autonomic nervous system (ANS) and thus a balanced response to various stimuli.

The Vagal Complex

Generally it can be said that all fear and anxiety disorders share the same hypersensitive amygdala response to a stimulus and disruption of regulatory circuits. The fear response engages the sympathetic nervous system (the fight-or-flight instinct) and disengages the ventral vagal branch of the parasympathetic system (the "social" system). However, if the perceived threat becomes overwhelming to the point of absolute terror, the sympathetic system can shut down and the dorsal vagal parasympathetic system activates, putting us into a dissociated *freeze* response. In this last-ditch effort to escape death by feigning death, the medial prefrontal cortex and anterior cingulate cortex shut down emotional arousal; the brainstem throws the body into shutdown (slowing the heart rate and metabolism and lowering blood pressure), and dissociation allows the sufferer mentally to go "elsewhere".

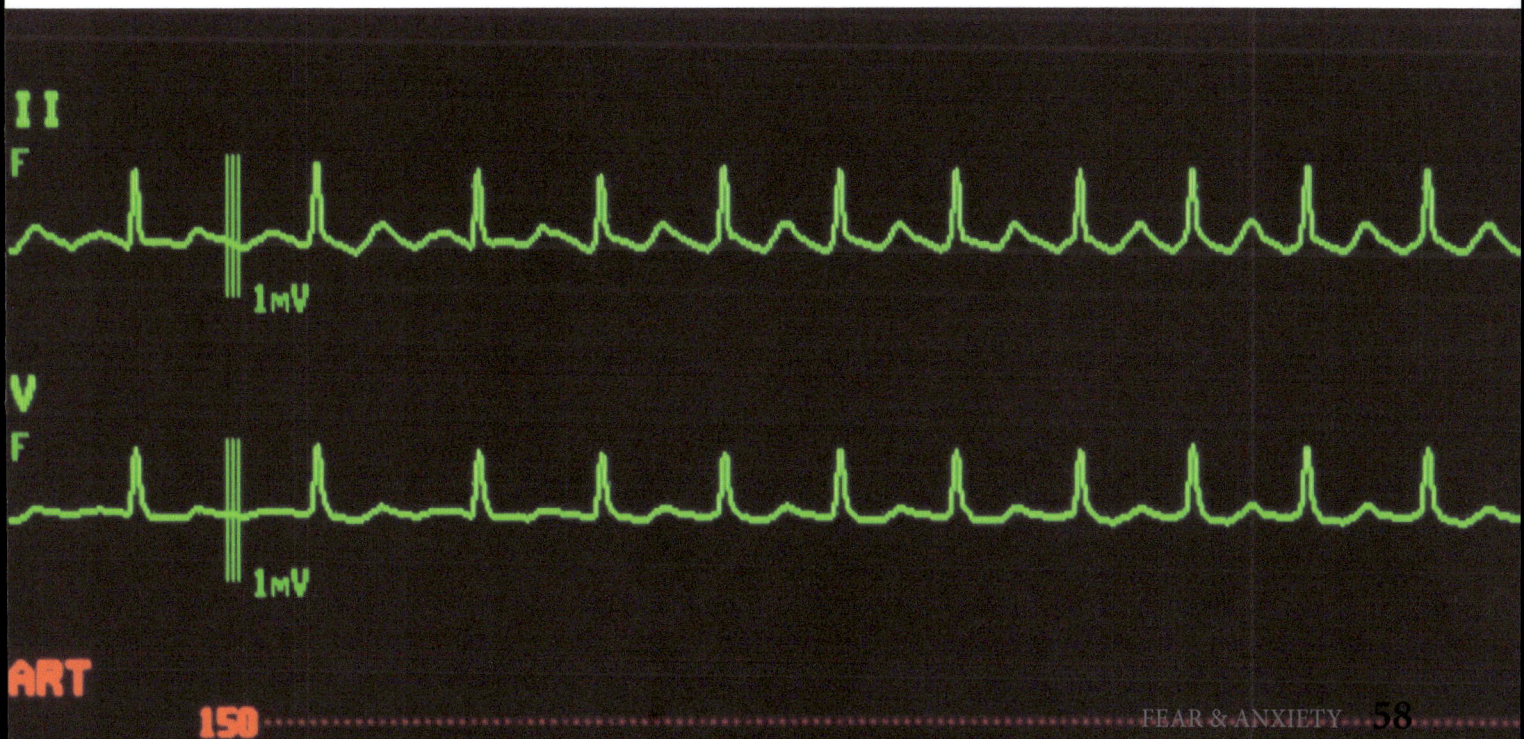

Approach & Avoid

So far, we have learned that the amygdala can act as an early-warning system for things that appear to be threatening, and that when the amygdala is triggered by an apparent threat, it starts a chain reaction of physiological responses to address the threat. First, corticotrophin-releasing hormone (CRH) signals the pituitary gland to release adrenocorticotrophic hormone (ACTH), which in turn signals the adrenal glands (situated above each kidney) to release adrenalin and then cortisol. This fear reaction takes place in what we call the hypothalamic–pituitary–adrenal (HPA) axis and is the best-known response to stress. But during a stress response the amygdala is simultaneously busy with other actions, such as signalling the locus coeruleus in the brainstem to release norepinephrine (NE), or noradrenaline. When the locus coeruleus is activated by stress, its increasing NE secretions alter prefrontal cognitive function, which has the knock-on effect of increasing motivation through the nucleus accumbens, increasing sympathetic and inhibiting parasympathetic tone as well as activating the HPA axis. Similarly, when NE is released by the locus coeruleus, there is greater activity in the right prefrontal cortex (R-PFC) and less activity in the left prefrontal cortex (L-PFC), hindering the latter's capacity to be verbally expressive in the face of growing anxiety. Excessive NE release can impair PFC function more generally and disinhibit the amygdala, leading to a state where the amygdala effectively "hijacks" the PFC. As a result, we are unable to rationalize the fear and anxiety we are feeling.

Experiencing fear and anxiety leads to the development of avoidant behaviour mediated by the R-PFC in order to avoid the triggering stimuli, whatever they may be. Continued avoidant behaviour has a rewarding effect (reinforced by dopamine), so that we become entrenched in the avoidance and end up enhancing and fortifying R-PFC activity at the expense of the more approach-oriented activity of the L-PFC. In effect, the more we avoid, and the more we allow the avoidant behaviour to develop, the harder it becomes to change.

Bolstering Top-Down Processing

Focused breathing technique is a common and easy way to begin calming an anxious student. A mindful breathing exercise, for example, has multiple benefits. Activation of the parasympathetic nervous system during long, controlled outward breaths, which calms the nervous system and helps put the brakes on the HPA

Amygdala

LeDoux's rats, which had learned to fear a specific tone, processed incoming auditory information from the thalamus directly to the amygdala—the small, almond-shaped fear learning centre seen here in this model of the limbic system and brain stem.

All sensory information from the thalamus first arrives at the amygdala—the fast "low road" of information processing.

axis, is one important benefit; L-PFC activation while the student pays focused attention to the sensation of breathing, with a corresponding perfusion of the PFC as blood flows back to the frontal part of the brain from the deeper limbic regions, is another. This blood flow helps to prevent hyperventilation and retain the right amount of carbon dioxide (CO_2) in the bloodstream. Note that excessive exhalation of CO_2 will produce many of the physiological sensations associated with panic, due to the lowering of blood pH (hypocapnic alkalosis).

Other techniques such as a body scan or progressive muscle relaxation exercise, or indeed any mindfulness exercise (meditation, yoga, prayer), will activate the L-PFC as the student pays focused attention—whether on *interoceptive* (within the body) or *exteroceptive* (outside the body) stimuli. For example, noticing one's breathing, heartbeat, muscle tension and other feelings, and then wrapping language around the sensations that are the focus of that attention, will activate the left hemisphere. This activation can restrict the right hemisphere from dominating with the impression of being completely immersed in anxiety, and create some mental distance from the physiological symptoms. As a result, the observing self can emerge, and a greater sense of control can begin to develop.

As the student practises focused attention, or mindfulness, stronger and faster neural control networks will be built from the PFC to the limbic system. Mindful breathing and other mindfulness exercises can be established in a daily routine to strengthen PFC–limbic networks, restore balance through a healthier level of activation in the left hemisphere, and maintain frontal-lobe

perfusion. With these bottom-up processes restored to a healthy level, the groundwork has been laid for effective work on top-down processes.

Cognitive approaches to anxiety address some of the errors in thought we are particularly prone to, such as polarization, catastrophizing, and automatic negative thoughts, all of which are associated with R-PFC-biased thinking. One of the keys to debunking cognitive misconceptions is to let your students know they need to give their PFC time to process what is happening rather than just go along with the amygdala's attempt to hijack the entire mental process. When negative or unhelpful automatic thoughts arise, they are more than likely a response to implicit memory activated by an overreactive amygdala. The student needs to take pause and think, "What is really going on here?" This gives the PFC time to become aware of the present moment, to appraise the current situation, and to decide on a more helpful, approach-oriented response as warranted by the current situation. Part of this approach orientation may take the form of reframing assumptions in a graduated way. For example, a student may be anxious and become panicky about an upcoming school camp. Stopping and appraising what is really happening in the moment, and taking time to think "I'm at home, on a Tuesday night, watching TV" can allow a better perspective. It enables the student to recognize, "There is no immediate pressure to cope with being away from home right now; I'm just with my family watching TV, and this is relaxing. This provides an opportunity to reframe the negative assumption of not coping at the school camp with "I'm learning to be more socially competent and I know the teachers are there to take care of us, I know I will be OK." For the student, cultivating such approach-oriented cognitions - and following up by actually going on the school camp and not cancelling - provides the exposure (controllable incongruence) that can rewire the brain towards an L-PFC approach bias. Even just imagining being OK on the school camp and imagining it to be a positive experience, can begin to stimulate the student's social brain.

On reading this brief review of "high road" and "low road" processing and the inherent tensions of the R-PFC/L-PFC (avoid/approach) axis to anxiety, the reader may be tempted to think of the R-PFC and bottom-up processes as the villain in this psychological drama. Don't be misled. The right hemisphere is imperative for a global perspective capable of tolerating the inevitable ambiguities of life, and bottom-up processes are vital to keeping us alive (see Iain McGilchrist's *The Master and His Emissary* for an expert and eye-opening exposition on the right hemisphere). But when normal flexible processing is hijacked by a hypersensitive alarm system, then restoring a healthy balance becomes a priority. As teachers, we can guide students toward this goal by working to increase parasympathetic tone and by introducing graded exposure (controllable incongruence) in safe environments, thereby establishing better L-PFC control over reactions.

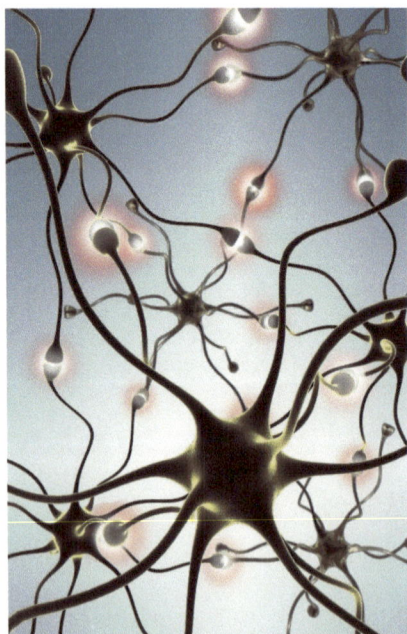

When someone is challenged to face a fear in a way that enables them to feel in control (what is called "controllable incongruence"), moderate amounts of stress hormones such as cortisol and glutamate help them to stay alert, energized, and engaged so that new learning is facilitated through the optimization of neural plasticity. On the other hand, when the challenge—or stress—is escalated, and levels of norepinephrine, corticotrophin-releasing hormone (CRF) and cortisol rise, the amygdala is overactivated, and the conditions for new learning are degraded. High levels of stress hormones will break down the synaptic connections of new learning, and in an attempt to keep us safe, the brain will revert to the old avoidant networks. This is because elevated and chronic stress raises glutamate levels excessively and overactivates the NMDA receptors responsible for long-term potentiation of new learning, damaging what could have been a new neural pathway.

Increasing Parasympathetic Tone

Basic "bottom-up" techniques can be used with clients to increase their parasympathetic tone and put the brakes on a runaway anxiety response. For example:

- **Stop and breathe:** Controlled, focused breathing, especially a long, deep outward breath, activates the parasympathetic nervous system, slowing the heart rate and allowing blood to perfuse the PFC as the client maintains a point of focus (their breathing).

- **Relaxed posture:** Sitting, lying and/or stretching in a relaxed and mindful way (yoga is great for ideas here) can defuse bodily tensions.

- **Mindful attention:** A focus on the here and now, whether the focal point is within the body (*interoceptive*) or outside the body (*exteroceptive*), activates the L-PFC and down-regulates the amygdala.

- **Observing without judgement:** Observing bodily sensations without making any judgement about self or symptom can allow the "observing self" to emerge, affording a degree of detachment from the symptoms of anxiety. This (healthy) detachment from the symptoms and the self can be enhanced by labelling bodily sensations and thoughts: "I can feel my heart is racing" or "I'm having the thought that things will not be OK".

PAIN

Professor Matthew Lieberman heads the Social Cognitive Neuroscience Laboratory at UCLA and is the author of *Social: Why Our Brains Are Wired to Connect* (Lieberman, 2013). He and his colleagues have done important work in discovering the neural underpinnings of social pain and how it correlates with physical pain. All of us would recognize that the language we use to describe social pain employs the same words and phrases commonly used to describe physical pain: "She broke my heart," "I'm so cut up about it," "He really hurt me," "They stabbed me in the back!" and so on—and the phenomenon appears common across cultures and languages. There is a strong linguistic overlap between physical and social–emotional pain. But is there an actual neural overlap? This is the question that neuroscientists like Professor Lieberman have been investigating: Can the social pain of rejection, exclusion, or ostracism share the same or similar neural mechanisms as physical pain?

One of the regions of the brain under investigation is the dorsal anterior cingulate cortex (dACC). You may recall from our section on The Neocortex that the anterior cingulate cortex (ACC) is the front part of the cingulate cortex, commonly understood to be employed in error detection, with the dorsal (top) part associated with cognitive processing and the ventral (bottom) part with emotional processing. Studies have suggested that the dACC is involved in processing the distress of both physical and social pain—rather like an alarm system that both detects a problem and elicits a response. The dACC seems to monitor for discrepancies between one's goals and one's most habitual or predominant responses. When there is an inconsistency, the dACC lets the lateral prefrontal cortex know that it needs to intervene with a contextually appropriate response. The Stroop test is a good illustration, in that when subjects are shown colour words in odd colours (e.g., the word "red" written in blue) and asked to state the colour rather than the word, the dACC detects an inconsistency with the prepotent response to pronounce the word rather than identify its colour (i.e., the correct answer for the word "red" written in blue is blue, but the tendency is to answer red). The dACC also functions to create attention-getting affective states such as pain, anxiety, and distress. Lieberman (2013) likens the ACC to an alarm system in that it can detect certain conditions (such as goal conflicts) and "sound the alarm".

As far back as the 1970s, the work of Jaak Panksepp and colleagues suggested that there was more than a metaphorical link between social and physical pain. These neuroscientists were looking at opiate receptor systems (the dACC is rich in receptors for endorphins, the brain's natural opioids) and found that both physical and social pain were modulated by such systems. Later studies found that even non-opioid pain relievers like Tylenol (acetaminophen) could ease social pain and that they reduced activity in the dACC (DeWall et al., 2010). The theory developed that since infant mammalian social needs are an issue of life or death—a baby mammal won't last long without social attachment—a system that monitors social–psychological proximity to caregivers is of vital importance. The idea was that a system that could detect an attachment breach and sound an alarm to elicit a reconnection would share some of the same neural processing as physical pain—

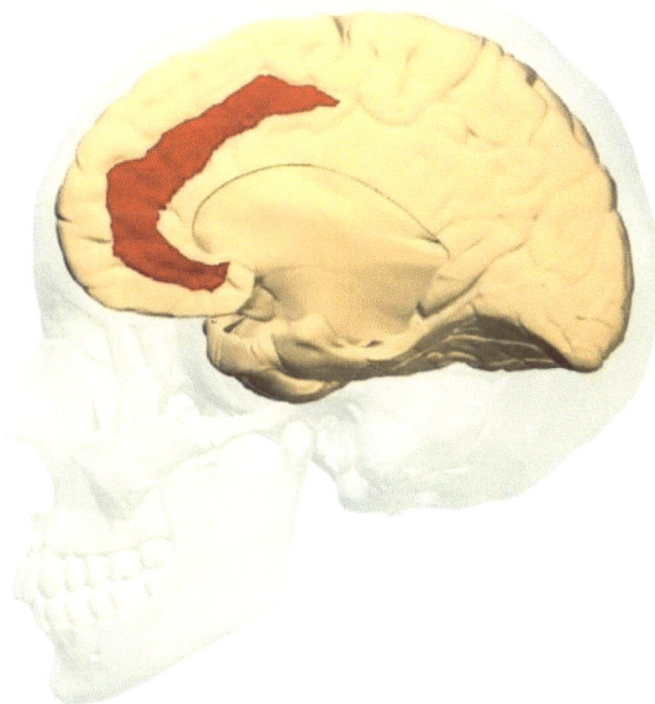

The dorsal anterior cingulate cortex is also know as Brodmann area 32 and plays a part in pain detection rather like an alarm system. 3D brain image from Anatomography

another trigger for a survival response.

It is an enticing idea that the brain responds to social rejection using the same circuitry that encodes physical pain, but it is likely not this way on a neural level. In 2014, Choong-Wan Woo and colleagues at the University of Colorado, Boulder (Woo et al., 2014) found that the two kinds of pain are processed in the same areas but with different neural representations. In fact, they found that the encoding of physical pain and social rejection occurred in distinct global (whole-brain) patterns as well as different patterns within the pain-processing regions. So there may be a sharing of regions when processing the two types of pain, but research suggests there are distinct neural representations for each (see also Iannetti, Salomons, Moayedi, Mouraux, & Davis, 2013).

The system of the brain involved in the perception of and response to physical pain is known as the pain matrix. It comprises the dACC, rostral (front) ACC (rACC), somatosensory cortex, insula, periaqueductal grey, and right ventral prefrontal cortex (RVPFC). The insula and somatosensory cortex are primarily concerned with the sensory aspect of pain, while the periaqueductal grey, rACC, and RVPFC are more concerned with the regulation of pain through the release of opioids and cognitive processing. The dACC seems to be involved more in the subjective aspect of distress. There is a high correlation between the sensory intensity and subjective distress of pain, but the two can be separated. In the 1960s, chronic pain sufferers would sometimes elect to have a cingulotomy (a lesioning of the anterior cingulate) that would significantly decrease the subjective aspect of pain, although the sensory aspect continued—they could feel the pain, but it didn't bother them. By contrast, in cases where the somatosensory cortex is damaged, they experience distress from pain but have difficulty perceiving where the pain is coming from. It seems sensory intensity and subjective distress are two different neural circuits.

In a fascinating study on social exclusion, Matthew Lieberman, Naomi Eisenberg, and Kipling Williams performed a neuroimaging experiment on subjects to see what regions would be activated during social rejection (Eisenberger, Lieberman, & Williams, 2003). The subjects were placed in an fMRI scanner and told they would be playing a ball-tossing computer game with others who were also in scanners, in order to work out the technical details of a new neuroimaging procedure called hyperscanning. In fact there were no other subjects in scanners, only a computer posing as the other subjects. During the first scan, the subject was told that there was a technical problem and that he or she could watch the other two players toss the ball between themselves but would not be able to join them. In the second scan, the subject was able to join in the game and was fully included, with a 50% probability of being

thrown the ball. In the final scan, the subject was initially included but after about 30 seconds was excluded from the ball throwing for the rest of the session—the appearance was that the other two "players" were having more fun tossing the ball to each other than including the (real) subject. After the scans, each subject filled out a questionnaire assessing the amount of social pain they experienced during the last scan.

During the exclusion trial, greater dACC, right insula, and RVPFC activity was observed than in the second scan when the subject was included in the ball tossing. There appeared to be a strong correlation between activity in the dACC and RVPFC and social pain. The pattern is similar to that in studies of physical pain, which have shown increased dACC, insula, and RVPFC activity. Further outcomes of such studies have indicated that the dACC mediates the relationship between self-reports of pain and RVPFC activity, substantiating the idea that the dACC produces the subjective level of distress but it is the RVPFC that intervenes to down-regulate the experience of such pain. Interestingly, the re-

searchers found that dACC activity was also elevated when the subject was told there was a technical fault and they were excluded from the game. Is it possible that we are sufficiently hardwired in our response to social exclusion that the mere suggestion of it will provoke an automatic response in our dACC "alarm system"? In this scenario, however, there was no increase in RVPFC activity, presumably because the subjects had no reason to think they were being deliberately excluded.

If social and physical pain do indeed share neural substrates, what does that mean for us? Naomi Eisenberger looked into the consequences of such an overlap when she examined the possibility that an individual's sensitivity to physical pain positively correlated with their sensitivity to social pain (Eisenberger, 2012). She discovered a significant correlation, showing that a greater sensitivity to physical pain went hand-in-hand with greater pain upon social rejection. Earlier findings reviewed by Eisenberger showed that subjects with a variability in the μ-opioid receptor gene OPRM1 (carrying the G allele), which is associated with greater

sensitivity to physical pain, also demonstrated greater sensitivity to social pain. Researchers had also tested to see if one sort of pain modulated the other, finding that physical pain tended to increase the sense of social pain, and vice versa (Eisenberger, 2012). Finally, as discussed earlier, some interventions that reduce physical pain, like Tylenol, can also reduce social pain (DeWall et al., 2010).

The pain of social rejection, it seems, is more than metaphorical. There are common neural regions that underpin social and physical pain, and the pain of a broken relationship may be as distressing as a physical wound. Eisenberger (2012) concludes:

> These findings encourage us to think more careful-ly about the consequences of social rejection. For example, whereas physically hurting another indi-vidual is uniformly frowned on and typically pun-ishable by law, rejecting someone else or inflicting social pain on someone is typically not held to the same standard. The work reviewed here suggests that our intuitions about and rules regarding social

pain might be misguided and that these experiences might be just as damaging as experiences of physical pain. In fact, with regard to both mental and phys-ical health, social pain-related experiences may be quite detrimental. For example, those who have ex-perienced the loss of a loved one (versus those who have not) are twice as likely to develop depression, and those who have experienced social rejection are approximately 22 times more likely to develop de-pression and do so more quickly. Moreover, patients with somatoform pain or fibromyalgia, who experi-ence pain with no medical explanation, report early experiences of social pain (emotional abuse, family conflict, and early parental loss), highlighting a po-tential link between these negative social experienc-es early on and later enhanced sensitivity to physical pain. Finally, although experiences of social pain are clearly distressing and hurtful in the moment, it is important to remember that these painful feelings after social exclusion or broken social relationships also serve a valuable function, namely, to ensure the maintenance of close social ties. (p. 133)

The Mu-Opioid System: The Brain's Natural Painkillers

As we have touched on above, the μ-opioid system can alleviate both physical and social pain. Opioid binding to μ-receptors has a reinforcing effect. It is part of the system responsible for addictions like that to morphine, but is also hypothesized to form part of the reward system that facilitates infant attachment. Studies continue to shed light on the role of μ-opioids in regulating social distress.

In 2013, a research team at the University of Michigan Molecular and Behavioral Neuroscience Institute developed an innovative methodology to test the brain's response to social pain by combining advanced brain scanning techniques (positron emission tomography, or PET) with an online dating model that incorporated scenarios of acceptance and rejection by strangers. In the study (Hsu et al., 2013) participants were asked to select people they might be interested in romantically from a wide range of photographs, just as in online dating—but then they were told these people were not interested in them! Brain activity at the moment of rejection was measured in the PET scanner and the results showed that the brain areas most active at this point were the same areas involved in physical pain. The personality of the participants proved a significant variable—for example, people who scored highly for the resiliency trait on a personality questionnaire tended to be capable of more opioid release during social rejection, especially in the amygdala, a region of the brain involved in emotional processing.

The importance of these findings is not merely theoretical; rather the research can help teachers understand student behaviours and resilience factors. It opens up an awareness of why some students seem to over-react in situations of emotional pain and others can 'cop it on the chin' and move on. It gives guidance when managing difficult behaviours as the knowledge raises awareness of the factors behind childhood behaviours, rather than the focus being solely on the behaviour itself.

DEPRESSION

How weary, stale, flat, and unprofitable
Seem to me all the uses of this world!

Hamlet – William Shakespeare

What Is Depression?

Depression comes under the umbrella of mood or affective disorders, in which individuals have difficulty controlling mood states. *The Diagnostic and Statistical Manual of Mental Disorders* (5th ed.; *DSM–5*; American Psychiatric Association, 2013) categorizes depressive disorders principally as follows:

- Disruptive Mood Dysregulation Disorder
- Major Depressive Disorder
- Persistent Depressive Disorder (Dysthymia)
- Premenstrual Dysphoric Disorder
- Substance/Medication-Induced Depressive Disorder

The manual also considers depressive states arising from medical conditions such as stroke, traumatic brain injury, Parkinson's disease, and others, with two further categories covering other specified and unspecified depressive disorders (American Psychiatric Association, 2013). To keep it simple, we will limit our focus here mainly to major depressive disorder (MDD).

Depression is marked by a deep sense of sadness and reduced motivation and activity levels. Most people suffering a bout of major depression experience a recovery phase—within 3 months for 40% of sufferers, and within a year for 80%. But some suffer chronic depression (dysthymia) that persists for years (American Psychiatric Association, 2013). Factors that influence risk and prognosis are temperament, environmental factors such as adverse childhood experiences and stressful life events, genetics, and physiological factors. According to the World Health Organization, depression affects an estimated 350 million people globally (WHO, 2016).

Brain Regions Involved in Depression

There are a number of brain regions implicated in affect regulation that can play a role in depressive disorders. They include the prefrontal cortex, anterior cingulate cortex, hippocampus, amygdala, and nucleus accumbens (Davidson, 2000, Davidson, Pizzagalli, Nitschke, & Putnam 2002; Grawe, 2007; Kandel, Schwartz, Jessell, Siegelbaum, & Hudspeth, 2012; Lambert & Kinsley, 2004). We will look at these areas, as well as the role of the lateral habenula and brain stem, in depression.

The Prefrontal Cortex in Depression

The prefrontal cortex (PFC) plays a dominant role in the determination of personality and temperament, guiding our behaviour on the basis of our goals and values. The PFC hemispheres appear to have different functions in this respect, with the left PFC tending towards positive goals and emotions in the form of an "approach" orientation while the right PFC specializes in avoidance goals and negative emotions (Davidson & Henriques, 2000; Grawe, 2007). Individuals with greater activation of the left PFC can experience more positive emotions in general than those whose right PFC predominates.

Depression often entails a generally underactive PFC, with hypoactivity more pronounced on the left than the right (Davidson et al., 2002). This results in a deficit of positive feelings and approach-orientated goal seeking accompanied by a surplus of negative ruminations. Processing of reward and punishment is also lateralized across the hemispheres of the PFC, with the left responding more strongly to rewards and the right to punishment. A study by Henriques and Davidson (2000) demonstrated that depressed individuals doing tasks that yielded rewarding, neutral, or punishing outcomes did not respond to rewards, whereas the control subjects did. This propensity to respond to punishment but not reward poses serious problems when trying to establish positive goals and rewards for depressed clients. However, this may be overcome by raising the overall level of activation of the PFC, thereby increasing reward processing. Antidepressant therapy has been found to increase dorsolateral PFC activity (Fales et al., 2009) and may be the most expedient way to get clients to engage in rewarding approach goals. This may not be the case, however, if there is a significant and habitual dominance of the right PFC over the left—pharmacological treatment with serotonin reuptake inhibitors (SSRI) has shown poor outcomes (Grawe, 2007).

The hypoactivation of the PFC that is typical in depression is also associated with reduced grey-matter volume along with volume decreases in the anterior cingulate cortex, orbital frontal cortex (Bora, Fornito, Panetlis, & Yücel, 2011; Grieve, Korgaonkar, Koslow, Gordon, & Williams, 2013), and glia cells (Grawe, 2007). These findings raise the question of cause and effect: Does reduced volume in these areas cause depression, or is it a result of being depressed? Is the decreased PFC blood flow and metabolism causing the reduced volume, or is it the other way around? As yet we don't know.

A recent study on childhood depression found that depression in this stage was associated with markedly increased rates of cortical volume loss and thinning across the entire cortex in comparison with the brains of non-depressed children (Luby et al., 2016). The study found that synaptic pruning of grey matter was particularly vigorous in adolescents who had experienced symptoms of depression during their childhood. In fact the researchers found marked decreases in the right hemisphere with only marginal effects in the left—a seeming paradox given that right dominance has been associated with depression. Whatever the case, it is certain that individuals who have undergone substantial change of this kind in the neural architecture will struggle to match the capacity of healthy individuals to motivate themselves toward approach-oriented behaviour.

The Anterior Cingulate Cortex in Depression

The anterior cingulate cortex (ACC) is an important area relaying information from the limbic regions to the PFC, providing integration for visceral, attentional, and affective information for self-regulation and adaptability (Thayer & Lane, 2000). The ACC is involved in attentional processing, and especially so when there is a high demand for the attention of executive functions as the individual is faced with conflicting demands, motiva-

Some Brain Areas Involved in Depression

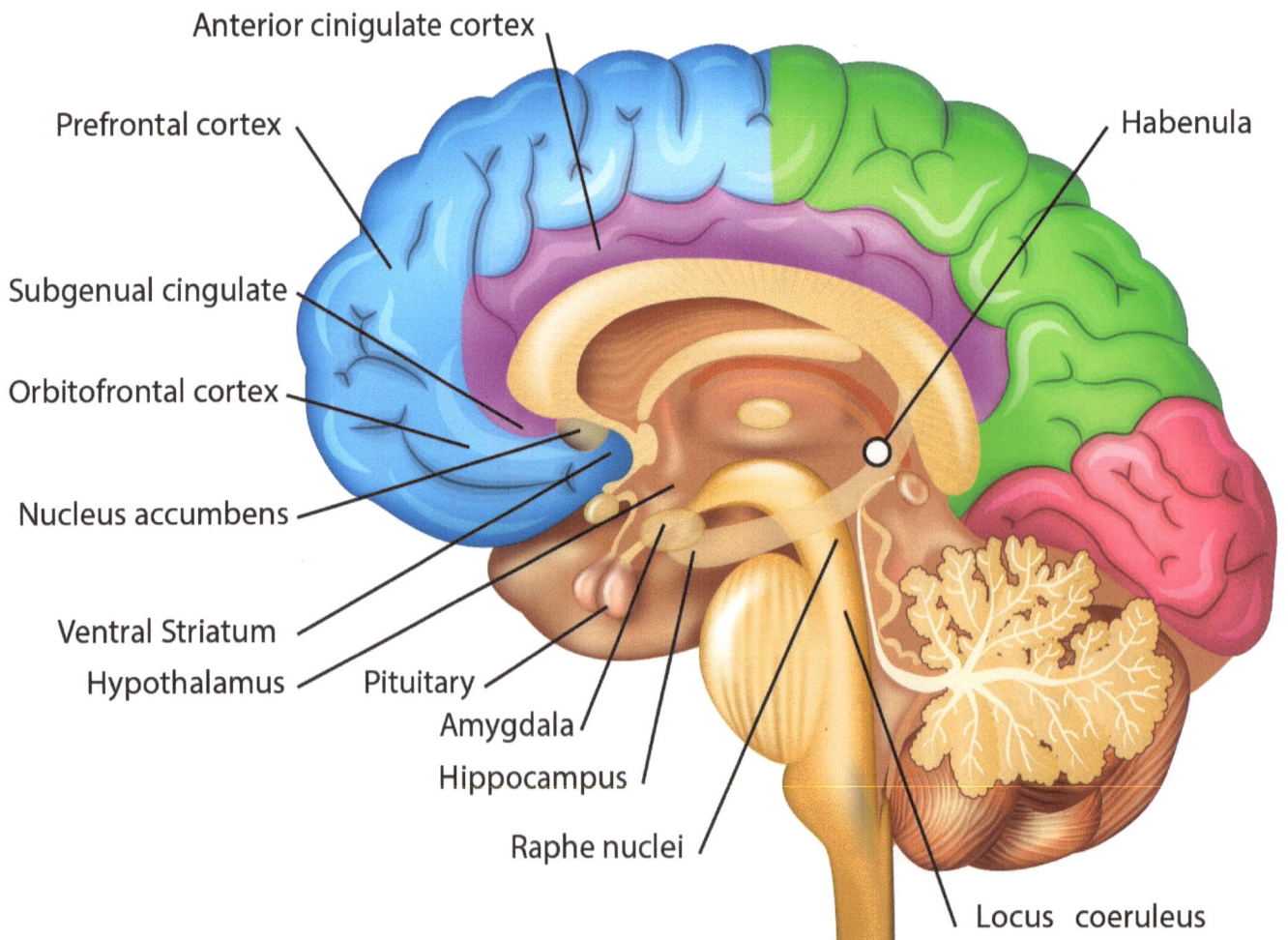

Anterior cinigulate cortex

Prefrontal cortex

Habenula

Subgenual cingulate

Orbitofrontal cortex

Nucleus accumbens

Ventral Striatum

Hypothalamus

Pituitary

Amygdala

Hippocampus

Raphe nuclei

Locus coeruleus

tions, and uncertainty (Grawe, 2007). When confronted with such difficult situations, the ACC ensures the right processing resources are made available: if things are not going the way we would like them to—producing a neural state of inconsistency—the ACC recruits areas such as the PFC to resolve such inconsistencies (Grawe, 2007).

In simplistic terms, depressed individuals have a chronically underactivated ACC, so that insufficient effort is made to recruit other brain resources when things are going wrong and something needs to be done about it. The demands of the environment can quickly overwhelm the individual whose ACC is not calling into action the right neural resources.

The ACC can be divided into two different functional areas: (a) the affect subdivision, encompassing the rostral and ventral areas connected with limbic and paralimbic regions—involved in regulating responses to stressful events, emotional expression, and social behaviour; and (b) the cognitive subdivision, comprising the dorsal regions closely connected with the dorsolateral prefrontal cortex—involved in processing cognitively demanding information (Davidson et al., 2002). Hypoactivation of the affect subdivision may blunt emotional experiencing and arousal, while hypoactivation of the cognitive subdivision may impair the recruitment and monitoring of executive functions to meet challenges.

Davidson et al. (2002) hypothesized that there may be two broad subtypes of depression, an ACC-subtype and a PFC-subtype:

> The ACC-subtype may be reflected phenomenologically in a deficit in the "will-to-change", as such individuals would not experience the conflict between their current state and the demands of everyday life. The PFC-subtype may fully experience such conflict and experience pronounced distress because the experience of the conflict between one's current state and the demands of everyday life are not sufficient to activate PFC-based mechanisms to organize and guide behaviour toward the resolution of the conflict. (p. 555)

The Amygdala in Depression

The amygdala is continually evaluating all incoming information for its importance to our safety and motivational goals and directing our attention toward those things with the highest emotional–motivational salience (Grawe, 2007). Because uncertainy can spell danger, the amygdala is particularly alert to uncertain and surprising information. A meta-analysis of studies on amygdala volume in MDD (Hamilton, Siemer, & Gotlib, 2008) found that medicated depressed individuals had significantly increased amygdala volume relative to healthy persons, whereas unmedicated depressed individuals showed a decrease in amygdala volume. The authors hypothesized that antidepressant-mediated increases in levels of brain-derived neurotrophic factor promoted neurogenesis—protecting the amygdala against glucocorticoid toxicity—but not in unmedicated cases of depression. In a more recent review (Schmaal et al., 2016), out of 1,728 MDD patients there was found to be a trend toward smaller amygdala overall.

The Hippocampus in Depression

The hippocampus has been found to have reduced volume in individuals with MDD, with the scale of reduction apparently corresponding to the duration of depressive states (Davidson et al., 2002; Grawe, 2007). Reduction in hippocampal volume is also a feature of bipolar disorder, anxiety disorders, obsessive–compulsive disorder, PTSD, and schizophrenia (Bremner et al., 1997; Buehlmann et al., 2010; Fusar-Poli et al., 2007; Geuze, Vermetten, & Bremner, 2005; Kempton et al., 2011; Shepherd, Laurens, Matheson, Carr, & Green, 2012). It may be that such reductions in hippocampal volume are a result of enduring stress. The hippocampus contains many glucocorticoid receptors and is therefore sensitive to stress hormones like cortisol. Chronically elevated cortisol levels due to sustained stress may result in the loss of neurons and glia in all the conditions noted above. However, it is possible that a reduced hippocampus exists prior to, and facilitates, depressive and anxiety disorders. More longitudinal studies are needed to establish a clearer cause-and-effect model.

The hippocampus is also involved in the hypothalamic–pituitary–adrenal (HPA) axis stress response. It normally provides negative feedback to the HPA axis to slow the release of cortisol in the stress response, but this capacity can be overridden and is compromised in the case of sustained stress and chronically elevated levels of cortisol damage, so that a harmful continuation of cortisol release continues.

The hippocampus is important for putting things in context and helping us to respond to events by regulating our emotions accordingly (Grawe, 2007). It plays a critical part in establishing a link between the memory of contextual information and whatever we are currently faced with. For example, the war veteran who hears a car backfiring engages his hippocampus to put the sound in context (hometown as opposed to Afghanistan), which helps him to make a situation-appropriate response (keep walking down the street as opposed to hitting the deck and calling for backup). In depressed individuals the hippocampus may not be helping to regulate emotional responses in a context-appropriate way, resulting in overly exaggerated or diminished responses.

A recent meta-analysis of brain alterations in MDD concluded that the hippocampus plays a key role in the pathophysiology of MDD and that hippocampal volume reduction is evident in both recurrent and early-onset MDD (Schmaal et al., 2016).

The Nucleus Accumbens in Depression

The nucleus accumbens (NAc), like the hippocampus, helps us respond to a changing environment in an appropriate and adaptive manner. It acts as a relay between the limbic and basal ganglia structures and is involved in motivation and behavioural responses—reinforcing hunger and pleasurable activities such as sex. Given that depression is marked by a diminished interest or pleasure in things that should be pleasurable (known as *anhedonia*), it is reasonable to assume that the NAc may play a role in depression (Naranjo, Tremblay, & Busto, 2001).

A recent study on adolescent depression and early-life stress found that NAc hyporeactivity was associated with a depressed adolescence (Goff et al., 2013). For someone who is unable to experience rewards, there is little motivation to change behaviour toward rewarding goals. The NAc acts as an important integrative hub for reward-mediated behaviours and may be adversely affected by chronic stress (Heshmati & Russo, 2015). An experiment applying deep-brain stimulation to the nucleus accumbens demonstrated an anti-anxiety effect in depressed patients (Bewernick et al., 2010).

The Habenula in Depression

The habenula is involved in multiple tasks such as reproductive behaviour, stress responses, pain processing, reward processing (especially in regard to negative rewards; Matsumoto & Hikosaka, 2007), and prediction errors (Bromberg-Martin & Hikosaka, 2011). It is extensively connected to the dorsal and medial raphe nuclei—a serotonergic region—and to the ventral tegmental area—a dopaminergic region. Studies of the lateral habenula that show heightened activity when rewards are withheld have led to the idea of a "disappointment

circuit".

Increased activity and reduced volume in the lateral habenula seem to be implicated with MDD, which may have functional consequences for the depressed person's ability to deal effectively with negative events (Savitz et al., 2011). Non-human studies have found that high lateral habenula activity promotes behavioural avoidance via the down-regulation of the serotonergic, noradrenergic, and dopaminergic systems and stimulation of the HPA axis. Habenula hyperactivity may influence the way we process motivationally important stimuli and result in abnormal emotional experiences and behaviours (Lawson et al., 2017; Stamatakis & Stuber, 2012)

The Brainstem in Depression

The dorsal raphe nucleus, as mentioned above, houses serotonergic (5-HT) neural networks that project into a host of brain regions including the PFC. This part of the brainstem has a huge impact on the central nervous system, as it projects serotonin pathways across the brain, releasing serotonin to mediate many processes including body temperature, blood pressure, respiration, hormone release, attention and arousal, uterine activities, aggression, food intake, sleep, and dreaming (Lambert & Kinsley, 2004).

For a long time it has been suspected that serotonin plays a role in depression and suicide. In a post-mortem study of mood disorders and suicide, it was found that those who had been diagnosed with MDD generally had a reduced dorsal raphe nucleus, yet suicide was associated with an increased dorsal raphe nucleus with a higher density but decreased size of serotonergic neurons (Matthews & Harrison, 2012). There is evidence that this seat of serotonergic activity is important in depression, but such post-mortem studies are rife with confounding variables, with only modest alterations in dorsal raphe nucleus morphology.

Another area of the brainstem that has an equally important impact on the rest of the central nervous system is the locus coeruleus (LC)—a major site for the synthesis of norepinephrine—which projects into the cortical, subcortical, and limbic structures (Malenka, Nestler, & Hyman, 2009). The LC noradrenergic system helps maintain vigilance in our responses to the environment and maintains arousal, attention, sleep–wake cycles, memory, and cognitive control, as well as playing a role in neuroplasticity and emotional responses (Benarroch, 2009). It is thought that the LC is overactive in MDD, and that antidepressants down-regulate the LC and its norepinephrine output while increasing serotonergic function (Ressler & Nemeroff, 2000). The big picture for depression, however, is complex, involving the modulation of many brain networks and neurochemicals. In the following half of this section we examine the role of neurochemicals, genetics, and neuroplasticity, to piece together a more accurate and holistic understanding of how depression affects the individual.

Neurochemicals in Depression

Evidence has mounted since the 1950s that serotonergic systems play a major role in depression. Central to this understanding early on was the observation that raising the level of serotonin appeared to reduce the symptoms of depression. The "monoamine hypothesis" of depression suggests that a deficiency in monoamines, including serotonin, causes the symptoms of depression. On the surface this logic appears reasonable, but it does not necessarily explain causality.

The monoamine hypothesis received support in the form of observations that the drug reserpine, which depletes monoamines, seemed to increase depressive symptoms. Armed with this knowledge, researchers looked at how to selectively increase synaptic serotonin levels, which led to the creation of selective serotonin reuptake inhibitors (SSRIs), more commonly known as anti-depressants.

During the 1970s and 1980s, there was also a focus on monoamine receptors and how receptor density and sensitivity changed in response to different therapies, especially antidepressants. Generally the body of research supported the hypothesis that depression is marked by impaired serotonergic and adrenergic activity, with effective drug therapy increasing one or both of these systems (Palazidou, 2012). We know that presynaptic serotonergic cells have autoreceptors that monitor the amount of serotonin released by the cell. These receptors regulate the amount of serotonin release in tandem with the reuptake transporters that take serotonin from the synaptic cleft and back into the presynaptic cell. Antidepressants, by blocking reuptake mechanisms and forcing more monoamines to stay in the synaptic cleft, increase the serotonergic activity of cells in a matter of days, and autoreceptors quickly adapt to the increase in serotonin. The firing rate of the monoaminer-

gic neurons is initially decreased to compensate for the increase in circulating monoamines, but the inhibition diminishes over time, and a therapeutic effect is felt by the patient (Lambert & Kinsley, 2005).

Another theory linking neurochemicals and depression rests on the catecholamine hypothesis introduced by Joseph Schildkraut (1965). This theory postulates that depression is a result of norepinephrine (NE) deficiency, and that an overabundance of NE leads to manic states. Although SSRIs had already produced clinically significant results in dealing with depression, the notion of a relationship between depleted NE and depression was supported by research (Delgado & Moreno, 2000; Nemeroff, 1998). It is worth noting that, as in the case of serotonin, NE depletion does not induce clinical depression in healthy people—the cause of depression appears to be more complex than simple imbalances in these levels. It is likely that depression may be a result of dysfunction in brain areas modulated by monoamine systems. The same probably holds for the involvement of another monoamine, dopamine, which has also been implicated in depression and anhedonia (Treadway & Zald, 2011).

Genetics in Depression

The early dominance of the monoamine hypothesis, which postulates that depressive symptoms are the result of decreased serotonin, noradrenalin, and possibly dopamine, has given way to alternative theories that consider neural dysfunction and genetic factors. In fact, a meta-analysis of major depression in twins concluded that the disorder is a familial one, albeit complex, arising from the combined effect of genetic and environmental influences (Sullivan, Neale, & Kendler, 2000). Epigenetic studies have been investigating how individual environmental factors modulate gene expression in depression. For instance, the 3A serotonin genotype (HTR3A-42C>T) is associated with grey-matter loss in the hippocampus and PFC in depressed individuals who have experienced early-life stress (Gatt et al., 2010). And just as we saw with the rhesus monkeys, human carriers of the 5-HTTLPR short allele are more prone to depression if they have suffered one or more earlier stressful life events, which lends further support to the idea that an individual's response to environmental stress is moderated by genetic makeup (Caspi et al., 2003; Karg, Burmeister, Shedden, & Sen, 2011).

Another line of research implicates brain-derived neurotropic factor (BDNF), which is involved in the growth of new neurons in the hippocampus and rep-

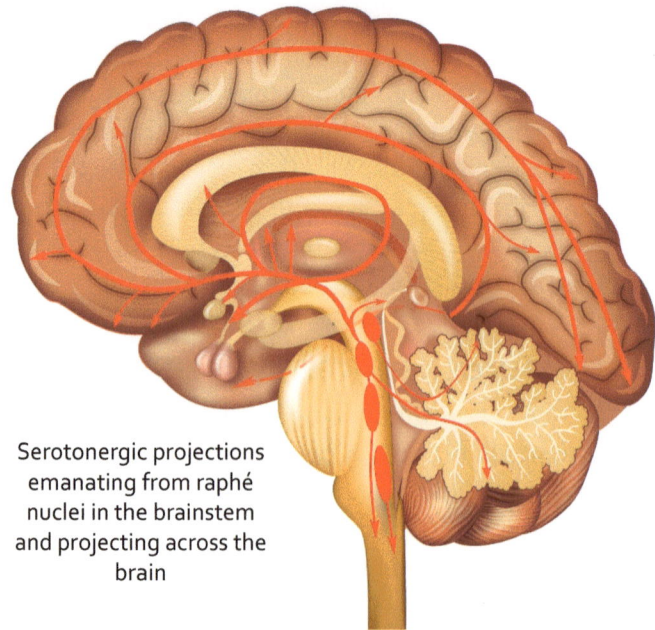

Serotonergic projections emanating from raphé nuclei in the brainstem and projecting across the brain

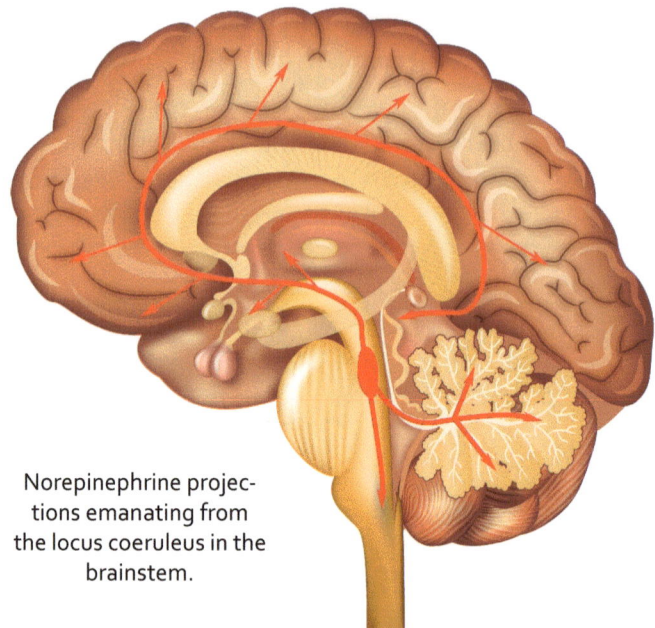

Norepinephrine projections emanating from the locus coeruleus in the brainstem.

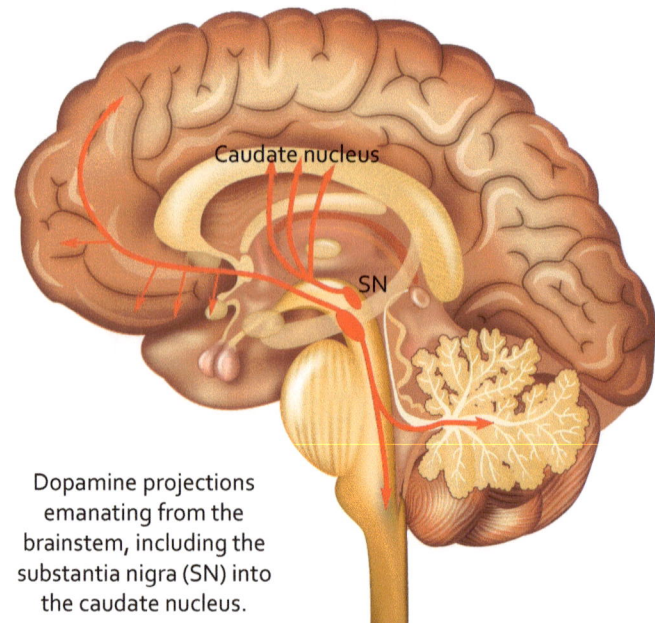

Caudate nucleus

SN

Dopamine projections emanating from the brainstem, including the substantia nigra (SN) into the caudate nucleus.

Stressed Rhesus Monkeys
and the Serotonin Transporter Gene

Studies on rhesus monkeys that investigated the impact of attachment (Suomi, 1999, as cited in Grawe, 2007) yielded some telling results: monkeys raised with peers, but without mothers, tended to be more impulsive and aggressive and drank more alcohol (made available as part of the experiment) as young adults than their peers. They also had lower levels of serotonin metabolite (5-HIAA) and higher glucose metabolism in their brains, making them hyper-aroused. These monkeys, with very poor attachment experiences, developed a biological system shaped by insecure attachment.

The researchers found that monkeys growing up without mothers had chronically lower serotonin levels, significantly affecting their social relationships and the capacity of female monkeys to be good mothers themselves. There seems to be a positive correlation between attachment relationships and serotonin levels that can have a calming effect on neural firing—animals with more serotonin available appear to do better socially.

The truly groundbreaking finding of these types of studies (see, e.g., Bennett, Abee, & Henrickson, 1998; Lesch et al., 1996) concerned experience-dependent gene expression: monkeys with poor attachment whose serotonin transporter gene (5-HTT) had the "short" HTT-allele (less efficient for expressing the gene) would have lower serotonin levels than monkeys with the "long" HTT-allele. Interestingly, monkeys with the short HTT-allele who did have normal attachment with their mothers did not have lowered serotonin levels—their genotype may have put them at genetic risk of serotonergic hypofunction, but secure attachment averted this genetic expression. On the other hand, monkeys who had the stronger genotype with the long HTT-allele, even though they may have had the disadvantage of a motherless upbringing, still had normal serotonergic functioning—their genotype protected them from the impact of not having a mother (at least in terms of serotonergic function). These findings, that favourable versus unfavourable life experiences can alter gene expression affecting areas like the serotonergic system, are important when we consider the environmental variables at play in cases of anxiety and depression.

resents an important mechanism of adult brain plasticity. Stress suppresses BDNF synthesis in the hippocampus, and depressed patients have been shown to have lower serum BDNF concentrations than healthy subjects. Antidepressants and electroconvulsive therapy seem to increase BDNF serum concentrations and reduce depressive symptoms (Piccinni et al., 2009; Shimizu et al., 2003). BDNF seems a good candidate for study in depression, as BDNF genetic variations influence brain areas related to mood (Palazidou, 2012). The Met allele BDNF genotype has been associated with abnormal secretion of BDNF, abnormal hippocampal neuronal function, and impaired episodic memory (Hariri et al., 2003) as well as smaller hippocampal volume (Frodl, Möller, & Meisenzahl, 2008). However, the evidence for the involvement of BDNF in the pathophysiology of depression is inconsistent and does not support a simple causal relationship between total brain BDNF levels and mood (Groves, 2007). Rather, the role of BDNF in modulating activity-dependent plasticity within emotional processing networks may be compromised in depression. In other words, BDNF may not control mood directly, but is critical in the process that determines how a plastic change influences mood (Castrén, Võikar, & Rantamäki, 2007).

Neuroplasticity in Depression

As discussed above, studies found that antidepressant medication rapidly increased the transmission at monoaminergic synapses, yet patients did not typically feel the therapeutic effects for some weeks after starting treatment. This points to something beyond merely the synaptic change elicited by the antidepressant. The neuroplasticity theory of depression suggests that the depressed brain has reduced plasticity in key areas such as the PFC, hippocampus, and amygdala, leading to neural and glial loss and pathology (Andrade & Rao, 2010). The theory suggests that depression is a disorder of the hardwiring of the brain rather than a chemical imbalance. In this context, antidepressants can protect against some of these neuronal architectural and connectivity changes that are at the foundation of the disorder (Castrén & Hen, 2013). Research demonstrating that stress and depression disrupt adult neurogenesis in the hippocampus, and research showing antidepressants' increased neurogenesis in the hippocampus, also support the neuroplasticity theory (Duman & Voleti, 2012; Eisch & Petrik, 2012).

Inflammation

It has been well established that the immune system is involved in the pathophysiology of major depressive disorder (Villanueva, 2013). Signalling molecules of the immune system, called proinflammatory cytokines, can elicit symptoms of anxiety and depression; typically, those with major depression will have elevated levels of circulating proinflammatory cytokines (Palazidou, 2012). It is interesting that in animal studies, researchers have been able to induce depressive-like behaviour and neutralize the effects of antidepressants by administering the proinflammatory cytokine interleukin-6 (Sukoff Rizzo et al., 2012), and people treated with interferon alpha (another cytokine) can develop depressive-like symptoms (Shelton & Miller, 2010). As the immune system activates an inflammatory response, it can deplete the body of the serotonin precursor tryptophan—a molecule that is used by the body to make serotonin. Inflammation may also influence noradrenergic activity, and it stimulates the HPA axis. Chronic physical illness or stress also releases inflammatory cytokines that can reduce glucocorticoid receptor function, which in turn can increase inflammation. In fact there are multiple causes for an inflammatory response, including obesity, multiple sclerosis, cardiovascular disease, and psoriasis (Shelton & Miller, 2010). Whatever the cause of the inflammation, it seems this process plays a role in depression.

The Gut

There is growing evidence that the interplay between the brain and the gut is of significant importance to well-being. In depression, the influence of the gut microbiota over brain chemistry and resulting behaviour is a variable we must take seriously (Villanueva, 2013). Recent studies suggest that the microbiota could activate our immune system and affect our central nervous system, delivering substances such as serotonin and gamma-aminobutyric acid (Evrensel & Ceylan, 2015). Such findings have led to the development of psychobiotic-based therapeutic strategies for mood disorders, and have directed research focus to the interplay between physical ailments such as irritable bowel syndrome and depression (Dinan & Cryan, 2013). We will examine this area in more depth in the next section of the guide, on the Brain–Body connection.

Elements Implicated in Depression

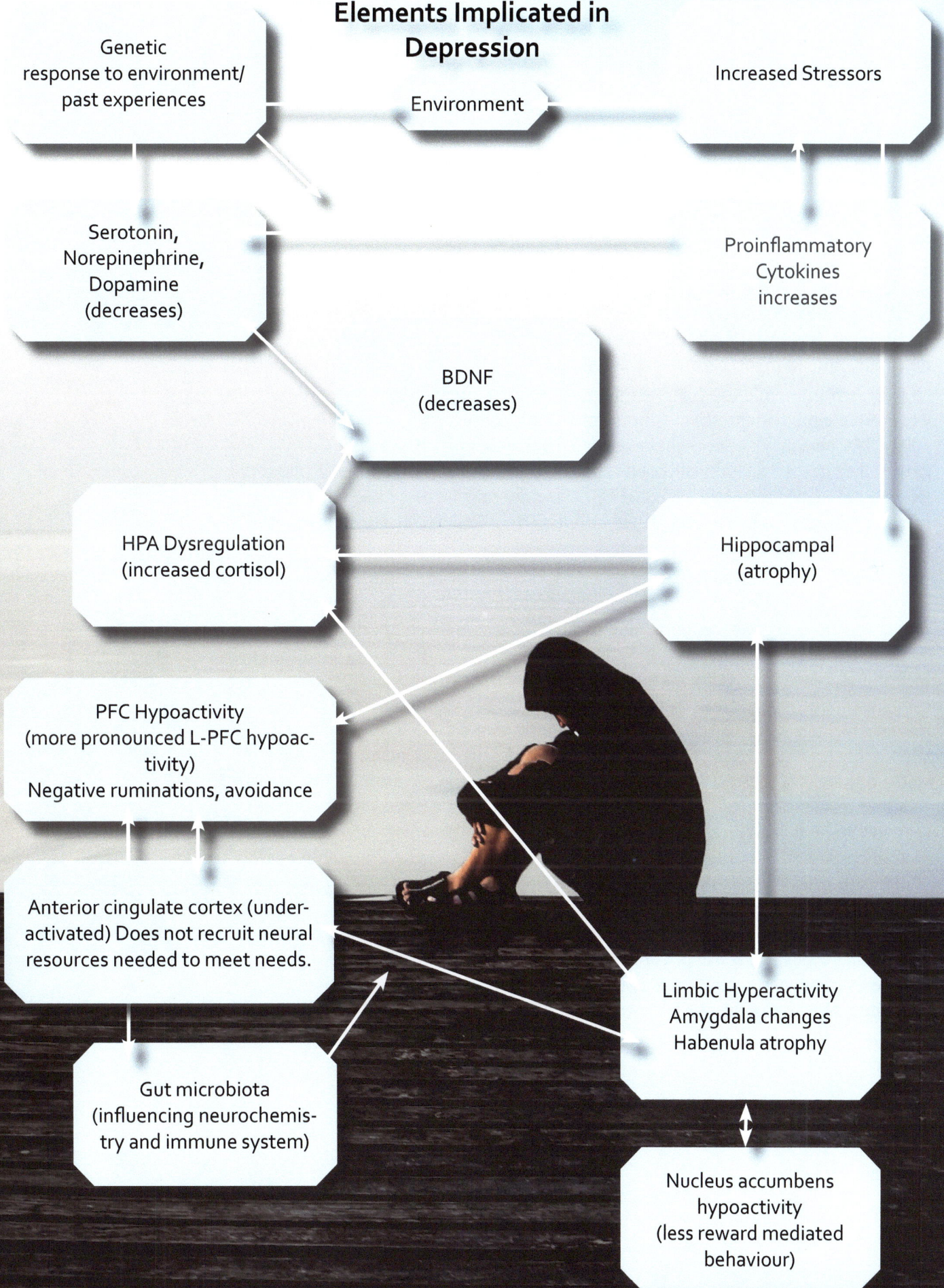

Genetic response to environment/ past experiences

Environment

Increased Stressors

Serotonin, Norepinephrine, Dopamine (decreases)

Proinflammatory Cytokines increases

BDNF (decreases)

HPA Dysregulation (increased cortisol)

Hippocampal (atrophy)

PFC Hypoactivity (more pronounced L-PFC hypoactivity) Negative ruminations, avoidance

Anterior cingulate cortex (under-activated) Does not recruit neural resources needed to meet needs.

Limbic Hyperactivity Amygdala changes Habenula atrophy

Gut microbiota (influencing neurochemistry and immune system)

Nucleus accumbens hypoactivity (less reward mediated behaviour)

Summary of the Pathophysiology of Depression

Depression is a complex phenomenon, from the social and environmental factors that prime our stress responses and express genes in different ways, to chemical balances, inefficient neural architectures, and lack of neural plasticity. There is no single, unified theory, nor a simple solution.

Research into childhood depression gives convincing evidence that children experience similar depressive symptoms to those observed in adults (Hallam, 2002). Teachers may notice depressive related behaviours such as acting out, negative self-concept, lack of positive affect, somatic symptoms and guilt/self-blame (Kovacs, 1981; Donelly and Wilson,1994). A child may feel worthless and inferior, fearful, anxious and would rather withdraw than interact socially with his or her peers (Hallam, 2002).

As teacher's we should be aware first and foremost of the complexity of the neurobiological, epigenetic, and environmental factors at play. School environments can inadvertently reinforce depressive tendencies when children feel excluded or teachers hold unfavorable attitudes towards students. Harsh discipline techniques, put-downs, embarrassment and sarcasm, lack of support for learning difficulties and not addressing peer bullying, can only exacerbate sad and depressive feelings. Conversely, the school environment can be a major player in supporting and assisting the child who shows depressive tendencies. Early identification of those that may be at risk of learning and/or behavioural difficulties to allow strategies and support to be put in place early in a child's school life is seen as essential (Ball, Finch, & Gettinger (2014). Equally important is the support of empathetic teachers who have an awareness of the difficulties depressed students face, so they are proactive in the development of caring and supportive student/teacher relationships, inclusivity (Cameron, 2014), and gentle nurturing to help provide a protective factor for students (McWhirter, 2013). Evidence has shown that a positive sense of connectedness results in positive adult reactions and peer acceptance, which is seen as most critical for sustained happiness in an individual's life (Lee et al., 2001; Townsend & McWhirter, 2005).

BRAIN–BODY

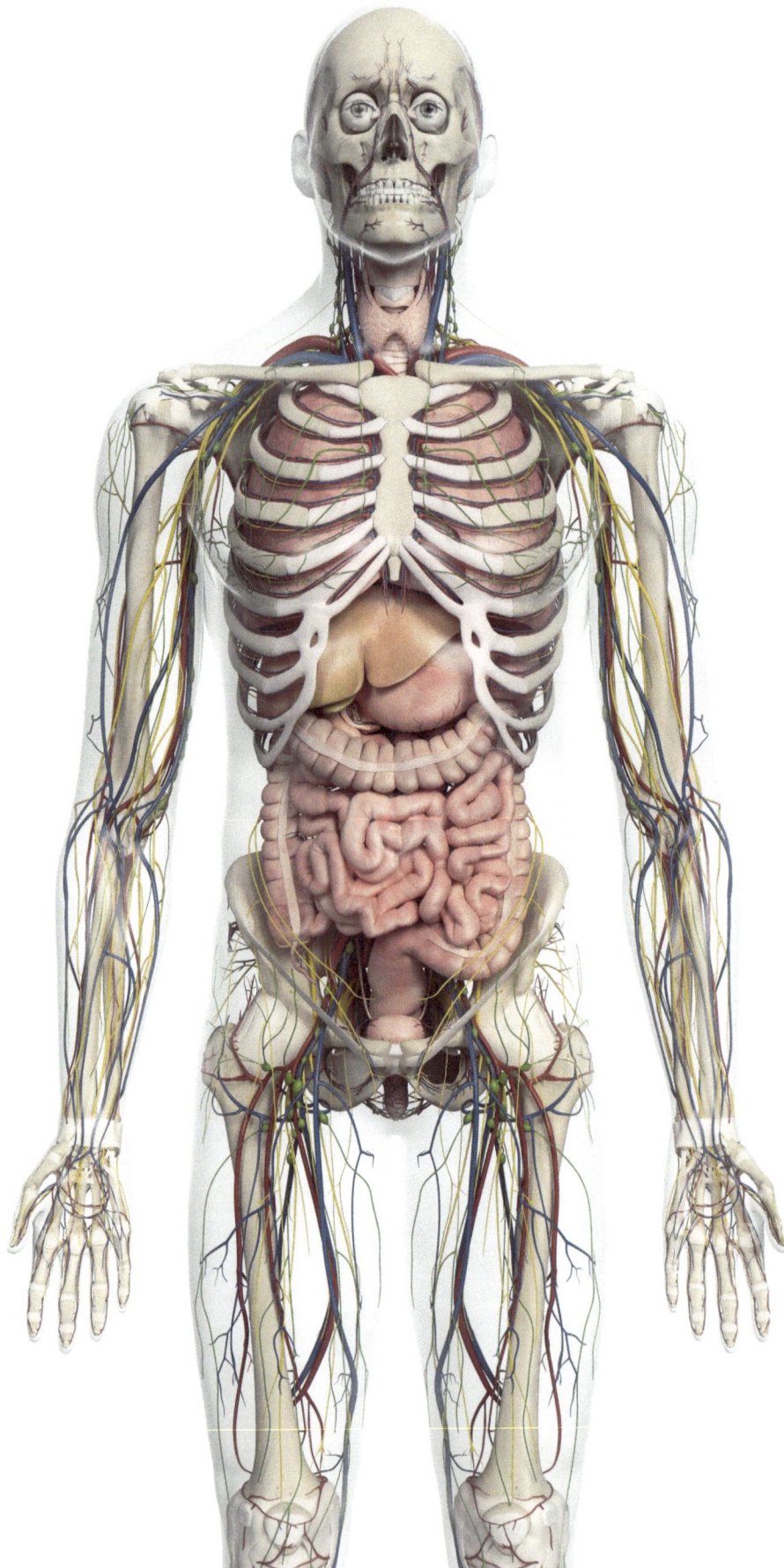

As a society we are becoming increasingly aware of the critical interplay between the systems of the body and mental health. Dysfunctions of the mind or body have a bidirectional effect, in ways more profound than we may have appreciated in the past. Research from the biological and psychological sciences is painting a more integrative picture of the brain–body connection than ever before. We are now gaining a more refined understanding of the way the central nervous system (CNS) and the rest of the body modulate each other, and how this insight can contribute to better treatment and prevention of mental disorders. In this section, while we touch on some of the body systems that have an effect on our mental well-being, we are really only scratching the surface of this wonderfully complex phenomenon of the brain–body connection.

The Heart

Thinkers throughout the ages have considered the heart to be the seat of the emotions and at the centre of spiritual life. William Harvey (1578–1657), an English doctor who was the first to fully describe the circulatory system that delivers blood to the body and brain, said, "Every affection of the mind that is attended either with pain or pleasure, hope or fear, is the cause of an agitation whose influence extends to the heart" (Rosch, 2015, p. 7).

In broad terms, our contemporary view of the heart is one of a complex and interdependent relationship between the heart and mind. Early studies of heart–brain communication were intent on explaining the influence of the brain over the heart, yet we now know there is more neural "traffic" from the heart to the brain than the other way around (McCraty, 2015a). In fact the heart communicates with the brain not only through the nervous system, but also through hormones, pulse waves created by heart contractions, and the electromagnetic field generated by the heart. At the forefront of the new science of the heart–brain connection has been recent research into heart rate variability (HRV), a measure of the nervous system's flexibility for emotional self-regulation.

In the 1960s and 70s, researchers John and Beatrice Lacey established scientific evidence that the heart communicates to the brain in a way that affects how we perceive and react to the world (Lacey & Lacey, 1974). German research by Velden and Wölk in the 1980s found that cognitive performance and cortical function are under the influence of the heart by means of afferent (heart to brain) inputs on neurons in the thalamus that affect the global synchronization of cortical activity (Velden & Wölk, 1987; Wölk & Velden, 1989). Importantly, the researchers identified the pattern and stability of these afferent inputs, which in turn have global effects on brain function. The heart, it seems, wields more control over the brain than we had supposed. Since these early discoveries there has been a proliferation of studies on HRV as a marker for physical and emotional well-being.

Simply put, HRV measures the variability in time between heartbeats. This, it turns out, is a good gauge of the interplay between the autonomous nervous system (ANS) and the heart. The parasympathetic branch of the ANS, via the vagus nerve, connects to the heart's pacemaker (the concentration of nerve cells in the sinoatrial node in the heart that initiates heart contractions) and exerts an inhibitory effect on heart rate. It is, as it were, the braking system for the heart. On release of the parasympathetic brake, the heart rate rises. This operation of the vagus nerve upon the heart's pacemaker occurs on a moment-by-moment basis, resulting in slight variations of timing between heartbeats. High HRV indicates that the heart is readily and flexibly influenced by the vagal brake, and this, it has been discovered, is a good indicator of our emotional flexibility.

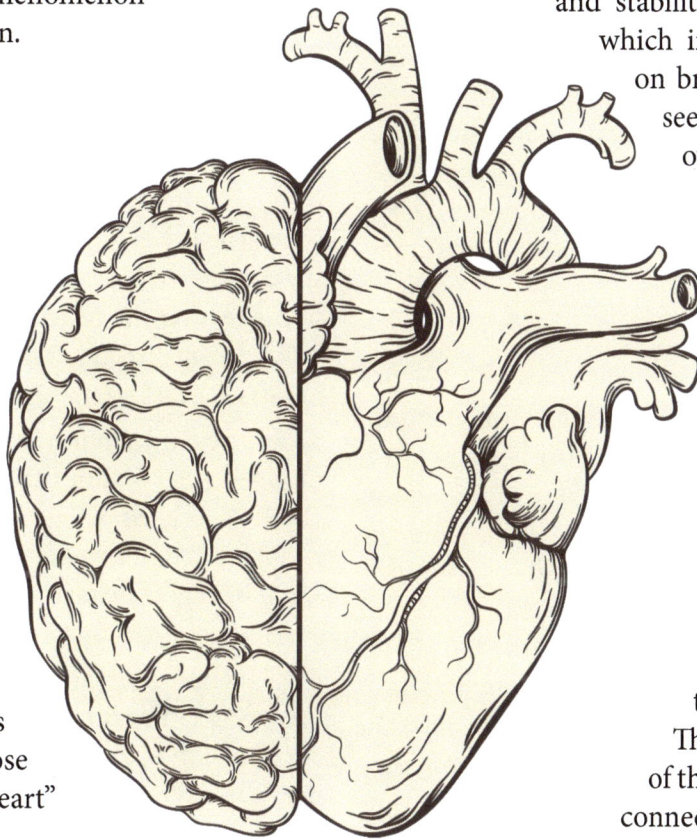

The heart influences the brain through four lines of communication:

1. **The nervous system**
2. **Hormones**
3. **Pulse waves**
4. **Electromagnetic fields**

The Intuitive Heart

Intuition is normally conceived as a cognitive–affective understanding, or "affectively charged judgments that arise through rapid, nonconscious, and holistic associations" (Dane & Pratt, 2007, p. 33). However, there may be other types of intuitive process where the heart informs the mind in unique ways. One such possibility lies in the capacity of our nervous system to sense electromagnetic fields, which the heart both produces and is sensitive to. This is referred to as cardioelectromagnetic communication:

> The heart is the most powerful source of electromagnetic energy in the human body, producing the largest rhythmic electromagnetic field of any of the body's organs. The heart's electrical field is about 60 times greater in amplitude than the electrical activity generated by the brain. This field, measured in the form of an electrocardiogram (ECG), can be detected anywhere on the surface of the body. Furthermore, the magnetic field produced by the heart is more than 100 times greater in strength than the field generated by the brain and can be detected up to 3 feet away from the body, in all directions, using SQUID-based magnetometers. (McCraty, 2015b, p. 36)

Psychophysiologist Rollin McCraty makes a fascinating exploration of the science of the electromagnetic sensitivities of the heart, including its apparently "nonlocal" or pre-stimulus knowledge and how this is communicated to the brain, in Chapter 7 of his book *Science of the Heart: Exploring the Role of the Heart in Human Performance* (Volume 2; McCraty, 2015b). Some of the intuitive capacity of the heart may be explained in the future by quantum neurophysics (Tarlacı & Pregnolato,

2016), and much remains speculative. Nevertheless, the interplay between the heart and mind is itself intuitive—as it is to anyone who has given the advice, "Listen to your heart."

The Polyvagal Theory

The polyvagal theory was put forward by Stephen Porges (2011). It proposes three vagal-mediated adaptive responses for different circumstances, namely safety, danger, and extreme threat to life. These responses are initiated by our *perception* of what is going on in our environment.

The first of these circuits is the ventral vagal complex (also known as the "smart vagus"), which downregulates the sympathetic "fight or flight" response so we can be social, engage in bonding, and emotionally self-regulate. This part of our nervous system is implicated in social communication on account of its effect on the muscles of the face, and in self-soothing/calming through inhibition of the defensive limbic system. The ventral vagal complex also influences heart rate: high vagal tone (strength of vagus response) has a suppressant effect on the heart's natural pacemaker; in the absence of vagal regulation, the heart's pacemaker rapidly increases heart rate.

The second circuit is the dorsal vagal complex, an unmyelinated circuit that is found in most vertebrates and is associated with primitive survival strategies. This is the branch of the vagus nerve that engages defensive "fight or flight" behaviour in the face of threats.

The third vagal mechanism acts through the dorsal vagal complex, which, in the face of an extreme threat to life, will feign death by producing neurogenic bradycardia (slowing of the heart rate) via the parasympathetic nervous system, manifesting in a freeze or faint. The bradycardia can be paralleled by apnoea—a response that may be adaptive for reptiles, but is potentially lethal for humans.

As mentioned previously, the initiation of any one of these three vagal responses is based on our perception of threat. This perception Porges calls *neuroception*—a subconscious neural process that distinguishes whether situations or people are safe, dangerous, or life-threatening. If there is no perception of threat, then the ventral vagal complex has control and we can be social and relaxed; we have good HRV, and all is well. But we all have different perceptions, or subconscious neuroceptions, about what is threatening and what is not, based on ear-

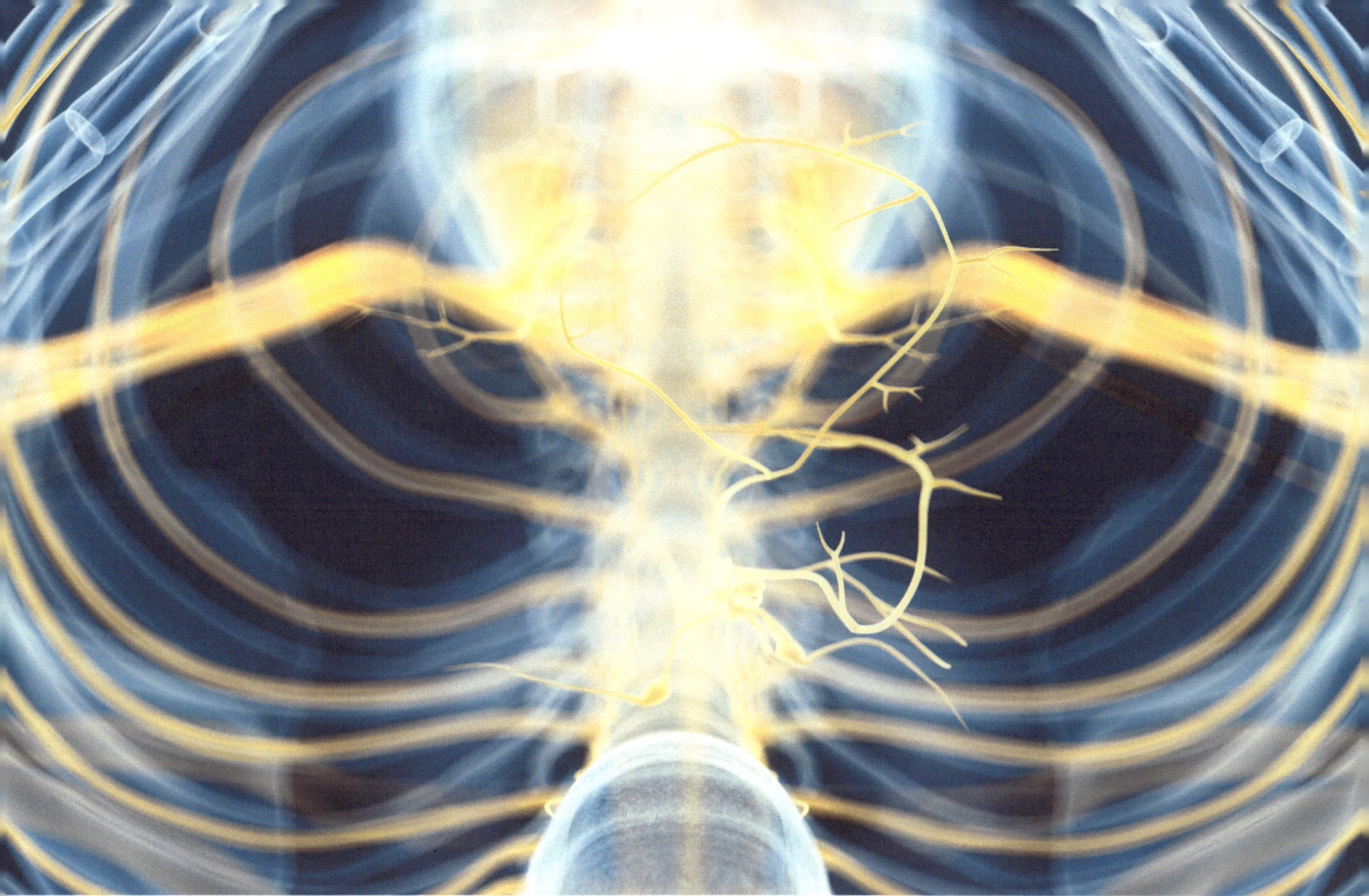

lier experiences. For an individual who has had mainly experiences of trauma, nothing in the world feels safe, and the default response is characterized by more frequent engagement of the dorsal vagal complex than is necessary to ensure actual safety. Lower HRV has been observed in individuals with post-traumatic stress disorder and borderline personality disorder (Meyer et al., 2016), rendering these people in a psychological state more prone to "fight or flight" than social engagement behaviours (Austin, Riniolo, & Porges, 2007).

The Gut–Brain Axis

The broad term *gut–brain axis* describes the bidirectional communication pathways of the central nervous system, the hypothalamic–pituitary–adrenal (HPA) axis, the autonomic nervous system, and the gut microbiota. Our bodies are host to an enormous population of microorganisms, collectively called microbiota or microflora, with the genomes in the microbiota termed the microbiome. These gut microbes outnumber the cells in our bodies by a factor of 10, contain 150 times more genes than our own (Gill et al., 2006; Qin et al., 2010), and comprise more than 1,000 species (Qin et al., 2010) and over 7,000 strains (Ley, Peterson, & Gordon,

2006). A growing body of research implicates the gut microbiome in the regulation of the CNS and behaviour in general. What we might term the microbiome-gut–brain axis, then, is a bidirectional communication network between the brain and gut modulated by neurochemicals and microbiota (Mawe & Hoffman, 2013; Mayer, 2011; Rhee, Pothoulakis, & Mayer, 2009).

Important findings in this research include that the microbial content of the gut is critical to the normal development of the HPA axis, brain-derived neurotrophic factor (BDNF, a key neurotrophin involved in neuronal growth), and expression of NMDA receptors in the cortex and hippocampus (Sudo et al., 2004). A number of studies have investigated changes in gene expression in the brains of "germ-free" mice—mice raised in a way that has significantly reduced their gut microbiota—finding decreased hippocampal expression of BDNF, which is important for brain plasticity, and alterations in normal neurotransmitter signalling (Mayer, Knight, Mazmanian, Cryan, & Tillisch, 2014).

There are several ways the gut microbiome influences the CNS, through humoral and neural routes (Bravo et al., 2011; Cryan & O'Mahony, 2011), and through neurotransmitter modulation such as elevating

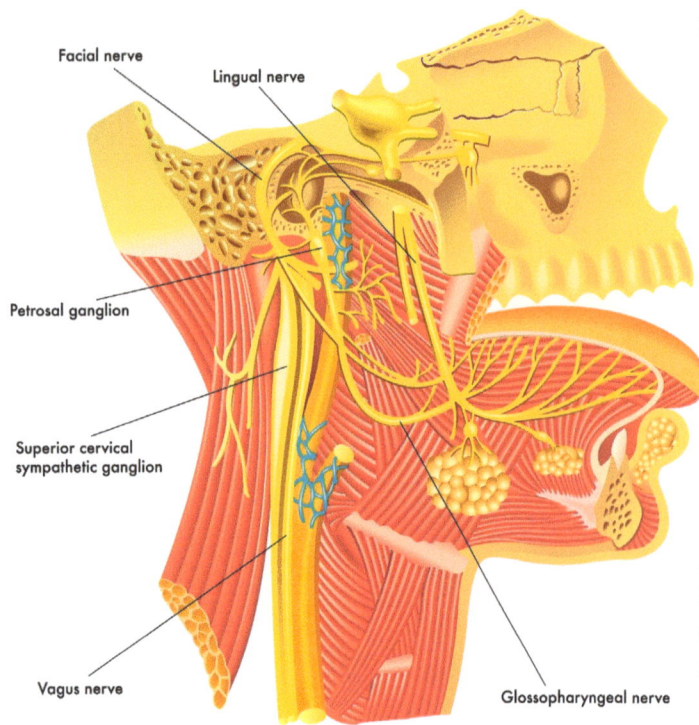

The vagal complex modulates bodily emotional responses.

plasma tryptophan—a precursor to serotonin (Desbonnet, Garrett, Clarke, Bienenstock, & Dinan, 2008). But the influence is not unidirectional. The CNS can change gastrointestinal motility, secretion, and intestinal permeability—actions that alter the gut environment for resident bacteria (Rhee et al., 2009). Stress can also induce permeability of the gut, allowing bacteria to cross the epithelial barrier, initiating a mucosal immune response that changes the composition of the microbiome (Kiliaan et al., 1998).

Researchers have been examining how to support the gut microbiome for normal brain function and experimenting with treatment for CNS disorders, in particular by the introduction of probiotics (Grenham, Clarke, Cryan, & Dinan, 2011). But this is a complex field involving not only many different species and strains of bacteria that elicit different effects in the gut, but neurochemicals and the CNS.

The Immune System

As we saw in the previous section on depression, the immune system is implicated in psychopathology, with inflammation being an important variable in major depression (Haapakoski, Mathieu, Ebmeier, Alenius, & Kivimäki, 2015). There is bidirectional communication between the brain and the immune system via many specialized pathways, such as the release of inflammatory cytokines in response to illness or other stressors. Cytokines can alter the function of serotonin, dopa-

mine, and glutamate in the brain, which play critical roles in depression. Stressful life experiences such as complex trauma may trigger long-lasting and systemic inflammatory responses. Childhood trauma can trigger such a response, affecting brain development and ultimately posing a risk of psychopathology (Danese & Baldwin, 2017).

Animal studies have found that psychological stress is communicated from the CNS to the immune system and from the immune system to back to the brain, releasing immune cells from the bone marrow. These immune cells, called monocytes, are released into circulation and provide inflammatory signals to the brain, with the potential to induce anxiety-like behaviour (McKim et al., 2016). Inflammation is a response that can be initiated by a multitude of variables including pathogens, stress, diet, and chemicals, all of which can prompt the release of inflammatory cytokines. The consumption of some foods, such as refined sugars, caffeine, alcohol, and anything triggering an allergic response, can initiate inflammation. There are also environmental and lifestyle factors, such as exposure to toxic metals, pesticides, herbicides, chronic stress, nutritional deficiencies, poor sleep, and ongoing infections, to name just a few. The cytokines released in an inflammatory response can cause oxidative stress to cells and shunt the serotonin precursor tryptophan toward the production of quinolinate, an excitotoxin in the CNS, which can lead to hindered neuronal function or apoptotic death (Guillemin, 2012).

There is still much to learn about the interplay of inflammation and mental health, but it is safe to assume that any chronic inflammation equates to a state of stress that is detrimental both developmentally and for our ultimate well-being.

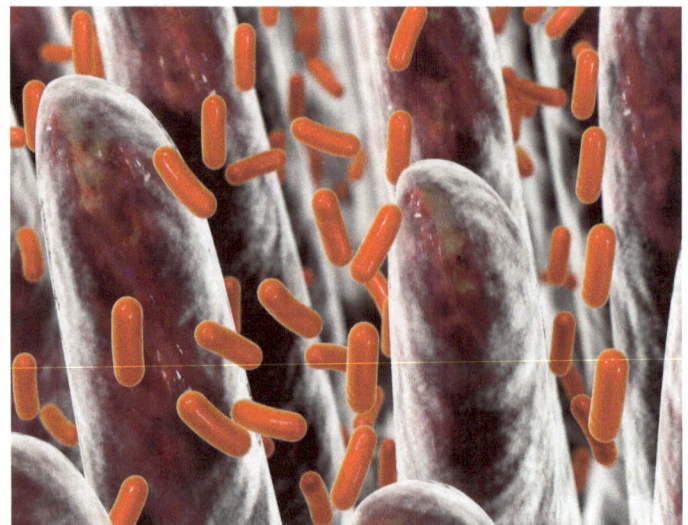

HEALTHY STATUS

Healthy CNS function

Normal Gut

Physiological levels of
inflammatory cells/mediators.
Normal gut microbiota.

STRESS/DISEASE

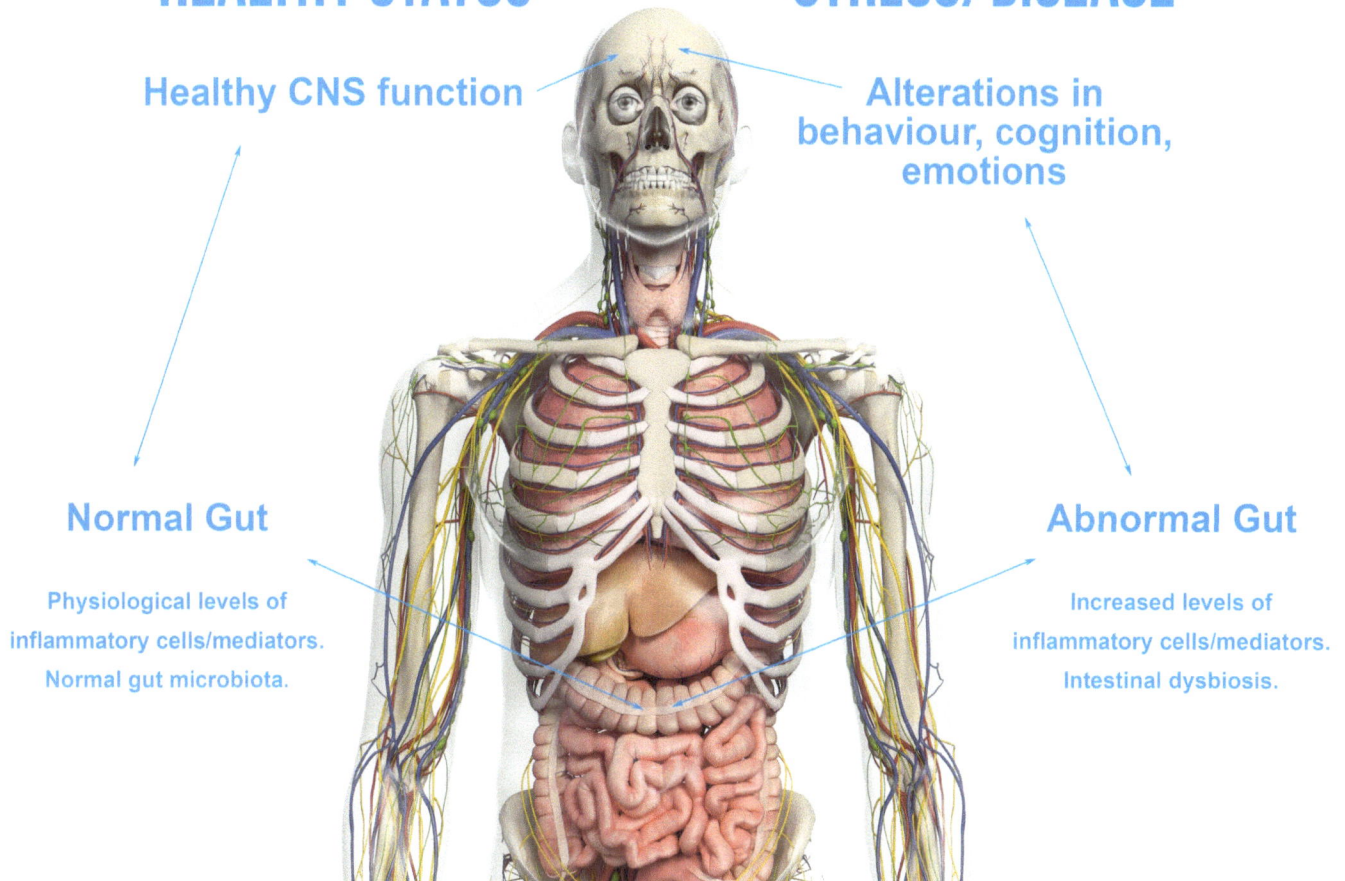

**Alterations in
behaviour, cognition,
emotions**

Abnormal Gut

Increased levels of
inflammatory cells/mediators.
Intestinal dysbiosis.

Brain–gut–microbe in health and disease (adapted from Grenham, Clarke, Cryan, & Dinan, 2011). A stable gut micro-biota helps establish normal gut physiology and appropriate signalling from the gut to the central nervous system. Poor gut microbiota health leads to inappropriate brain–gut axis signalling and negative CNS states. Stress signals originating from the CNS also negatively impact gut function and microbiota.

The Following Strategies Can Help Reduce Inflammation*

- Exercise—20 to 30 minutes of exercise at a minimum of 3 times per week.
- Rest—practise good sleep hygiene and get enough sleep.
- Stress Management—use relaxation techniques you enjoy; include deep-breathing exercises.
- Diet—focus on omega-3 fatty acids, alkaline-producing content, and whole foods rather than refined foods. Avoid saturated fats.

*Consult relevant professionals for exercise and diet strategies.

MEMORY

All through our lives we are on an insatiable learning quest that we call memory. We continually store information, either consciously or unconsciously, and draw on that learning to be animated and have a sense of who we are and what the world is. It is a never-ending cycle of encoding, storage, and retrieval (Baddeley, Eysenck, & Anderson, 2009). When you think about it, this process of encoding and storing experience as memory is everything to us. We are born into the world ready to learn, ready to memorize, and in fact have already started the learning quest in the womb (Partanen et al., 2013). Without memory you cannot talk, walk, or move in any meaningful way; you would know no past; you would have no concept of self or place—no concept of who you are, where you are, or what surrounds you. From the unconscious reflexes and motor control that allow you to walk with little conscious effort to the complexities of advanced cognition such as solving equations in theoretical physics, memory is the indispensable operant. Memory links our past with our present and allows us to project into the future—it absolutely influences our next move. Our lives, and the memories our lives are built on, are uniquely crafted by the complex interplay of our individual neural architecture and genetic expression immersed in the experience of our environment.

The epigenetic process—where our experience of the environment alters the way in which genes are expressed—is another fascinating aspect of memory. But it is a complex subject, and too large for our brief study of memory here (for a study on epigenetics for therapists, see Peckham, 2013). For now, our focus here are the networks and molecules involved in memory encoding, storage, and retrieval.

Ever since Paul Broca, in 1861, discovered that damage to a particular part of the left frontal lobe (now known as Broca's area) produced deficits in language, there has been a quest to discover the discrete parts of the brain that mediate specific cognitive functions, including in this quest the prevailing question: "Are there discrete brain systems devoted to memory?" Certainly, in the last few decades, there has been significant progress in our understanding of learning and memory. Eric Kandel, who received the Nobel Prize for his research on memory, and whose outstanding career and discoveries are documented in his book *In Search of Memory: The Emergence of a New Science of Mind* (Kandel, 2006), is perhaps the foremost of the many researchers who have given us a much more sophisticated understanding of memory processes. Kandel's work, famously with the elegant sea slug *Aplysia californica*, has uncovered some of the secrets of learning and memory, most notably the mechanisms of memory consolidation and neural plasticity. Kandel identified two problems: the *systems* problem of memory (Where in the brain is memory stored?) and the *molecular* problem of memory (What are the mechanisms of this storage?).

When addressing the systems problem we can divide memory into two broad categories:

1. **Short-term memory**—momentary memory that is processed in the temporal lobe and hippocampus before being transferred into long-term memory or discarded. This transient memory can also be manipulated by the prefrontal cortex—a process known as *working memory* (a distinction can be made between short-term and working memory, see Aben, Stapert, & Blokland, 2012)—before it is either lost or integrated into long-term memory. Short-term memory can be thought of as a transient representation of goal-relevant knowledge (Kandel, Schwartz, Jessell, Siegelbaum, & Hudspeth, 2012), an important part of our consciousness. We can further divide short-term memory into verbal and visuospatial information that is coordinated by *executive control processes* that allocate attention to the different memory systems.

2. **Long-term memory**—memory that can persist for years and is encoded in the cerebral cortex. Long-term memory is further divided into:

Riding a bike without having to "think about it" utilizes your procedural memory function.

a. *Explicit (declarative) memory*—the memory of facts and events, and people, objects, and places, processed in the medial temporal lobe and hippocampus. This sort of memory requires conscious effort to recall. For example, the legendary spatial memory held in the hippocampus of London taxi drivers actually enlarges their hippocampus, full of London street information, ready for conscious recall. Explicit memory is mediated by the processes of encoding, storage, consolidation, and retrieval, and the elements of this form of memory are distributed among many brain regions that can be accessed independently (Kandel et al., 2012).

b. *Implicit (procedural) memory*—the memory of skills and habits of the neocortex, striatum, amygdala, cerebellum, and reflex pathways that do not require conscious attention to recall. These are the memories that encode the automatic part of our behaviour—walking and talking, and all the special skills we have learnt. Implicit memory can be further categorized as:

- Priming—the improved perception of a word or object by prior experience, processed in the neocortex;
- Procedural—skills and habits processed in the striatum;

Types of Memory

Memory Type	Description	Key Brain Areas
Sensory	Neural traces from sensory input lasting less than a second	All sensory input going to specific sensory areas of the brain.
Short-term	The holding of a limited amount of information for less than about 18 seconds without manipulation or rehearsal (Revlin, 2012), and may be limited to 5–9 discrete bits of information at any one time (first proposed by Miller, 1956).	Hippocampus; subiculum
Working	A prefrontal cognitive capacity responsible for the transient holding, processing, and manipulation of information (Diamond, 2013)	Dorsolateral prefrontal cortex
Long-term explicit	The conscious memory of facts and events, also known as declarative memory; can also be divided into episodic (autobiographical events and experiences) and semantic (facts, concepts) memory.	Medial temporal lobe: perirhinal, entorhinal, and parahippocampal cortices; hippocampus
Long-term implicit	The unconscious memory of skills and tasks, also known as procedural memory; can be further divided into priming, procedural, associative learning, and non-associative learning	Neocortex (priming); striatum (procedural); amygdala (emotional responses in associative learning); cerebellum (skeletal musculature in associative learning); reflex pathways (non-associative learning)

The division of memory types below follows the Atkinson-Shiffrin model (Atkinson & Shiffrin, 1968), also known as the multi-store or modal model of memory. The Atkinson-Shiffrin model defines discrete types of processes, as opposed to the levels-of-processing model (Craik & Lockhart, 1972), which assumes a continuum of depth of mental processing, from shallow perception to deeper semantic memory.

Glossary

cyclic adenosine 3',5'-cyclic monophosphate (cAMP): An important "second messenger" for intracellular signalling, such as transferring into cells the effects of hormones that cannot pass through the plasma membrane, for the activation of protein kinases.

CRE (cAMP recognition element): A promotor element that CREB-1 binds to in a chain of interactions to promote gene transcription.

CREB-1 (cAMP response element binding protein 1): An activator-type transcription factor that stimulates transcription upon binding to the CRE—a key element involved in turning on gene transcription. In the case of memory formation, the interaction between this activator type and the repressor type (CREB-2) initiates the emergence of long-lasting synaptic enhancement, that is, memory consolidation (Wagatsuma et al., 2006).

CREB-2 (cAMP response element binding protein 2): A similar transcription factor to CREB-1 but inhibits the transcription of downstream genes. When CREB-2 is relieved of its repressive function, and CREB-1 is activated, it produces a cascade of new gene expression for the consolidation of memory.

CBP (CREB-binding protein): A CREB protein involved in transcription.

MAPK (mitogen-activated protein kinase): A protein kinase (an enzyme that modifies other proteins by adding a phosphate group to them) that is involved in many cellular responses to stimuli and regulates a number of cellular functions including gene expression.

PKA (protein kinase): An enzyme that modifies other proteins by adding a phosphate group to them, resulting in functional changes in the target proteins.

Transcription: The first step in gene expression, where segments of DNA are copied to RNA (single chain nucleotides that convey genetic information to direct synthesis of specific proteins) to produce a primary transcript followed by various modifications to yield functional forms of RNAs.

- Associative learning—classical and operant conditioning such as fear learning in the amygdala and the learning of motor skills in the cerebellum; and

- Non-associative learning—habituation and sensitization along reflex pathways (Kandel et al., 2012).

Explicit memory processing involves four related yet distinct operations (Kandel et al., 2012):

1. *Encoding.* For incoming information to be remembered it must be "well-encoded", or what might be termed "deep" encoding (Craik & Lockhart, 1972). Encoding involves attending to the new information and associating it with prior knowledge. Motivation to remember (which may involve more focused attention) is correlated with deep encoding; sleep and dreaming may also play a part in encoding memories, as the experiences of the day are processed and associations made while you sleep.

2. *Storage.* Neural mechanisms, and the resulting neural architecture, retain the learning over time—learning that may last a lifetime. There seems to be an almost unlimited capacity for long-term storage, unlike working memory that can only hold a few bits of information for a limited time.

3. *Consolidation.* Once neural connections are established to hold the memory trace, consolidation makes the connections more stable. This involves the expression of genes, protein synthesis, and changes in the synaptic connections.

4. *Retrieval.* The recall of stored memories is a constructive process that brings together the various elements of a memory and reconstructs them into a perception of the thing remembered. Recall uses a range of strategies such as comparison, inference, supposition, and guessing, and using the new information to generate, or recreate, a memory that seems coherent and consistent with our other memories and perceptions. Because memory retrieval is a constructive process it is open to distortion and also, as we will learn below, open to reconsolidation in a form different from what was originally encoded or even from what was last reconsolidated. In other words, memories can change.

What then are the mechanisms that allow the storage of memory to occur? Kandel and others have discovered that repetition is one mechanism whereby the information being received is converted from short- to long-term memory through altered gene expression and the growth of new synaptic connections. These changes, which we call *experience-dependent neuroplasticity*, require protein synthesis to create more permanent synaptic connections between neurons. When there is repeated activation of a neuron, the second messenger system within the cell causes changes in the cell nucleus, where the genes are located, and this works in distinct ways for explicit and implicit memories. Second messengers are small intracellular molecules that are produced after the first neurotransmitter has activated the receptor. Second messengers activate intracellular signaling pathways that amplify the signal and activate or inhibit transcription factors, inducing a cellular response.

It is also important to note that one-trial learning (a single exposure to a stimulus) can happen when there is strong emotion involved—as in a traumatic event, for example. As anyone who has been traumatized by a single transient event (such as being held up at gunpoint) can attest, that one event can form a remarkably stable

and enduring memory. There may, however, be cognitive processes going on after the event that persist to consolidate the memory of such a trauma.

To take an example, let us look at long-term implicit memory formation (consolidation) that involves changes in chromatin structure (the DNA double helix packaged around proteins called histones) and gene expression. The following is a somewhat simplified version, with many details and regulatory factors omitted. (Those wishing to know all the detailed interactions are encouraged to read Chapter 66 of Kandel et al., 2012.) When there is repeated activation of a set of neurons (e.g., practicing scales on the piano), there is a prolonged rise in cAMP (see Glossary) due to repeated application of serotonin. This, in turn, activates protein kinase (PKA) that does two things: first, it translocates into the cell nucleus to turn on CREB-1 to activate gene transcription while activating mitogen-activated protein kinase (MAPK), which turns off the inhibitory gene repressor CREB-2. Then, once activated, CREB-1 influences downstream genes and stimulates the growth of new synaptic connections. These new connections consolidate a memory that is lasting.

In the case of explicit (declarative) memory, repeated stimulation of neuronal circuits again establishes a consolidated memory. Like implicit memory, explicit

memory uses modulatory transmitters and CREB-mediated switches to initiate downstream gene expression to grow new synaptic connections. But unlike implicit memory, it employs NMDA receptors and the dopaminergic system to activate a cAMP/PKA pathway within the neuron, triggering the cascade of events that results in a more stable connection. (Once again, for full details on explicit memory consolidation, see Chapter 67 of Kandel et al., 2012).

Students have been known to take amphetamines or other dopamine-enhancing drugs when cramming for exams to heighten explicit consolidation by supercharging the front end of that process. The reverse is also conceivable: drugs that short-circuit the cAmp–PKA–CREB pathways may limit the consolidation of traumatic memories if administered in a timely manner. Trauma sufferers should approach the use of drugs to enhance the dopaminergic (explicit memory) or serotonergic (implicit memory) systems with care for possible negative consequences. For example, a study investigating the link between chronic stress and PTSD found that stress enables a serotonergic memory consolidation process that was not present in unstressed animal subjects (Baratta et al., 2016). The results of this study showed that chronic stress causes proliferation of 5-HT2C receptors in the amygdala that bind to serotonin, thereby creating a heightened sensitivity to serotonin and stronger memory consolidation. This finding suggests that antidepressants such as Prozac and other selective serotonin reuptake inhibitors (SSRIs), when given to recently traumatized individuals, may actually promote stronger traumatic memories (Trafton, 2015).

In ageing and memory loss there may be a compromise in the cAMP process. Kandel (2012) suggests there are two ways to boost memory—either increase the dopaminergic input in the case of explicit memory systems, or slow down the degradation of cAMP by introducing a drug (e.g., Rolipram) that inhibits phosphodiesterase, which would normally break down cAMP. For example, Alzheimer's disease activates inhibitory constraints on the cAMP cycle, and in experiments with mice it has been found that Rolipram restores learning. In the case of Alzheimer's, however, other strategies are available that aim to reduce the toxicity of beta-amyloid to nerve cells (beta-amyloid is the main component of toxic plaques that are believed to play a central role in the development of Alzheimer's disease), rather than boosting the cAMP system (Kandel, 2012).

The Hippocampus

Any discussion of memory, especially explicit memory, would be incomplete without a consideration of the hippocampus. The hippocampi are structures in both hemispheres of the brain, at the base of the temporal lobes, that are likened to the shape of two seahorses—hence their name (from the Greek *hippos*, "horse"). They encode explicit memory, such as the conscious learning of facts taught at school, as well as spatial information, and help to make sense of new information based on previously learned information (Cozolino, 2013). Each hippocampus has slightly different functions: damage to the left hippocampus is associated with difficulties

memory. Yet H.M. could engage in tasks that required practise to improve, such as drawing a figure from its reflection in a mirror, and his ability on the task did improve: he was able to learn the motor coordination skills required to do the task well. This means he could still consolidate implicit memory, but he could not recall actually practising the task—an explicit memory.

Concerning its function in memory, Robert Moss (2016) describes the hippocampus not as a *storage* device but rather an *association* device, because of its role in bringing together various elements stored in the cortex into a coherent and meaningful recall. He conceives discrete bits of information (learning) as stored in cor-

Memory works better when there is context, and the hippocampus puts things in context when encoding and reassembling memory.

in forming new verbal memories, while damage to the right hippocampus produces deficits in other forms of nonverbal memory (Moss, 2016). Memory works better when there is context, and the hippocampus (considered as a whole) puts things in context when encoding and reassembling memory. The hippocampus is active when we navigate space or recollect personal events, and it negotiates the large overlap of spatial/navigational and autobiographical information needed to give us orientation. There are even cells in the hippocampus named "place cells" (O'Keefe & Dostrovsky, 1971) that respond to a certain spatial location to help orient us.

One subject who has famously contributed an enormous amount to our understanding of memory and the role of the hippocampus is a patient named Henry Molaison, commonly known as "H.M.". In 1953, at the age of 27, H.M. had the medial portions of his temporal lobes removed to treat epilepsy. Following this bilateral medial temporal lobectomy, which included most of the hippocampus, H.M.'s seizures were all but eliminated; he seemed to have normal perceptual and motor abilities, and his intelligence actually increased (Pinel & Barnes, 2014). However, the surgery had devastating amnesic effects: H.M. had a memory for events long predating surgery, some retrograde amnesia for events up to two years prior to surgery, but a total inability to form new long-term explicit memories. After surgery he could not remember people, places, events, or experiences for longer than his working memory would allow. The lesson learned from H.M. was that the medial temporal lobes (including the hippocampus) play a critical role in memory, specifically in storing and recalling long-term

tical columns: when we need various bits of information to recreate a memory, cells in the hippocampus are activated and, through the thalamus, connect to various cortical columns to activate those bits of memory simultaneously. Thus, the hippocampus does not itself hold the bits that recreate the memory; instead it coordinates the synchronized activation of those bits held in the cortex. He offers the following example to illustrate:

Quiroga et al. (2005) described a cell in a patient's hippocampus that consistently activated each time different pictures of Jennifer Aniston were shown, but the same cell did not show such activation to other pictures of objects or animals, or other famous faces. This gives the impression that the cell is the location of the memory. However, my belief is that the visual facial recognition of Jennifer Aniston and the associated word columns of her name occur in separate cortical circuits. For those circuits to be consolidated as an association memory (i.e., her name with her face), the single hippocampal neuron is needed to reactivate the separate circuit columns and the common column in the perirhinal cortex. When shown her picture, the visual column tied to her face activated the common column that in turn activated the hippocampal cell. This explanation fits well with the finding that patients with anterograde amnesia caused by hippocampal damage retain long-term memories that occurred years before they developed the amnesia. Thus, if you know Jennifer Aniston by sight and have future damage resulting in the loss of the hippocampal cell that was involved, you will have no problem recognizing her face and giving her name provided the cortical columns in the circuits relating to her remain intact. (Moss, 2016, p. 18)

Establishing long-term memories that are capable of recall without hippocampal intervention may be possible through the association of circuits between the critical cortical bits—integrative connections of colour, sound, emotion, spatial information, and other bits that are all stimulated at the same time upon recall.

Eleanor Maguire, Professor of Cognitive Neuroscience at University College London, has been exploring with colleagues the way the hippocampus encodes and recreates memory. One of the interesting questions posed by Maguire (2008) was, "Can patients with hippocampal damage and amnesia imagine fictitious experiences?" Similar brain areas are activated in both the imagining of a fictitious experience and the recall of a real episodic memory: we draw on what we know to imagine what we have not experienced. Maguire describes a study of people with hippocampal damage who, when asked to imagine a scene, were unable to do so effectively. They could come up with some of the elements but could not construct a vivid and coherent scene. It was the spatial connectedness of the scene that was wanting in these subjects: there was discontinuity and little ability to create a spatial backdrop in their imagination. Due to the damage in the region, the normal contribution of the hippocampus in recalling various elements and holding them together in context was not available to them.

The concept that consolidation of memories progresses from short-term to long-term has been challenged in a recent study in *Science* suggesting that short-term memory in the hippocampus and long-term consolidation in the cortex form simultaneously (Kitamura et al., 2017). The researchers proposed that the simultaneously formed long-term memories remain "silent" initially but gradually mature, changing in anatomy and physiological activity, until the long-term cortical memory is fully recallable. Using mice and a technique called optogenetics, whereby target cells can be turned on or off with light, the researchers mapped the development of a fear memory. After just one day, memory of the fear event was detected in the cortex. This finding is contrary to the standard theory of memory consolidation (that memories transfer gradually over time), because the memory had already formed. According to this study, memories are formed rapidly and simultaneously in the prefrontal cortex and the hippocampus: "They're formed in parallel but then they go different ways from there. The prefrontal cortex becomes stronger and the hippocampus becomes weaker," said Mark Morrissey, a co-author on the paper (Trafton, 2017, para. 18). This finding, if supported, will add greatly to our understanding of the functioning of the brain and memory formation.

Recall and Trauma

State-dependent recall describes a phenomenon where our current internal state, if it replicates that at the time a significant event was encoded, can set in motion a spontaneous recall of that memory. A traumatized individual may have the memory of trauma come flooding back when he or she experiences increased heart rate, breathing, or emotion that closely resembles the original response to trauma. In fact, just about anything that matches the original internal experience can trigger some aspect of what the individual went through emotionally and physiologically at the time. Even body posture may be a catalyst for state-dependent recall.

In the case of childhood traumatic events, it has often been observed that explicit memories are difficult to recall, while implicit emotional memories flood the PTSD sufferer—until there is a change of context in the individual's life, potentially years later, that triggers an explicit recall of the event. However, as Dan Siegel (2012) has noted, delayed recall of explicit autobiographical memory is subject to (unintentional) creative licence:

Although delayed recollection may be quite accurate, explicit memory is exquisitely sensitive to the conditions of recall. Recounting the elements of explicit autobiographical memory is a social experience that is profoundly influenced by social interaction. Thus what is recounted is not the same as what is initially remembered, and it is not necessarily completely accurate in detail. . . . actual events can be forgotten, and non-experienced "recollections" can be deeply felt to be true memories. (p. 80)

Our minds can be extremely suggestible, and every act of retrieving a memory can be altered by social context and new information. We can be convinced a memory is totally accurate when in fact it may be quite different from its original consolidation (which itself may not have been a completely accurate representation of what really occurred).

Memory Reconsolidation

Memory reconsolidation is a process in which a memory is modified at the level of its neural encoding. It is a substantive change brought about by new learning. The concept of reconsolidation is based on the understanding that when a memory is retrieved from long-term storage, it is held in a labile (unstable) state in short-term memory while it is being utilized (Nader & Hardt, 2009). This process may be a way in which

new information is integrated into an existing memory trace—a kind of maintenance of consolidation intended to keep retrieved memory up to date.

The work of Bruce Ecker and colleagues (Ecker, Ticic, & Hulley, 2012) has demonstrated that emotional memories can be strengthened, weakened, altered in their details, or completely nullified and cancelled through a reconsolidation process—thereby bringing about a true unlearning of an emotional memory. Reconsolidation is a natural, neural process that can transform an acquired behaviour or emotional response by fundamentally revising the memory associated with it (Ecker, 2015).

It is implicit memory that is mostly involved here, in the form of emotional learning, such as how to avoid particular vulnerabilities and sufferings. These memories, or learnings, are often attained without awareness, entirely within the implicit learning system, in the presence of strong emotions. Accordingly, they can prove powerful and durable. All sorts of emotional and traumatic experiences form implicit emotional learnings whose purpose is essentially adaptive—to help us cope with life as we perceive it. But they frequently become maladaptive later in life when we no longer need to respond in the same self-protective patterns. The child who needs to do outstanding work to attain her parents' love and approval may carry that learning into adult life and become a workaholic, not realizing that her behaviour is more a desperate attempt to meet a basic emotional need than a reflection of her passion for work. The very behaviour that helped her adapt to circumstances as a child now alienates the people she most wants love and affection from. There is no conscious realization that this is the case: it is implicit, an automation. Such encoding is mainly in the subcortical regions that store implicit, tacit, emotionally urgent, procedural knowledge, rather than the neocortical regions involved in explicit memory, which store conscious, episodic, autobiographical, declarative knowledge (Ecker, 2015).

Memory and the Classroom

Understanding memory recall and the emotional effects relating to our experiences is particularly relevant to the educator.

The emotions we feel when we experience a situation affects our memory and recall of the experience (Schneck, 2011). As teachers, we often wonder why parents don't show up for parent/teacher interviews or they don't want to come into the school to discuss their child. For many parents, school is a place where unpleasant memories were created and the memories associated with these strong painful emotions prove powerful and durable (Shneck, 2011).

This highlights the fact that schools need be places of emotional safety, where memories of pleasure and not pain are created. The memories made in classrooms should be associated with the emotions of joy and happiness, surprise and wonder, rather than emotional memories of fear, anger and sadness. Schools that nurture, encourage, support and have a respectful environment are places where the memories taken away are memories of positive teacher/student relationships, safe connections and enjoyable learning. A place where students are encouraged to try new things and feel success, because they are welcomed and valued. Memories of fear are reduced when the classroom teacher actively reduces stress and anxiety, by showing empathy, understanding and relationship, thus increasing the feelings of safety for students and their parents.

Memory and retrieval of information

Research on memory retention indicates that 70-90% of new learning is forgotten with 18-24 hours after the lesson (Sousa, 2011). For some student's the retention may be even less. How well an individual learns and how long it takes to retrieve information is dependent on a number of factors. Firstly, how the new information is linked to prior learnings. The context in which something is learned determines retention, as the brain remembers best when facts and skills are linked to authentic contexts (Tokuhama-Espinosa, 2014). The mood of the student, and the emotional connection, at the time of learning plays a large role in what is recalled. And finally, the adequacy of the cues given when recall is needed (Sousa, 2011; Smith & Moynan, 2008; Tokuhama-Espinosa, 2014 a).

Students that recall quickly are able to answer class questions more often, gaining teacher recognition and approval, and cementing a feeling of close attachment with the teacher. For those students that retrieve information more slowly, the story can be quite the opposite. Their retrieval process stops when those first hands go up, lowering self-concept and stimulating feelings of inadequacy, isolation and disconnect from the teacher and often with the rest of the class (Sousa, 2011).

Tokuhama-Espinosa, (2014 a) reminds us that learning and memory is enhanced by challenge, but inhibited by threat. Many students feel a sense of threat and fear when they can't keep up with teacher expectations and the pace of learning. The more they feel they are behind, the more overwhelming school and learning can seem. A teacher may never knowingly promote a sense of fear, however, sometimes the classroom environment can appear threatening when a student is not given adequate time to complete a task. Often times threats are perceived when a teacher reminds a child that play, lunch or privileges will be

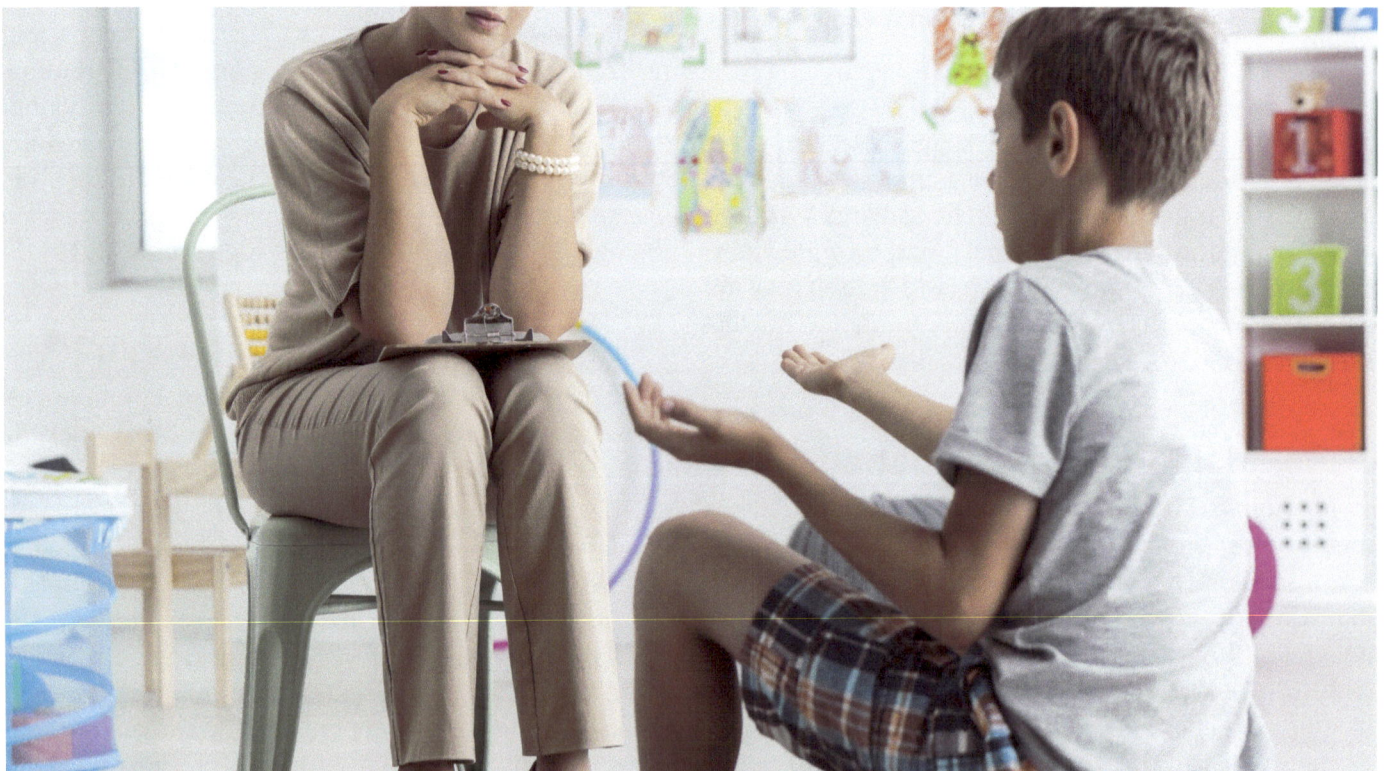

withdrawn if work is not completed. Many children stress when the fast-finished children are rewarded with stickers and sweets, fun activities and praise and the students that take longer to recall information are reprimanded and continually told to hurry up.

Experiences of fear and anxiety severely affects memory and dampens new learning. A child's brain will do what it can to protect the body from feeling pain or fear, as protection and survival is paramount. When children feel, they are not coping, falling behind, or simply feel stress, they will adopt behaviours to avoid and stop the emotional turmoil within. The toilet will be seen as a safe place to visit; pencils will need sharpening and re-sharpening or they will become ill and need to lie down. Stress affects what can be recalled. A classroom environment that arouses fear is not one to enhance learning. The classroom will be remembered, but not for what was learned or the knowledge gained. What will be remembered will be the pain of the classroom experience, rather than the knowledge the teacher tried to impart.

Memory and discipline

Too often teachers find themselves in situations where they cannot seem to obtain 'the truth' or a so-called 'accurate' story about a certain behaviour issue. Memory and recall is affected by many variables, one of which is the emotional ties to the social experience at the time, and the implicit need to avoid particular vulnerabilities and sufferings. If the teacher intensifies the stress a child feels when being challenged about certain behavioural situations, the intensity and/duration of that stress interferes with the student's ability to retrieve memories. The child feels threatened and the fear response is triggered, preparing the body for action. Instead of the discipline issue being resolved, we find the situation can escalate as children may react with violent outbursts, or retreat into protective withdrawal behaviours.

TEACHING FOR SUCCESS

Teaching children and young people is known to be one of the most rewarding of occupations, due partly to the satisfying pleasure a teacher feels when students participate enthusiastically in the learning process, and a classroom of eyes light up as new knowledge is grasped.

However, this is not always the case. Teachers are also driven to various levels of distress, irritation and disappointment as they deal with unmotivated and disruptive students. They struggle with students who show disrespect or respond to instruction and guidance with outbursts of anger or defiance. It is not uncommon to hear teachers declare that more time is spent controlling and disciplining students than there is time to teach curriculum concepts.

Many students, also, struggle with the school environment and find school loathsome, stating that they only attend class because it is compulsory. Truancy is on the rise for multiple and cumulative reasons. There is a common denominator of students feeling frustrated and uncared for (Australian Law Reform Commission, 2013) due to an atmosphere of distress and fear that pervades many school environments.

Success in the classroom requires more than knowing *what* works and *how* to implement strategies. When educators understand the neuroscience of *why* certain methods are successful, how the brain processes and remembers new information, along with the blocks and triggers that inhibit successful learning and enjoyment of the school experience, teachers can evaluate current methods and implement strategies to ensure all students are given the best of opportunities (Sousa, 2010). But the benefits are twofold. As the joy of learning and being at school is resuscitated, there is fulfilment, delight and satisfaction for the teacher.

In a rapidly expanding economic world where success and business proficiency require top performance and elevated accountability, the need to push and stretch employees, meet deadlines, and increase productivity is at the forefront of every staff meeting and business review. This same expectation of proficiency extends to educational facilities, with funding and expansion of services dependent on growth in student numbers, and with an educational "product" that boasts high academic results in order to equip students to survive in the business world.

Teachers feel continually pressed into meeting another deadline, peaking student academic performance and providing extra-curricular activities to satisfy parental wishes and administrative demands.

Teaching methodology and best practice have been the subject of robust discussion for decades. We have moved from textbooks to computers, where the potential for knowledge is now limitless with the use of smartboards, smartphones, tablets and numerous online courses (Cook, 2014). The advance in technology has provided teachers with attractive and innovative audiovisual aids and teaching resources intended to make teaching more effective and to excite students to learn. However, recent studies reveal that it is not an increased availability of resources or revolutionised teaching aids that make learning successful (Schenck, 2011). Nor is it the bribes, rewards or incentives frequently used to cajole students in an attempt to improve behaviour or school performance (Kohn, 1999). While there are no absolute formulas or ultimate solutions to the complexities confronting today's educators, increasingly fruitful research in the neurobiological sciences suggests that a student's success at school is determined by the interaction between the teacher and the student and the emotional safety the student experiences within the school environment (Caviness, 2001; Schenck, 2011).

Learning begins the moment a child is born, with young minds receptive and sensitive to absorbing myriad experiences of the world in which they are raised. Brain development begins with cell growth in the brain stem (the survival brain) and progresses to the limbic system (the emotional brain), followed by the outer cortical regions of the cerebrum, the area of perception and cognition (Damir, 2009). As environmental sensory information is received and processed, influential memory systems and behaviours are developed according to the fulfilment or the violation of four basic psychological needs: the need for a sense of belonging and attachment, the need for control, the need for pleasure as opposed to hostile or fearful situations, and the need for a healthy self-esteem (Grawe, 2007; Arden & Linford, 2009). The basic needs, as outlined by Epstein (1990), are not isolated needs but are intrinsically linked and influenced by one another in determining the emotional wellness of an individual (Grawe, 2007).

As a child develops, its senses filter every family ex-

perience, relaying messages to the brain to interpret how the experience is to be understood, with responding consequential behaviours (Howard, 2013). Children who enjoy family environments of nurture, care and safety develop secure attachments that positively affect their future relationships and foster a keenness to approach new challenges and situations (Grawe, 2007). Securely attached children move into the social school environment with relative ease and will have the emotional stability to manage classroom learning and playground issues with little or no difficulty (Howard, 2013). However, mistreated children—those whose safety has been compromised emotionally, physically or socially—experience continuous, uncontrollable incongruences, since negative feedback loops have been established from infancy, resulting in a fear of new experiences and excessive emotional reactions to relatively minor changes or unpleasant situations (Grawe, 2007).

Early childhood behaviours of approach or avoidance become particularly evident once a child reaches school and there are certain expectations regarding social independence, appropriate behaviours and learning ability. Many learning centres expect students to be able to achieve at certain levels and meet certain criteria, thereby fitting into a particular grade or learning environment. However, Schenck (2011) reminds teachers that nothing is ever quite in sync, as students enter school already genetically wired and are emotionally influenced by the range of early life experiences they have been exposed to (Peckham, 2013; Tokuhama–Espinosa, 2011). With current research suggesting that the interdependence of cognition and emotion is responsible for guiding all learning and retention (Sousa, 2010), it is a concern that many children experience heightened states of stress within the family environment before they reach the school gate (Howard, 2013) and are then expected to sit, listen and learn.

Threatening environments (either real or perceived) compromise the feeling of safety and intensify negative emotions due to an overproduction of adrenalin and cortisol. Behavioural inhibition systems (BIS) are triggered and neural activity is impaired, resulting in the reinforcing of avoidance schemas geared towards surviving uncontrollable incongruences (Grawe, 2007; Rossouw, 2012a; Siegel & Bryson, 2012). The social environment of the school can either further distress or calm an anxious child, depending on teacher reactions and the safety the child feels within the classroom (Sousa, 2010). Unless the child's anxiousness is down-regulated, the brain will persist in protecting him or her from harm (Sousa, 2010). Distressing situations up-regulate a fear response; blood flow increases in the emotional centre of the brain, and there is reduced blood flow to the prefrontal cortex where problem solving and decision making occur (Grawe, 2007). The emotional centre of the brain (the limbic system) takes over, activating survival instincts of fight, flight or freeze. Resulting behaviours often prompt reactions from the teacher that are confusing to the child or felt to be unjust or inappropriate in response to the embarrassment, fear or shame being experienced (Cozolino, 2013; Howard, 2013; Siegel & Bryson, 2012).

While it is appropriate and necessary for negative behaviours to be addressed, a proactive teacher responds with compassion and offers emotional safety in a nonthreatening environment free of retaliatory anger, putdowns and humiliation. Teacher criticism, verbal abuse and alienation only add fuel to an already heightened emotional state and result in an escalation of anger and an intensity of negative behaviours from the child (Cozolino, 2013; Howard, 2013).

Children are not "hardwired" but need help to develop self-control and emotional regulation, and this is best achieved through role modelling, genuine forgiveness and unconditional care (Howard, 2013). Recent neuroimaging studies show the amygdala responds not only to danger or fear, but positive emotional influences and nonthreatening conditions also increase metabolic activity through the amygdala to the prefrontal cortex, allowing an opening of neural networks to assist in successful learning (Sousa, 2010). A warm, caring relationship between the student and teacher is central to motivation and positive learning (Schenck, 2011); but the positive relationship holds even higher significance. A supportive, nurturing mentor in a child's life can shift the trajectory of negative behavioural development and move it in a positive direction, despite the family violations a child may have experienced (Grawe, 2007; Howard, 2013; Tokuhama–Espinosa, 2011)

ATTACHMENT

We are born social creatures, and our brains require connections with other people to develop wellbeing and equilibrium (Siegel, 2006). The basic need for attachment is critical to all individuals. We thrive on a sense of belonging, personal significance, and the consciousness that we are genuinely cared for (Grawe,

2007). Secure attachments, or feeling part of a "tribal" community (Cozolino, 2013) is imperative to the well-being of students. Genuine teacher care provides an environment of security and trust, releasing oxytocin and opiates that prompt a down-regulation of negative emotions, thereby calming and relaxing a student, stimulating neuroplasticity and a readiness for learning (Baumeister & Leary, 1995; Grawe, 2007; Pawluk, 1998). It is in the connections students make with their teachers that behaviour and emotions are positively or negatively affected, either motivating students to learn, or causing an anxiousness that shrinks neural branching to the detriment of both the learning process and the retention of knowledge (Grawe, 2007; Tokuhama–Espinosa, 2011).

Positive relationships are formed when teachers loosen up their rigid rules, laugh with their students, and take proactive steps to become warm and supportive—speaking in affirming tones, demonstrating genuine care, showing an interest in their students' lives and giving empathy when students are struggling (Schenck, 2011). Many who teach or are in administrative roles mistakenly take their position of responsibility and make it into a position of power. Teachers are entrusted with the responsibility of guiding and nurturing young lives, giving them a sense of personal significance (Pawluk, 1998), but in accordance with the fundamental principle of care: *primum non nocere*—the first thing [is] to do no harm. Harsh, unbending attitudes give a teacher a sense of power, often termed the locus of control (Schenck, 2011), but it is a misplaced power if it violates the basic needs of the students in their care.

PLEASURE

Learning and decision making are influenced by the state of our emotional well-being, resulting in a positive or negative effect on how and what we learn and retain

(Tokuhama–Espinosa, 2011). Research has shown that it is the fun and enjoyable activities, those with variety and creativity, that motivate students to want to learn (Kohn, 1993). It is unfortunate that in our current education systems, many classroom practices raise negative emotions, diminishing the love of learning, by pandering to a culture that values performance and academic success at any cost (Morelan, 2002). We have become obsessed with accountability and standardised test scores; so much so that enthusiasm for creativity has waned in classrooms, and time-poor teachers are often adopting practices that are not always conducive to student well-being and learning enjoyment (Tokuhama–Espinosa, 2011).

When a classroom fails to be fun and strong negative emotions are experienced, learning is blocked and the retention of information is inhibited (Lopez & Alipoon, 2001). Learning occurs when students enjoy the classroom environment and feel positive towards their subjects and learning tasks, experiencing the pleasure of personal fulfilment in their own abilities (Grawe, 2007; Morelan, 2002).

CLASSROOM ACCEPTANCE

The feeling of acceptance and "being valued" is regarded as the most important of human motivations and is necessary for a healthy self-image (Grawe, 2007; Prochaska & Norcross, 2010). Positive self-esteem is directly related to environmental experiences and the human language interactions individuals have on a day-to-day basis (McNeil, 2009). It is the language we hear from others, and the silent, nonverbal cues associated with human interactions, body language and mirror neurons, that influence our thinking and form our individual beliefs (Schore & Schore, 2007). What a student believes a parent or teacher thinks about him or her greatly impacts personal motivation, efficiency and general well-being (Tokuhama–Espinosa, 2011).

Parents and teachers who show acceptance of a child only on condition, using power to control behaviours, giving bribes or rewards when marks are satisfactory or when a child performs to a set standard, lead the child to believe that his or her worth is dependent only on doing the "right" thing (Grawe, 2007; Kohn, 1999). These children develop a self-esteem based on conditional approval and instinctively attempt to always please others (Prochaska & Norcross, 2010). Other children simply live up to the language they have experienced and become "bad" kids, actively striving to maintain or verify their negative self-image in an attempt to protect their self-esteem (Grawe, 2007). It is common for a child to become stuck in a self-fulfilling prophecy of negative behaviours, due to a negatively developed self-confidence and low self-efficacy (Grawe, 2007). These children present in the classroom as the ones who are continually in trouble, the ones that teachers find it difficult to attach to, and the ones who receive the brunt of criticism and punishing reactions (Grawe, 2007). Unfortunately, it is the "unattractive" students, the ones we find most difficult to love, who are the very ones who need a teacher's care and attention. They need affirming language and caring attitudes so as to change their negative view of themselves and begin to form neural pathways of acceptance of themselves and others (Grawe, 2007). Teachers who understand children's poor behaviour as stemming from the violations and inappropriate emotional nurturing they have received can be proactive and put in place strategies to care for and value these students rather than perpetuate the unfavourable experiences they continually live with (Arden & Linford, 2009; Grawe, 2007). A teacher's encouragement of student effort, no matter how small the progress, builds positive mental images that prompt the release of dopamine and serotonin, leading to intrinsic motivation: the desire to learn more, do better, experiment and try new ideas—all of which assist in long-term learning and subsequent retrieval (Grawe, 2007; Schenck, 2011).

CHOICE EMPOWERS

While learning content is often not negotiable, *how* a student learns can and should be. Taking time to understand individual students' strengths and weaknesses maximises their learning potential, as the teacher can potentially provide a choice of opportunities for each child to experience success (Schenck, 2011). This does not necessarily mean a separate activity for each child. Teachers are stressed, time-poor and constrained by a regime of standardised tests and prescribed curriculums (Morelan, 2002); to cater to the myriad of individual needs seems impossible. Choice involves a teacher relinquishing some control and providing the students with more autonomy in their learning (Schenck, 2011). Establishing classroom environments free of rigidity, presenting problems that are open-ended, encouraging students to explore, experiment and try new ideas, adopting activity-based learning where the students can move throughout the classroom, and providing safe and caring support when mistakes are made all foster accountability and shift the responsibility for ownership of learning to the student (Baldoni, 2005; Maulana, Opdenakker, den Brok, & Bosker, 2011).

Schenk (2011) describes choice as "creating a thirst" (pp. 145–146), a motivating power within students, which is dependent on student expectations and the anticipated benefits of success (Porter, 2007). When a student is motivated, neurons and synaptic connections are stimulated, causing rapid-fire activation that results in a thickening of the dendritic branches. This in turn reinforces learning and enables information to be retrieved at a later time (Lopez & Alipoon, 2001; Arden & Linford, 2009).

However, there is an understandable fear among teachers that introducing creative activities and options will increase workloads and result in a loss of classroom control (Anonymous, 1996). It has been argued that creative teaching activities that provide choice and individual expression are most relevant for primary school-aged children; it is expected that students entering high school know the importance of learning and should have the maturity to embrace it. Unfortunately, both rational thought and cognition of responsible behaviours develop around the age of 24 (Sousa, 2010). Young people tend to live for the moment, with limited cognitive ability to determine how important their education will be in the future but a strong desire for acceptance and personal power over their lives (Geldard & Geldard, 2010). Teachers who understand that students don't respond well to authoritarian control minimise frustrations and the number of behavioural issues they encounter (Schenck, 2011). While firm boundaries and routines are necessary and should be maintained, evidence has shown that student motivation is heightened when teachers work alongside students, encouraging and supporting, rather than in a directive, authoritarian role, implementing punishments and rewards to enforce compliance (Cook, 2014; Kohn, 1993).

Learning that takes place under stress results in performance based only on fear (Rossouw & Henson, 2013). The heightened anxiety a student feels when they fail, suffer ridicule (real or perceived), or find themselves in a fearful situation causes a cascade of stress hormones to flow through the limbic system. Blood flow drains from the logic and reasoning centres of the brain resulting in a fight or flight reaction, which often plays out in negative behavioural tendencies (Kohn, 1993; Siegel &

Bryson, 2012). The anterior cingulate cortex (ACC), often known as the "conflict monitor", plays a crucial role in an individual's engagement with the environment and the conscious experiencing of emotions (Grawe, 2007). High levels of stress deactivate the ACC, causing an up-regulation of fear and anxiety that results in irrational and illogical thinking (Grawe, 2007); if the negative environment persists, a child's responsiveness will shut down, resulting in students passively withdrawing and not engaging in class, and/or displaying behaviours such as seemingly not caring or not having the energy or willpower to attempt to change (Dutton, 2007).

However, there is no denying that some students do not respond to care, creativity or kindness towards them. They annoy, disrupt and make a teacher's life miserable in their quest to undermine any attempts at successful teaching and the learning of others. Frequently teachers have shown support, but they have felt the brunt of cruel attacks. Cozolino (2013) suggests kind acts from teachers can trigger emotional sadness in neglected students and that they attempt to punish them for the parents they never had (Howard, 2013).

When aggression and serious relational difficulties disrupt the classroom, violating the safety of others, teacher attitudes can determine whether negative behaviours escalate and spiral out of control or settle into a state where the student is ready to listen and use the incident as a learning platform (Siegel & Hartzell, 2004). As emotional energy rises and abuse is hurled, it is a normative reaction for a teacher to raise his or her voice, yell back and make demanding statements. Unfortunately, this approach escalates the fear and negative behaviour to a higher level as both the student and the teacher fight to maintain control (Cozolino, 2013).

Calming the limbic system and regulating the amygdala's fight-or-flight response is an essential first step in regaining control. It is not "giving in" to a student's wishes, but rather it offers emotional safety, empathetic support, and an understanding approach so as to facilitate new neural communications (Rossouw, 2012b). It is tempting to berate, to demand respect, to insist the child apologise or simply to eject a student from the classroom. However, when a student feels his or her basic needs of control, pleasure, attachment and self-esteem are being threatened, he or she will respond and react negatively and illogically, because the immature child brain is unable to think beyond the emotional pain being experienced (Siegel & Bryson, 2012).

Adults can experience similar reactions when their work environment lacks democratic input, if there is social and emotional disconnection in the staffroom, or if the culture they work in fails to be supportive of their basic needs (Cozolino, 2013). Emotional safety is essential for everyone and directly impacts an individual's wellness and performance (Weinberg, 2013). Wise classroom teachers and exemplary schools grasp the importance of developing a community where students feel safe by providing genuine support for every individual, without bias or prejudice, recognising that the value of care given to students surpasses any high academic achievement or economic advantage.

CONCLUSION

Recent findings in neuroscience have significant implications for the future of both classroom teaching and school management as a whole, with informed educators adopting brain-based approaches to ensure students experience physical and emotional safety in the context of positive and supportive teacher–student relationships (Williams, 2012). While genetic makeup and early environmental experiences have a significant influence on development (Peckham, 2013), it is understanding the brain's plasticity—the student's ability to develop positive neural change and their potential for growth—which can and should motivate teachers to teach with the highest expectations of learning for every student, irrespective of prior experiences, since there is no limit to the adjustments the brain can make (Doidge, 2010; Tokuhama–Espinosa, 2011). Adopting strategies to down-regulate classroom stress and provide protection against humiliation, fear, or damage to self-esteem is essential for truly effective change and for learning to be beneficial for all students (Tokuhama–Espinosa, 2011). These are the conditions under which learning will prosper; which can alter a child's brain and influence the future trajectory of every student.

KITCHEN GARDEN PROGRAM

Plants and gardens are vital elements in human well-being and have long been recognised for their healing, pleasure, and reward (Capaldi, Passmore, Nisbet, Zelenski, & Dopko, 2015; Townsend & Weerasuriya, 2010). Engaging children in gardening and horticulture has become increasingly popular, and many schools are adopting a kitchen garden program as part of the curriculum (Block et al., 2012). The programs are seen to have a positive impact on student engagement, social connections, self-esteem, confidence, and general health and well-being (Blair, 2009; Block et al., 2012).

Neuroscience research advocates the necessity of children spending time away from artificial light and outdoors, stating fresh air and sunshine are vital elements to enhance brain development and help balance brain functions (Laakso, Porkka-Heiskanen, Alila, Peder, & Johansson, 1988; Nedley, 2009. Along with being outside is the importance of exercise, which is vital for the production of essential neurochemicals that assist with stress reduction, positive mood, sleep hygiene, and general well-being (Henson & Rossouw, 2012; Kendler, 1996; Nedley, 2009).

Due to the success of the Stephanie Alexander Kitchen Garden Program (www.kitchengardenfoundation.org.au; see Alexander, 2009; Block et al., 2012; Brien, 2014), it was hypothesised that a similar program could be beneficial in a therapeutic day program to enhance the mental and physical health of children currently in foster care who have experienced abusive trauma. The aim of the study was to determine the usefulness and reliability of such a program in terms of the behaviours and emotional regulation of children who have a predisposition to heightened behaviours when memories are triggered.

Care of Abused Children

Children who have experienced an environment of abuse and neglect are some of the most vulnerable and needy in society (Howard, 2013). Their basic needs have been violated, resulting in insecure attachments (Grawe, 2007), and the child is left feeling highly vulnerable and without trust due to the insecurity and harm they have experienced from significant adults (Howard, 2013; Krueger, 2013). The violation of safety significantly affects the wellness of a young developing brain (Jensen & Nutt, 2015) and leads to the adoption of brain schemas of protection, played out either as withdrawal and disassociation or as hyperarousal, high anxiety, and demand-

ing behaviours when memories are triggered (Grawe, 2007; Howard, 2013; Rossouw, 2014). In these circumstances, inner resilience can be significantly impaired, impacting emotional self-regulation and the capacity for successful socialisation (Howard, 2013).

Child safety organisations commonly recognise that in order to protect children from domestic abuse there is a duty of care to remove the child or children from the abusive situation and place them in a foster home (Fisher, Kim, & Pears, 2009; Maher et al., 2009). However, even in a safe foster home—an environment that can help remediate the effects of maltreatment—many children still feel anxious and unsettled (Fisher et al., 2009). Although abused, such children feel a level of sadness living apart from their biological parents and siblings, with many experiencing placement instability as a result of a mismatch of a carer with a child. These situations can result in multiple foster placements, requiring repeated adaptions by the child, and resulting in unintended negative consequences (Chaffin & Friedrich, 2004; Fisher et al., 2009).

Recognising that traumatised children in foster care have a higher risk of poor developmental, psychosocial, and mental health outcomes (Fisher et al., 2009), programs have been set up in order to assist and support children who have been subjected to abuse (Macmillan et al., 2009). One such program involved introducing a gardening and cooking component to therapy sessions. A kitchen garden program not only teaches children important life skills, but a garden environment is also recognised as being a positive setting to calm and down-regulate heightened emotions (Block et al., 2012; Capaldi et al., 2015).

Supporting Literature

Research studies, both qualitative and quantitative, give overwhelming evidence promoting the benefits

of garden programs for children (Blair, 2009; Block et al., 2012; Peddie, 2015). Kitchen garden programs can provide pleasurable experiences; importantly, they also assist in building confidence by connecting and integrating potential at-risk children as well as enabling children who are struggling academically and/or behaviourally to experience "success" (Block et al., 2012).

The physical and mental benefits of children and adults getting outdoors cannot be overstated (Capaldi et al., 2015; Fenwick, 2012; van Praag, Fleshner, Schwartz, & Mattson, 2014). Fresh air and exercise assist in the treatment of anxiety, panic disorder, depression, and anger (Kruger et al., 2010; Nedley, 2009). Exercise and fresh air stimulate the production of brain-derived neurotropic factor (BDNF), a vital neurochemical needed for down-regulating the stress response and relaxing the impulsive brain (Doidge, 2015; Etherington, 2012; Henson & Rossouw, 2013); and sunlight is an important source of Vitamin D, which is needed for the pro-

duction of melatonin that can assist in relaxation and sleep (Nedley, 2009; Thomas, 2014). Researchers have also discovered that sunshine and soil microbes boost serotonin production (Paddock, 2007). Serotonin is essential for strengthening immunity, improving mood disorders, and reducing anxiety and depression (Etherington, 2012; Nedley, 2009; Thomas, 2014; Wilson, 2014), and the friendly bacteria in soil may act in a similar way to antidepressants (Paddock, 2007).

While it could rightly be argued that taking a walk or playing outside would have the same physiological effect, the added advantage of a kitchen garden program is that it engages *all* the senses and evokes an enchanted curiosity in things that sprout, grow, and produce something edible. In their evaluation of the Stephanie Alexander Kitchen Garden Program, Karen Block and colleagues (2012) convey the enjoyment the children feel coupled with the development of a healthy sense of pride and satisfaction as garden produce is harvested.

Themes	Sub-themes	Categories
Development and learning	• Skills acquired	• Safe practices • Clean-up techniques • Setting table
	• Knowledge learned	• Basic gardening skills • Basic cooking skills
Engagement	• Engaged	• Motivated • Task-focussed • Enjoyment
	• Disengaged	• Disinterested • Withdrawn
Behavioural expression	• Calm and regulated engine	• Cooperative • Calm • Positive attitude
	• Heightened engine	• Irritable • Aggressive • Noncompliant
Personal growth	• Positive growth	• Resilient • Teamwork • Social connectedness • Respectful

Table 1
Themes Arising From Routinely Collected Clinical Data for a Kitchen Garden Program in TDP.

Note. "Engine" is the term participants use to explain the emotional regulation of their body.

Responsibility is nurtured while children care for the growing plants, and enthusiasm is heightened when children harvest and transform the produce into delicious food (Alexander, 2009; Holden, 2008).

The activity of gardening incorporates exercise and play (Etherington, 2012). Many children live sedentary lifestyles with a growing dependence on screen time often used to give parents and carers a break from difficult children (Must & Tybor, 2005). If children are not engaged in team sports, they baulk at suggestions of doing exercise and quickly lose stamina when attempting it. On the other hand, a garden provides a perfect opportunity for children to get offline and outdoors (Thomas, 2014). Ideally, a kitchen garden program will foster long-term interest so that exercise and outdoor activities become a natural part of daily life.

One must acknowledge that the success of a kitchen garden program goes well beyond the program itself. While there is enjoyment and satisfaction in growing fresh produce, it is the ability to maintain a safe, nurturing, and affirming environment that contributes to the positive emotional experience for the children. Rossouw (2014) highlights the importance of a safe and nurturing environment for any learning to take place. This is especially relevant in the case of children who have experienced abuse, and who often struggle to connect with others and build trusting relationships as a result (Geldard, Geldard, & Foo, 2013). Working as a team in a garden program helps build social connections with peers, and turn-taking and sharing skills are enhanced (Block et al., 2012).

Connecting with the earth and nature can assist in mindfulness-based techniques that help children understand they can control their thoughts and their behaviours (Thomas, 2014). Aside from the curiosity outdoor gardening activities evoke, many lessons can be drawn from nature. For example, seeing how nature adapts and adjusts to changes in seasons can be applied to childhood situations of loss, trauma, and recovery (Bilton, 2014; Thomas, 2014).

Children who have suffered trauma may find learning difficult as a result of being in a hyperalert state most of the time (Cozolino, 2013; Howard, 2013). Current research suggests that stress is down-regulated when children are engaged in natural forms of exploration (Thomas, 2014), and a kitchen garden environ-

ment can provide a sense of relaxed safety (Blair, 2009; Block et. al., 2012). The program is seen as a pleasurable adventure (Block et. al., 2012), stimulating the release of serotonin, associated with relaxation and calm feelings (Wilson, 2014), and the motivating neurochemical dopamine, both of which open neural pathways and a readiness to learn (Henson & Rossouw, 2013; Rossouw, 2014). There is a cumulative positive effect of self-esteem enhancement as children are affirmed and given opportunities to engage in the garden and cooking processes (Blair, 2009).

Putting Theory into Practice

Karen Ferry was involved in a recent study that tested the literature and evaluated the effectiveness of a kitchen garden program for children in a therapeutic day program (TDP). The aim of the study was to determine the usefulness and credibility of a kitchen garden program as it relates to behaviours and emotional regulation for children in foster care, and whether heightened children would down-regulate when in the garden environment.

Routinely collected clinical notes, written after each session by the staff involved in various aspects of the program, formed the data that was then evaluated, using a qualitative thematic analysis. It was recognised that there were significant limitations to the study in regards to the number of participants and time frames. A more comprehensive study would need to include a range of therapy environments across broader populations and include an evaluation of the transferrable benefits of the cooking and gardening program when a child was in their routine school or home environment. However, despite the limitations, there were interesting and informative findings to be considered when analysing the effectiveness of a kitchen garden program as a tool to help children who have suffered abuse and trauma.

Results

The study identified four significant themes: development and learning, engagement, behavioural expression, and personal growth, described in Table 1 (page 111).

Knowledge and learning of life skills was paramount. The children were taught and engaged in: basic kitchen and gardening safety, simple cooking skills, gardening tasks, cleaning activities, washing dishes and dining-room manners. Most children were willing to try new foods, and there was a high level of engagement, motivation, and enjoyment, particularly when the cooking groups shared their prepared foods with the rest of the group or took produce home to share with their foster families. The program provided opportunities for children to try new activities and use equipment that was new to them.

Children who suffer abuse commonly struggle with self-efficacy due to the negative interactions they have experienced and the language they have heard (Grawe, 2007). Because of low positive self-regard, they commonly lack social skills and find making friends difficult (Geldard, Geldard, & Foo, 2013). The kitchen garden program provided opportunities for safe interactions, connectedness with other children, and working as a team. It was noted that connecting with caring, supportive, and nurturing staff enabled trust attachments to develop, and the more connection the children had with the staff, the more they were willing to participate, explore, and become involved. Feeling a sense of belonging and acceptance enhanced personal value and allowed a healthy sense of pride and positive self-esteem to develop. The praise, affirmation, and encouragement given by the staff to the children served to counteract negative personal attitudes, and the children began not only to change their own negative self-talk but also to affirm each other. These findings concur with studies conducted by Block et al. (2012) identifying the significant benefits of a kitchen garden program as leading to a personal sense of achievement, healthy pride, and enhancement of self-esteem.

Providing the children with challenging but achievable activities developed potentials beyond their current attained levels ("controllable incongruence"), promoting growth and the development of new neural struc-

tures (Grawe, 2007). Words such as *attempted*, *tried*, *completed*, *achieved*, and *showed resilience* were clearly evident in the clinical notes. The data also reported that even those participants who found gardening or cooking challenging, and therefore did not engage in or enjoy the activities as readily as others, still showed significant resilience and felt proud of their achievements.

When the children were outside in the garden or engaged in cooking activities there was an air of calm and excited enjoyment. The activities were enjoyable, and the advantages of being outside in nature were apparent, in accordance with the research showing that fresh air and exercise down-regulate anxiety, panic disorders, depression, and anger (Krueger, 2013; Nedley, 2009). It was noted that initially a few of the children became more heightened when outside, sensing a freedom they were unfamiliar with. However, when these children were given a responsible job, within suitable boundaries, they quickly calmed and became cooperative and enjoyed working along with the other children.

The study highlighted the benefits of having a safe outside area for children to go to when they are feeling stressed or heightened. There were occasions during the therapeutic day program when memories were triggered and a child became frustrated and angry. Individual behaviours of protection were quickly adopted. Howard (2012) describes how children who have suffered trauma histories have a very low threshold for stress and become either disinhibited (hyperaroused) or inhibited (hypoaroused) when triggered. It was common for a child either to withdraw into a corner or hide under tables, blankets and cushions, effectively disengaging from others, or to become hyperaroused and display demanding and aggressive behaviours. Tables were often upturned, toys smashed, books ripped, and violence towards staff was common. However, it was also noted that there was a significant calming effect when these children were led outside into the garden area. Some chose a favourite tree to climb, others sat amongst the plants, but for many their curiosity and inquisitiveness was quickly aroused by things in the garden—insects were found, soil was dug, or garden produce was picked and tasted. Regardless of the activity of gardening, simply being outside provided distraction and refocus, and calmed heightened emotions.

Implications for Practice

The study concluded that a kitchen garden program is a useful tool to help children regulate heightened emotions. For some individuals it could become a life-long tool, as finding peace in a garden environment and learning to down-regulate stress and anxiety without the cost and side-effects of pharmaceuticals can be positive. Additionally, many children in the program who struggled academically found they were skilled in certain kitchen procedures, suggesting that cooking could eventually be an employment opportunity and possible trajectory into a career path. There were also opportunities to explain nutritious food choices to children throughout the program, and a positive awareness of food options and nutritious snacks was created as the children engaged in the gardening activities. These findings are also highlighted in the researched evidence, which suggests that kitchen garden programs can have a positive impact on children's food choices and assist them in making positive decisions in the future (Block et al., 2012; Brien, 2014).

Creating a kitchen garden environment in an office therapy room (or inner-city school setting) could be challenging due to the limitations of space and resources. Nevertheless, where space is limited a therapist (or teacher) might consider a miniature indoor garden, pot-plants, window-boxes, or even vases of flowers with lemon, mint, rosemary, and lavender to promote sensory stimulation. Having a bird-feeder outside the window, or a nature table that contains objects from the natural world would arouse curiosity, particularly if the natural items were changed regularly. Providing a sand tray for children to enjoy with their hands and feet, or simply growing seeds in a cup, can all become part of a soothing and calming experience that begins to heal the senses and connect the body and spirit (Drewes, Bratton, & Schaefer, 2011; Kottman, 2014). Food preparation can be introduced even when resources are limited, since many recipes do not require stoves or elaborate kitchen equipment. Food preparation is an expressive therapy that can increase self-esteem, ego, nurturing, and grounding (Drewes et al., 2011).

Future Considerations

It is interesting to note that the garden environment had a calming effect on most children in the study, but not all. There were those who found the gardening activities frustrating due to physical disabilities; for others, gardening was not "their thing", and they struggled to engage fully. Those with OCD tendencies detested getting their hands dirty due to contamination fears, and some children simply preferred other activities. Providing the children with a choice of activities and changing the activities frequently stimulated interest and reduced the "I'm bored" comments so commonly expressed by children who have had enough!

In evaluating the results, consideration must be given as to the type of garden that has the greatest positive effect. Research indicates that highly structured and controlled gardens lacking intimate spaces or places to explore and dig in the soil can hamper creativity and stifle imaginative play (Blair, 2009). The study highlighted the need for the garden area to have a variety of things to do and look at for the garden to be successful. For example, the program should include things to decorate, pools of water, sensory areas, hidden objects, and items of interest to cater to a range of needs and curiosities. Providing an element of choice in what to plant, where to plant, how a pot can be decorated, what else could be added to a garden environment provides opportunity for a child to have some measure of control. Control and orientation is a fundamental human psychological need, which is robbed from a child when they suffer abuse (Grawe, 2007; Rossouw, 2014). A kitchen garden program could fail if the program is too directive, or run by staff that are more concerned about getting jobs finished and done correctly, rather than allowing for mistakes and enjoyment.

Conclusion

A kitchen garden program for children who have suffered abuse can be evaluated as a positive lived experience. A child's involvement in the garden was shown to be a useful and credible strategy to down-regulate stress and anxiety whenever they became highly anxious or excitable. The program enhanced self-esteem and self-efficacy. It gave knowledge and learning, enjoyment, and opportunities for social connections to develop as the children worked together.

Wilson's (1984) biophilia hypothesis states that humans have an innate love of nature. After this study it was clearly evident that nature holds an innate love, curiosity, and respect for little humans!

DOMESTIC VIOLENCE

Domestic violence has been an alarming and destructive feature of our society for decades, but only recently has there been significant public recognition of this injurious practice. Traumatic and considered one of the most life-threatening public health concerns, domestic violence affects not only adult partners but also any children present in the relationship (Aoun, 2012). Studies clearly indicate that children suffer serious emotional, psychological, social, behavioural, and developmental consequences when exposed to aggression and violence within the family home (Reynolds, 2014).

Family violence, domestic abuse, or intimate partner violence (IPV; Hester, 2006; Sousa et al., 2011) has been defined as a pattern of behaviour that is used to gain or maintain power over an intimate partner, and includes behaviours that frighten, intimidate, manipulate, hurt, humiliate, blame, injure, or wound someone (Davis, 2008). It includes physical, sexual, and emotional abuse, threats, and economic manipulation or deprivation (Aoun, 2012). Domestic violence is a complex weave of factors involving parents, children, and often extended family members (Bancroft, Silverman, & Ritchie, 2012), but attention has primarily been focused on the adult victims or perpetrators, with little recognition afforded the children who are exposed to and witness the abuse (Aoun, 2012).

Childhood exposure to domestic violence includes any situation where children see, hear, or are directly involved in or experience the aftermath of assaults that occur between their caregivers, whether the aggression is perpetrated by a male caregiver, the child's mother, or bidirectionally through reciprocal acts of violence and unresolved parental arguments (Evans, Davies, & DiLillo, 2008; Jeffries, Field, & Bond, 2015). The effects on children living in volatile family situations vary, with some children appearing to remain relatively unscathed while others present with a range of adjustment and psychopathological problems (Hornor, 2005). How a child copes is often determined by individual temperament, the child's overall perception of the violence, age and gender, cultural norms, the type of violence witnessed, and whether the child is also a victim (Evans et al., 2008; Hornor, 2005; Nicklas, 2010; Sternberg, Lamb, Guterman, & Abbott, 2006). Irrespective of individual responses, over two decades of research has concluded that domestic abuse does have a negative and destructive impact on children that effects a child's overall development, contributing to emotional maladaptation and problematic behaviours (Evans et al., 2008; Hester, 2006; Reynolds, 2014).

The brain experiences incredible growth between the ages of 0 and 3, with neural connections and brain structures responding and adapting to the individual's environment (Grawe, 2007). Traumatic experiences leave an indelible mark on an infant brain, as it is during these significant stages of brain development that the brain organises responses, and behavioural schemas are formed (Aoun, 2012; Grawe, 2007). Exposure to domestic violence at this age is highly impactful on account of the trauma being at the hands of the child's trusted caregivers (Aoun, 2012; Howard, 2013; Sousa, 2009); however, parents are frequently unaware of the detrimental impact their fighting has on their children (Aoun, 2012). Infants are extremely sensitive to the emotional states of their caregivers (Aoun, 2012). A child relies on secure attachments, safety, and care as they explore the world and learn about social interactions (Baker & Jaffe, 2002). Parents involved in partner violence can be unable to effectively or consistently respond to the needs of the child, leading to inhibited growth patterns, failure to gain appropriate weight, and delays in reaching developmental milestones (Hornor, 2005).

When parental fighting violates the security of a child's home, the child perceives their world as unpredictable, insecure, and threatening. The fear and insecurities they experience cause an overwhelming sense of powerlessness, as they are unable to stop the parental conflict (Medina, 2014). Grawe (2007) describes this sense of powerlessness as a loss of control. Having a sense of control is one of the most fundamental psychological human needs, and is satisfied when a person feels comfortable and safe in their current situation with available options for future safety and survival (Rossouw, 2012). It is also essential to have an accurate view of a situation. Being confused and not understanding what is going on in one's environment can be highly disconcerting, particularly when it involves personal safety and survival (Grawe, 2007). When the basic need of control and orientation is violated, an individual instinctively adopts protective behaviours in order to escape the stressful or traumatic situation (Grawe, 2007). Some young children can be seen to cover their ears, put their hands over their eyes and bury their head, perhaps believing that if they can't see and can't hear, the danger will cease to exist. Others clench their fists, cry, or withdraw to a safe corner, often curling into the foetal position for comfort. Many plead for the fighting to stop, while still others simply remain rigid, stunned, and silent.

As the child grows into a preschooler, exposure to family violence erodes and undermines cognitive development (Nicklas, 2010). Withdrawal behaviours, anxiety, and clinginess are frequent, and the child tends to be more irritable and unsettled, suffering emotional instability (Hornor, 2005). Nightmares and bed-wetting commonly occur, often adding to parental frustrations and heightening negative reactions (Aoun, 2012). By the time the child reaches school age, the constant stress affects learning and commonly manifests in emotional and social difficulties (Sterne, 2009), with many children re-enacting the violent behaviours they see in the home during their play experiences with others (Hornor, 2005; Zavala, Melander, & Kurtz, 2015). A child of early school age often begins to feel responsible for the home violence (Hornor, 2005; Reynolds, 2014), becoming torn between helping the parent who is abused and keeping the family secret (Hornor, 2005).

Teenagers too are not immune to the effects of domestic violence, and react to stressful situations with extreme emotion (Jensen, 2015). When confronted with crisis situations, they experience intense levels of fear and anger due to the underdeveloped cortical regions of the brain where problem solving, reasoning, understanding, and evaluation occur (Rossouw, 2012). There is a notable difference in responses to stress and trauma between teenagers and adults. In adults, the rush of adrenalin and cortisol is modulated after a short period of time by the hormone tetrahydropregnanolone (THP), which has a calming effect to help down-regulate the stress and anxiety, but in teenagers the effect of THP is the opposite, causing an increase in anxiety and reducing their defence against stress (Jensen, 2015).

The physiological and psychological changes that occur during the teenage years signify a somewhat difficult time, even for a child who lives within walls of nurture, support and security (Brackenreed, 2010). Adding family violence to the equation undoubtedly aggravates teen fears and insecurities (Coleman & Hagell, 2007). Teenagers tend to withdraw and become inhibited. Many are hypervigilant, readily misinterpreting innocuous environmental stimuli as dangerous (Aoun, 2012). They are prone to personality and eating disorders, self-mutilation, suicide ideation, and delinquency, and have a higher vulnerability to depressive conditions and anxiety. (Aoun, 2012). This period is often associated with rage, rebellious behaviours, relationship issues, truancy, and drug and alcohol abuse (Aoun, 2012).

Studies conducted by Kitzmann et al. (2003) found that children who witness family abuse experience the same level of negative psychosocial outcomes as children who are the direct recipients of physical abuse (The Australian Domestic & Family Violence Clearinghouse, 2011). The emotions of fear, hate, anger, and panic trigger the survival centres of the brain, the limbic system, and the brain stem, causing a release of adrenalin and cortisol which activates the instinctive "fight, flight, or freeze" response (Howard, 2013; Jenson, 2015; Perry, 2000). Physiological symptoms are evident: increased heart rate, dilated pupils, quickened breathing, a slowing down of digestion, sweaty palms, and the inability to think rationally due to the release of the stress hormones which assist the body in protective behaviours (Howard, 2013; Medina, 2014). When a child experiences intense and frequent emotional trauma, the stress response remains in a state of high alert, continuing to escalate until it eventually breaks over a certain threshold where nuclei in the hypothalamus are activated, causing hypothalamic–pituitary–adrenal (HPA) axis activation and the release of cortisol (Grawe, 2007). The surge of cortisol adds to the already heightened emotional response, particularly in the hippocampus, adversely affecting learning and memory (Jensen, 2015), as the neural terminals in the hippocampus are particularly sensitive to cortisol, resulting in a degeneration of the axons and neural receptors (Grawe, 2007). The excess stress undermines the ability of the individual to adapt to environmental changes (neuroplasticity), making the brain less flexible (Daliman, 2007; Grawe, 2007). In order to protect against and escape emotional pain, the lower brain survival systems respond, and

the individual adopts an avoidance behaviour which, if practised often enough, becomes a scaffold for handling future emotional stressors (Grawe, 2007; Teicher et al., 2003). Children who witness domestic abuse can suffer intense terror, fear of death, and the fear of losing a parent (Aoun, 2012). Their behaviours become agitated and disorganised, and depending on the severity, the duration, and the proximity of a child's exposure to family violence, it is not uncommon for a child to exhibit symptoms consistent with post-traumatic stress disorder (PTSD; Hornor, 2005), where the violence is commonly re-experienced and the child suffers nightmares, flashbacks, and severe anxiety (Keeley & Storch, 2009). Constant stress causes excessive growth in parts of the amygdala while the hippocampal volume becomes shrunken (Davidson & McEwen, 2012), predisposing the child to long-term and often irreversible learning and mental health problems (Jensen, 2015; Pittenger & Duman, 2008).

Influences of domestic abuse on child education

It is important to note that not all stress is negative or harmful. Studies consistently advocate that exposing children to moderate stress when they are supported by an emotionally available adult is beneficial in the childhood years, as it enhances hippocampal learning and stimulates memory formation (Dolby, 2007; Jensen, 2015). Children who experience moderate levels of stressful discomfort become highly resilient, as the repeated mastering of controllable stress enables the development of self-soothing behaviours and builds tolerance levels (Coleman & Hagell, 2007; Grawe, 2007; Monahan, 2011). Resilient children approach new situations rather effortlessly, as they have developed a certain emotional security and a level of social orientation, making adaptation to school life relatively easy (Grawe, 2007). When confronted with stressful situa-

tions at school, such as the introduction of new learning, classroom changes, or notice of a test, in place of an unhealthy stress response that could cripple the cortical regions of the brain and render the child incapacitated, a well-functioning stress response energises and motivates (Howard, 2013; Jensen, 2015).

Child witnesses of violence have a heightened sensitivity to emotional stimuli and suffer the effects of excessive fear and anxiety, anger, frustration, and sadness (Aoun, 2012). They are unable to manage even low-intensity stress (Rossouw, 2012) and respond with aggression and antisocial behaviours or internalised behaviours of anxiety, depression and a reluctance to try new things (Grawe, 2007; Hornor, 2005).

Traumatised children suffer physiologically, often being continually tired and physically exhausted, as a volatile home situation keeps them in an unrelenting state of fear and alert (Cook, Ciorciari, Varker, & Devilly, 2009; Reynolds, 2014). Distressed children regularly feel ill and commonly express vague somatic complaints, particularly headaches or stomach aches (Grawe; 2007; Hornor, 2005). Obesity, hypertension, and asthma are also more prevalent due to the strong comorbidity of psychological disorders and physical conditions (Aoun, 2012; Nedley, 2009).

Teachers are often unaware of the home situation of children, so that the impact of domestic violence goes unrecognised (Sterne, 2009). A child may appear deficient in learning ability, when in fact the stress they experience raises cortisol levels, blocking memory and preventing any absorption of knowledge and or recall of learned material (Aoun, 2012; Reynolds, 2014; Sterne, 2009). Studies conducted with children living in emotionally unstable homes revealed they did not perform as well in *any* academic area, with standardised test scores for math and reading found to be significantly lower than for chil-

dren living in a supportive and safe family environment (Medina, 2014).

When a child struggles academically, negative and disruptive behaviours often represent an attempt to avoid the humiliation and shame commonly associated with inability (Cozolino, 2013; Grawe, 2007). Many children resort to violence as a way to solve conflicts and cope with humiliating situations, emulating parental role models that suggest aggression is an acceptable way to resolve uncomfortable situations (Withers & Russell, 2001). These behaviours lead to teacher impatience and frequent disciplinary reactions (Grawe, 2007). However, many disciplinary methods used in the school setting, particularly those of manipulation or coercion, parallel negative parental responses and have the effect

of quickly snapping a child into shut-down and withdrawal mode (Cozolino, 2013; Schenck, 2011). Neuroscience research has shown how the amygdala "remembers" threatening and painful situations (both physical and emotional) and reactivates the fear response when it recognises a pattern from a past experience, applying it to a present situation (Rossouw, 2014). A student may overreact to a gesture, words spoken, a command, a facial expression, a feeling, or any number of stimuli, triggering a memory that causes the amygdala to activate and instinctively shut down the cortical, "thinking" regions of the brain, making learning impossible and giving rise to irrational behaviours and outbursts (Rossouw, 2014; Tokuhama-Espinosa, 2011).

The positive influence of the school environment

The future can look very bleak and disheartening for a child suffering in a home where there is domestic abuse. However, a family does not exist in isolation; there are many stakeholders in educating a child (Benson, Leffert, Scales, & Blyth, 2012; Tokuhama-Espinosa, 2014; Withers & Russell, 2001). The importance of the school environment cannot be ignored, given the compulsory hours a child spends within its gates and the quality of interactions that occur there (Tokuhama-Espinosa, 2014). There is strong evidence for the benefits of a school environment that fosters both physical and emotional safety (Cozolino, 2013).

Schools are often the first port of call for children in distress (Sterne, 2009), and teachers can be proactive in assisting families to seek help from professionals in order to ensure that children are not in imminent danger (Coulter & Mercado-Crespo, 2015; Murray, 2015). Schools also have the opportunity to facilitate programs to support students who have not benefitted from nurturing family environments, helping them to find strategies for effective communication, self-awareness, and conflict resolution (Monahan & Steinberg, 2011; Plummer, 2012; Sterne, 2009). Studies have shown that inter-adult violence indirectly impacts child adjustment by disrupting parent–child relationships, inhibiting effective parenting practices (Maughan & Cicchetti, 2015). Therefore, schools can work with family health centres to introduce programs that provide parenting strategies and strengthen child–parent attachments (Rowe & Stewart, 2011; McWhirter et al., 2013).

One of the greatest impacts on a child's development is the quality of the classroom teacher (Tokuhama-Espinosa, 2014). Aside from providing the kind of teaching that can propel students to excel academically, a teacher is in a position to give compensatory nurturance to students who are caught in unpleasant family situations (Benson et al., 2012). It is important to acknowledge the realities of the classroom environment today, where teachers are often struggling to meet the needs of the 20–30 children in their care (Sousa, 2009). But teachers don't have to "go it alone". Studies show that suitable adult mentors from outside the school environment have a positive effect on student relationships and can help ease the pressure teachers face (Sousa, 2009).

Recent neurobiological research recognises that student performance and learning is affected by an individual's emotional and physical state (Immordino-Yang & Damasio, 2007). Students simply cannot learn when they are stressed and anxious (Brackenreed, 2010; Cozolino, 2013, Schenck, 2011; Sousa, 2009). A teacher is highly influential in these circumstances, able to either heighten or down-regulate student stress due to mirror neurons that help us process emotions (Schenck, 2011). Neurobiological evidence suggests our brains are highly social and that we are influenced by our connectedness with others, absorbing and integrating input from other people via the brain's mirror neuron system (Siegel, 2006). It is thought that we perceive another's expression and then create an internal state that "resonates" with that of the other person (Siegel, 2006). When a teacher displays emotional warmth and pleasant facial expressions and calmly connects with students, mirror neurons activate and students begin to imitate the teacher's positive and calm emotional disposition, improving their overall well-being (Cooper, 2011; Schenck, 2011).

Just as the amygdala responds to danger, fear, and anger, it also responds to positive emotions (Sousa, 2009). Teachers can develop positivity in the classroom by fostering an atmosphere of inclusiveness and belonging characterised by a strong sense of trust, respect, value of individuals, group identity, and connectedness (Cooper, 2011; Cozolino, 2012; Schenck, 2011). "Belongingness", or feeling attached, is a most fundamental psychological need (Allen & Bowles, 2012; Grawe, 2007; Rossouw, 2014). A sense of belonging in a safe classroom environment provides students with peer support and establishes positive teacher–student relationships, which assists in lowering psychopathological stress and acts as a protective factor against future risky behaviours (Cozolino, 2013; Lumpkin, 2008; McWhirter et al., 2013). Student confidence and self-esteem are enhanced (Benson et al., 2012; Cameron, 2013; Cozolino, 2013; Withers & Russell, 2001), a factor particularly pertinent for children who witness domestic violence, as they frequently suffer feelings of shame, guilt, and low self-efficacy (Aoun, 2012; Hornor, 2005; Jensen, 2015).

Qualities of personal warmth and supportiveness build emotional security and support academic engagement (Cooper, 2011; Rietz, 2001). When a student experiences a non-threatening environment, the positive emotional influence down-regulates stress. Once stress is reduced and pleasurable feelings are increased, the neurotransmitter dopamine is released. Dopamine motivates behaviours, and as a student masters various levels of achievement, be they academic or behavioural, more dopamine is released, strengthening memory circuits and neural connections; thus learning occurs (Sousa, 2009). A student who feels confident in his or her learning ability develops a sense of personal satisfaction, wins teacher approval, and improves in social competence, the combination of which acts as a protective factor in the face of stressful challenges (Grawe, 2007; Monahan & Steinberg, 2011).

Conclusion

A student's perception of life can become severely negative as a result of information built from the environmental influences he or she is exposed to (Schenck, 2011). Many students come to school burdened by the trauma of exposure to domestic violence, which not only affects their perception of school but colours all of their dealings in peer relationships and interactions with teachers, thus affecting their academic learning (Howard, 2013). Childhood life experiences are potent (Davidson & McEwen, 2012), with neuroscience research clearly demonstrating that trauma associated with abusive family environments where children are witnesses to the abuse has serious effects on brain development (Aoun, 2012).

However, we must remember that a child is not "hardwired" (Jensen, 2015). The plasticity of the brain allows for reorganising, correcting, pruning, and strengthening neural pathways (Sousa, 2009). When parents fail to offer an environment of emotional safety, the skills, attitudes, and behaviours imparted by a supportive and caring teacher can become the pivot for the building of new neural pathways. Despite a child's home circumstances and the impact of early environmental influences, a nurturing and safe school environment can provide an enriched learning context, devoid of stress, to guide a child's trajectory into positive educational possibilities and future wellbeing.

PSYCHOLOGICAL NEEDS

Now that we have explored some of the basics of the brain, it is important to put this "wetware" in context with the basic principles of mental functioning. To understand the broader mental functions from the standpoint of their neural underpinnings gives the teacher a sophisticated appreciation of a child's struggles. It also crucially sheds light on why certain teaching strategies work and why others may not work so well in any given circumstance. The meta-framework known as neuropsychotherapy represents a multidisciplinary perspective that equips the teacher with a mature understanding across the spectrum from basic neural communication and networks to psychological needs and how we go about enhancing and protecting them. This final section brings together the elements into a bigger picture that I hope will serve you well in your classroom practice and inspire you to learn more.

Klaus Grawe developed a view of mental functioning that combined insights from mainstream contemporary psychology with an understanding that "the goals a person forms during his or her life ultimately serve the satisfaction of distinct basic needs" (Grawe, 2007, p. 169). Influenced by Seymour Epstein's cognitive-experiential self-theory (Epstein, 1973, 1980, 1991 1993, 1994, 1998; Teglasi & Epstein, 1998), Grawe defined four key psychological needs that provide the motivation for behaviour: the need for attachment, the need for control/orientation, the need for pleasure/avoidance of pain, and the need for self-enhancement (Grawe, 2007; see also Epstein, 1994, p. 715 for the origins of these four needs). Implicit motivational schemas, which we will discuss below, are designed to satisfy these four psychological needs via either approach-driven (primarily cortical processes) or avoidance-driven (primarily limbic processes) behaviour in what Epstein describes as an emotionally driven experiential system (Epstein, 1994). Here we explore these basic psychological needs:

Motivational Schemas

A motivational schema is, at root, a neural network developed to satisfy and protect basic needs. Schemas can be broadly divided into two classes: approach schemata and avoidance schemata (see figure below). Approach and avoidance schemata operate on different neural pathways (Grawe, 2007). If an individual grows

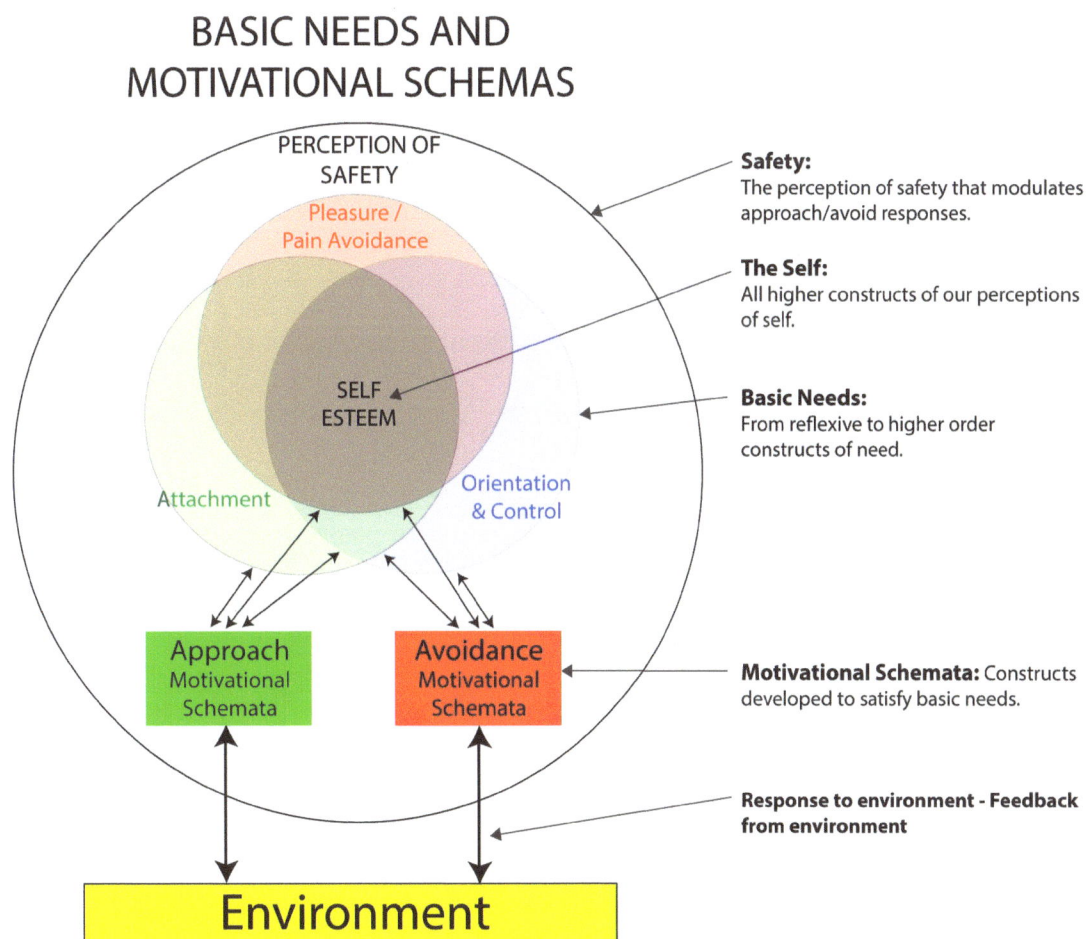

BASIC NEEDS AND MOTIVATIONAL SCHEMAS

PERCEPTION OF SAFETY

Pleasure / Pain Avoidance

SELF ESTEEM

Attachment

Orientation & Control

Approach Motivational Schemata

Avoidance Motivational Schemata

Environment

Safety: The perception of safety that modulates approach/avoid responses.

The Self: All higher constructs of our perceptions of self.

Basic Needs: From reflexive to higher order constructs of need.

Motivational Schemata: Constructs developed to satisfy basic needs.

Response to environment - Feedback from environment

up in an environment where needs have been met, especially during the critical early attachment phase, then approach schemas of interacting with the environment are likely to develop, resulting in approach-oriented behaviour. Conversely, an individual whose needs are continually threatened and violated is likely to develop avoidance schemas that will motivate insecure, anxious, and avoidant behaviour. Bowlby's (1973, 1988) attachment theory furnishes a critical understanding of the foundation of mental schemata, explaining how securely attached children develop primarily approach motivational schemas and insecurely attached children develop avoidance motivational schemas.

Approach and avoidance motivation has a long history. The concept first appeared in the writings of Greek philosopher Democritus of Abdera (460–370 B.C.E.), broadly seeking to explain behaviour as directed either toward positive stimuli or away from negative stimuli (Elliot, 2008). The full spectrum of approach–avoidance motivation includes such orienting exteroceptive reflexes as the startle response, salivary reflex, and pain withdrawal. But for the purposes of neuropsychotherapy, approach and avoidance schemata are psychological orientations toward or away from stimuli (whether concrete objects, events, and possibilities or abstract subjective representations) that may or may not have a corresponding somatic movement or action. Furthermore, "movement toward" can represent either *gaining* something positive that is currently absent or *keeping* something positive that is currently present (in functional terms, "continuing toward"). Likewise, "movement away" can represent either *getting away* from something negative that is currently present or *keeping away* from something negative that is currently absent (in functional terms, "continuing away from"; Elliot, 2008, p. 8).

The consistency theory model conceptualizes all behaviour as the product of approach and avoidance motivations. The somewhat binary nature of this view may appear over-simplistic at first glance, but its complexity lies in the fact that many approach and avoidance schemata can be operating in parallel (as in the case of motivational discordance; Grawe, 2007) and in a hierarchical manner (Elliot, 2006), to service not only our basic psychological needs but also physiological reflexes as we navigate our experiences of the world.

According to consistency theory, there are three ways the mental system can experience inconsistency: through *approach incongruence*, *avoidance incongruence* and *discordance*. These upset the neural harmony of the system, creating a system demand to reduce such stress or dissonance.

Approach incongruence. If an individual tends towards avoidance motivational schemas—that is, if there is an established neural propensity to avoid perceived threats to basic needs rather than seek to satisfy those needs—he or she can experience incongruent signals due to unfulfilled approach schemas. To illustrate, consider a teenager who has recently changed schools and has a desire to join in the school's drama group. However, fear of rejection and ridicule prevents her from signing up to the drama classes and auditioning for the school play. The avoidant motivational schema is well established to protect her from the pain of rejection that she has experience at her previous school, and prioritizes the maintenance of whatever self-esteem and control over circumstances she has.

However, there is at the same time, a desire represented in another motivational schema to approach, to fulfil the passion she has for acting, to feel belonging and the thrill of being on stage. It is when this latter desire is suppressed or overridden by the stronger avoidance schema that the individual experiences approach incongruence.

Avoidance incongruence. When attempts at avoidance ultimately fail, and what was feared actually happens, the individual experiences avoidance incongruence. To continue the previous illustration, if the teenager does sign up and audition for the school play and is, after all, rejected, ridiculed and embarrassed, she will experience avoidance incongruence - the very undesired consequences her avoidance schema had motivated her to protect herself.

Discordance. Discordance occurs when two or more motivational schemas are activated simultaneously and are incompatible with one another. Following through with our example, the student auditions for the play, but the character is at odds with her religious or moral world view. This is not an incongruence between perception and goal but rather two incompatible goals being activated simultaneously.

Incongruence and discordance, and the affect that accompanies them, can occur implicitly or explicitly and create inconsistency in the system. Continual inconsistency can impair an individual's effective engagement with the environment and lead to increasingly avoidant tendencies, stress, negative emotions, anxiety, and a range of serious mental difficulties, as limbic survival mechanisms dominate to protect the individual who is descending into a highly complex state of stress.

The consistency model conceptualizes behaviour as

an attempt to attain or protect the object of basic needs through motivational schemas that have been shaped by earlier experiences (in particular of attachment), in a way that provides agreement with the individual's perception of the world and internal model of the world and him or herself.

There are current attempts to refine Grawe's model so that the basic psychological needs are portrayed in a less linear fashion and are seen as overlapping in their neural arrangement, with the superimposition of the basic needs yielding a higher-order construct of "self". The figure below shows a refinement by Rossouw (2014) in which the higher-order construct of "self" emerges from the neural milieu of needs and motivational schemata.

Attachment

John Bowlby (1973, 1988) demonstrated convincingly that the basic need of an infant is the physical proximity of a primary attachment figure, ushering the importance of attachment into mainstream psychology. Bowlby (1973) articulated the basis of his attachment theory in three central postulates that could be summarized this way:

- A child with an available, trusted caregiver will be less anxious than one without such a caregiver.

- Trust or lack of trust in the availability of the caregiver will translate into a similar expectancy of relationships later in life.

- The expectations a child has of a caregiver are relatively true of the actual experiences of the caregiver.

Bowlby referred to this theory of attachment as the internal working model, a concept taken from Kenneth Craik, who proposed that an organism carries a "small-scale model" of external reality in its head (Wallin, 2007, p. 26). In essence, early dyadic relationships, especially with primary caregivers, form implicit memories from which a child constructs schemas, or ways of understanding and interacting with the world. A parent's approach to his or her infant shapes the very structure of its developing brain through proximity and gaze (Schore, 2012). As Bonnie Badenoch has put it, "What is alight in the parental brain lights up in the newborn brain. It is as though the parent is passing on the family's emotional legacy in regards to relationships through these initial firings and wirings" (Badenoch, 2008, p. 53).

Mary Ainsworth, a colleague of

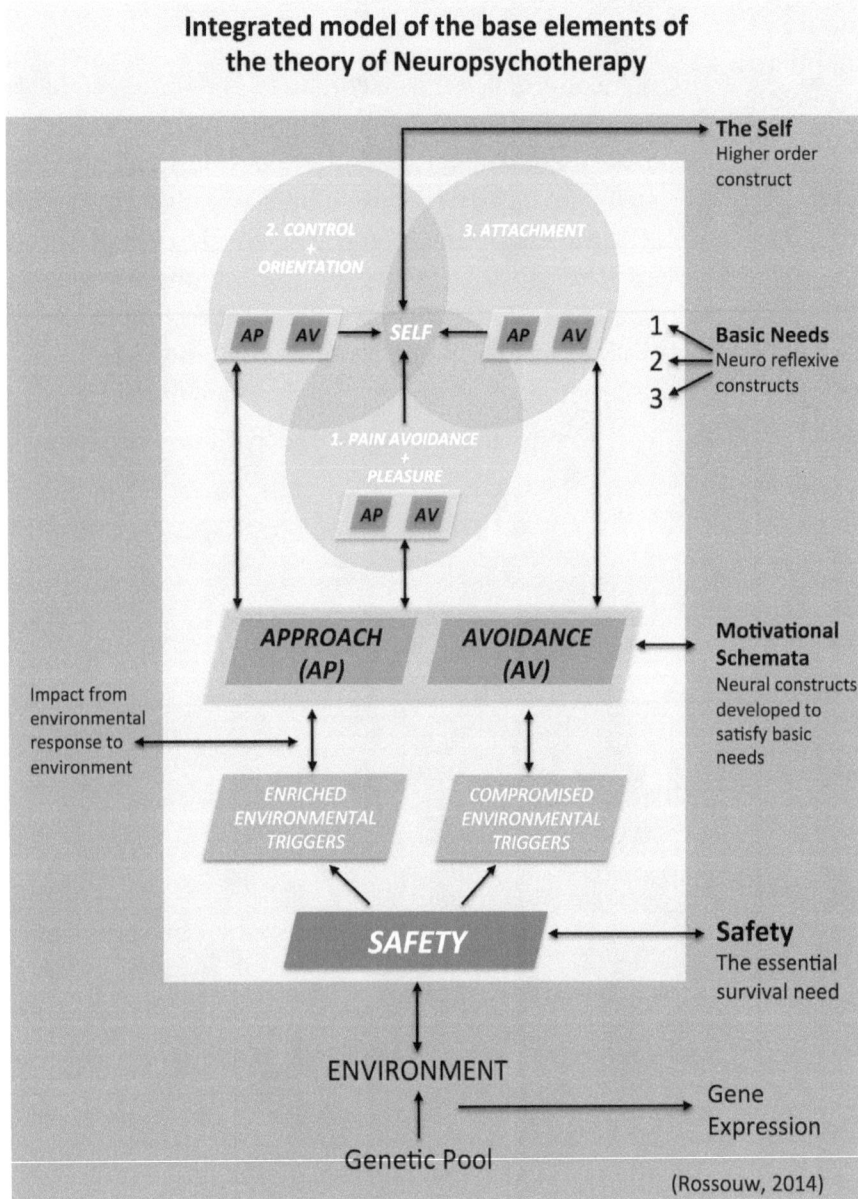

Integrated Model of the Base Elements of the Theory of Neuropsychotherapy (Rossouw, 2014, p. 57)

Bowlby, developed an empirical method for assessing attachment in infants called the Strange Situation Protocol, based on Bowlby's attachment theory (Ainsworth, Blehar, Waters, & Wall, 1978). Ainsworth observed the behaviour patterns of young children when they were separated and then reunited with their mothers in a controlled environment. Several attachment styles were identified at this point: secure attachment, insecure-avoidant attachment, and insecure-ambivalent attachment (Ainsworth et al., 1978; Badenoch, 2008). Later, Mary Main and colleagues (Main & Solomon, 1986) identified another style they called insecure-disorganized/disorientated attachment.

Unsurprisingly, the children who were found to thrive in life were those who had formed secure, rather than insecure, attachment patterns. Attachment patterns start to form in the first months of life—a time when brain development is extremely rapid, the sympathetic nervous system is dominant, and right-hemisphere limbic learning is critical (Badenoch, 2008)—and they lay the foundation for the motivational schemas that ultimately drive behaviour.

Orientation and Control

Epstein (1990) characterized the need for orientation and control as the most fundamental of all human needs. According to Powers' (1973) perceptual control theory, this need plays out in a pervasive striving for perceptions of reality that are consistent with the individual's goals, and this striving is a major driver of behaviour and mental life. If we want to be respected or to be financially secure, we will act towards achieving a sense that we are. To attain such a goal requires control over our environment, or at least our perception of the environment. Grawe (2007) added that control was not only about manipulating or regulating the environment or relationships to achieve goals, but also about maximizing the number of options we are free to act upon. How we then choose to take up the options available to us will be determined by our motivational schemas.

A sense of control begins in infancy, in the context of attachment, with the child having the volition to manipulate the environment to meet his or her needs. An infant crying when hungry has the desired outcome of summoning Mother who has food. If the child cries for food and no food comes, there is an incongruence (the gap between what the child needs and what she per-

ceives she has), and with such a violation of the need for attachment there is a corresponding violation of the need for control. A satisfaction of the need for control, on the other hand, causes a reduction in distress, which in turn strengthens the sense of control.

There is a component, or an understanding, of control that can be described as the need for orientation—that is, to have an accurate appraisal of a situation, and to understand what is going on. To gain such clarity about one's situation, and what can be done to improve it, is an important aspect of control. It is a common experience in psychotherapy to see a better sense of control gained simply through understanding a situation with greater clarity.

Pleasure Maximization and Pain Minimization

Freud, in his theory of personality, postulated a single fundamental need that he characterized as the pleasure principle: the need to maximize pleasure and minimize pain (Freud 1920/1959). Epstein (1994) considered this a core need, as did Grawe (2007).

The basic premise of this need is that we are motivated to attain pleasant experiences or states and avoid unpleasant or painful ones. These states may be physical, psychological, emotional, or social. Neurologically there is an automatic, implicit evaluation of experience as either "good" or "bad", to the degree that there is a continual monitoring of our experiences (one aspect of this process is known as feedback-related negativity; see

The prefrontal cortex (PFC) is the most underdeveloped region of the brain at birth, and its architecture is developed in response to our experiences as we grow. It is highly adaptive, shaping the way we see ourselves and the world as we experience life. The capacity of the PFC to regulate emotions by inhibiting sympathetically driven, survival-orientated neural networks while increasing calming parasympathetic vagal activity is dependent on its early development. Experiences of abuse, neglect, and trauma typically result in a PFC less capable of emotional self-regulation. Conversely, experiences of caregivers who sensitively help navigate emotions, soothe, and demonstrate self-regulation—essentially creating emotional safety—foster the development of a PFC capable of regulating the limbic system and providing a flexible sympathetic/parasympathetic balance.

Psychotherapy is an opportunity for a less well developed PFC to gain the skills of emotional self-regulation that may not have been instilled in childhood. This kind of therapy is literally about rewiring the brain so that the PFC has stronger mechanisms of control over the fear-driven emotional brain areas like the amygdala, and can apply the parasympathetic "brake" more readily and flexibly via the vagus nerve to the heart, increasing heart-rate variability (we will discuss heart-rate variability in a later section). Psychotherapy can help us be more aware of our habitual anticipation of threat and to choose new experiences that make us feel safer and more flexible in our responses. In short, we can choose to change the heart–mind connection (Peckham, 2015).

Hajcak, Moser, Holroyd, & Simons, 2006; Nieuwenhuis, Slagter, Von Geusau, Heslenfeld, & Holroyd, 2005). Humans have a motivation to maximize experiences of the good and limit the bad, even in the case of suffering "for the greater good"—the denial of some pleasures to attain something of greater worth. What constitutes "good", "pleasurable", "beautiful", and the like is dependent upon the individual and how his or her experience is consistent with the satisfaction of the other basic needs. Grawe contends that the individual is in a maximal state when his or her "current perceptions and goals are completely congruent with one another, and the transpiring mental activity is not disturbed by any competing intentions" (2007, p. 244). This maximal state—a state of pleasure—is comparable to Mihaly Csikszentmihalyi's (1991) concept of "flow", which describes our intrinsic motivation to align our perception of experience with our intentions.

Just how a person will size up the world around him is dependent on both his prior experience and his momentary state. For example, a hot drink on a very hot day may be evaluated more negatively than an ice-cold drink, and vice versa on a cold day; this is a state-dependent evaluation. By contrast, the experience of going on a roller-coaster is likely to be far less state-dependent—one individual may evaluate it as bad and another as good, according to each person's prior experience with roller-coasters. The relearning of taste preferences is a complex process influenced by motives such as social compliance and positive self-evaluations, yet the same automatic evaluative process is in play. The development of a taste for wine, for example, may be motivated by a need for social acceptance (attachment and self-esteem), but ultimately becomes an automatic preference for wine as part of the neural evaluative process.

When a situation is evaluated either positively or negatively, it triggers an approach or avoidance tendency, meaning that our mental activity is primed in a certain direction. For example, someone who evaluates New York cab drivers as bad on the basis of past negative experiences may be primed to "jump" at the sudden lane changes made by the driver. Another person with a more positive evaluation of New York cab drivers may not be startled or fearful at all at the same sudden lane changes. This motivational priming is essentially an orientation of the motivational system toward either approach or avoidance behaviour in response to certain cues in our environment.

Mental processes transpire more easily and quickly when the good/bad evaluation is compatible or synchronized with the behavioural approach–avoidance orientation. In other words, when evaluations and behavioural orientations are consistent, the mental system works more efficiently and with less stress.

Self-Esteem Enhancement

The need for self-enhancement or self-esteem has been called the "master sentiment" (McDougall, 1936, p. 224) and "the basic law of human life" (Becker, 1971, p. 66). It is the only one of the four needs that is distinctly human. Self-esteem has been defined as "an individual's subjective evaluation of her or his worth as a person. If a person believes that she is a person of worth and value, then she has high self-esteem, regardless of whether her self-evaluation is validated by others or corroborated by external criteria" (Trzesniewski, Donnellan, & Robins, 2013, p. 60). However, there has been debate over the

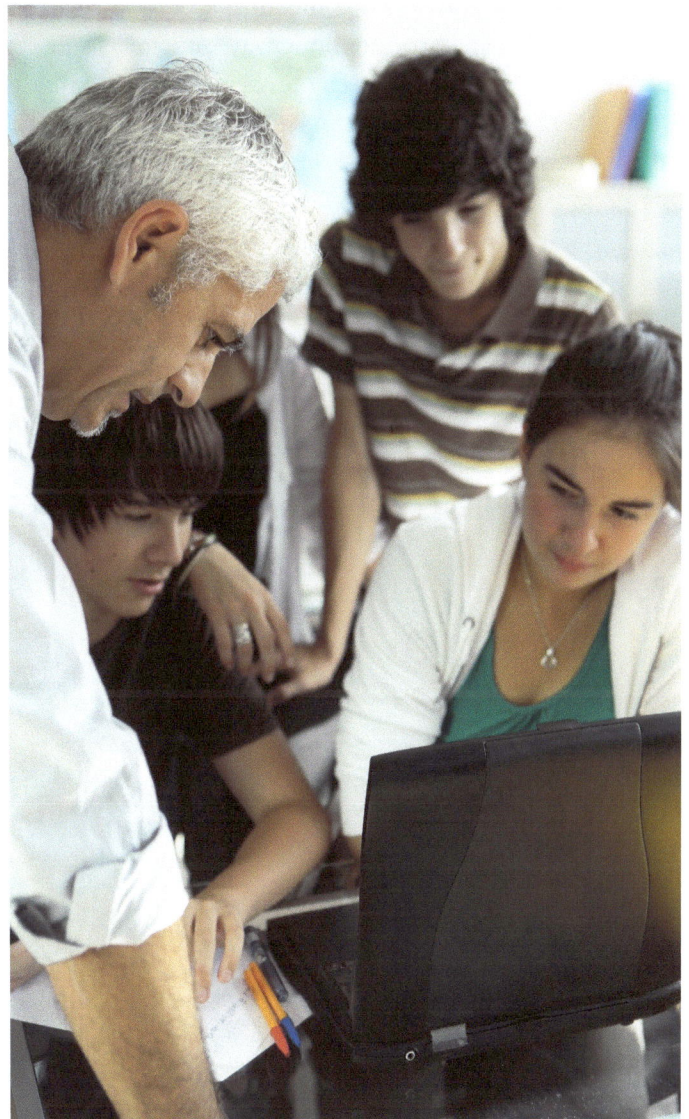

importance of this construct, with some arguing that self-esteem is essential (Orth, Robins, & Widaman, 2012) and others considering it of limited value in that it is likely a reflection of other processes (Boden, Fergusson, & Horwood, 2008, Zeigler-Hill, 2013). The self-esteem that Grawe conceptualized as a basic need is a global one that is secure and congruent as opposed to unstable, narcissistic, or discrepant (see Park & Crocker, 2013). Nevertheless, it is possible that self-esteem is a complex construction emerging from more fundamental needs—an outcome of self-perception, and indeed of a perception that may be culturally driven and fail to qualify as a basic need (Dahlitz & Rossouw, 2014).

In some cases, to preserve the greatest number of needs, one need may be "sacrificed". For example, the maintenance of low self-esteem may be an avoidance pattern utilized to fulfil another need such as preventing pain or preventing loss of control, or to protect existing self-esteem from further degradation. Alternatively, avoidance of high self-esteem may win the individual acceptance, thus meeting a need for attachment—which, in a roundabout way, satisfies some aspect of self-esteem. In these scenarios the tendency to self-esteem enhancement can be regarded as part of the approach system, and self-esteem protection can be regarded as part of the avoidance system. The exact reasons for an individual maintaining low self-esteem may be complex, but in context with other needs, it is safe to assume this is a compromise aimed at achieving overall need fulfilment/protection as best the individual can.

Those who do satisfy the need for enhanced self-esteem are characterized by better mental health. These individuals will take opportunities to enhance their self-esteem through approach motivational schemas. They will evaluate themselves more positively than objective observers—in fact it has been found that an unrealistically positive perception of self satisfies the self-esteem enhancement need and is itself a good indicator of overall mental health. Mentally healthy individuals also have a skewed perception of their place in social context, often seeing themselves as "above average" within the general population. Indeed, striving for an absolutely realistic self-evaluation may not be in their best interests for mental well-being. Depressed individuals, however, who have a more pessimistic view of reality, do not share this delusion and are prone to further mental problems. Operating out of avoidance schemas, these individuals experience life, and take on roles, in a way often detrimental to self-esteem.

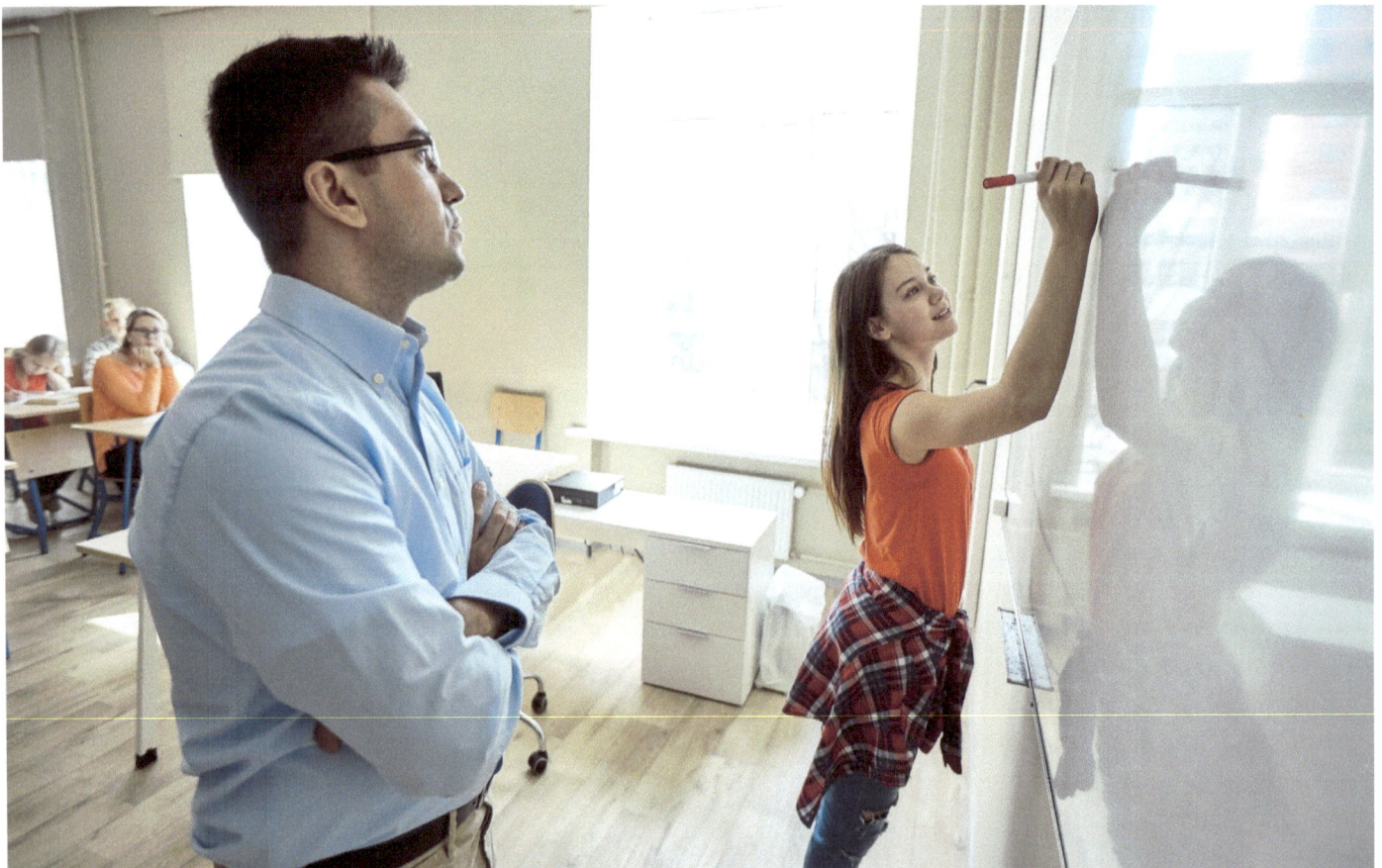

Approach/Avoid Networks

A view of mental function based on the binary notion of approach and avoidance motivational systems can prove useful. We are either "approaching" to apprehend something, or we are "avoiding" to preserve and protect. Such approach/avoid systems operate independently of one another and have independent neural substrates and mechanisms (Grawe, 2007). They can be activated in a parallel fashion, although equally strong systems will tend to mutually inhibit each other. As we have learnt earlier, there are significant differences between the left and right hemispheres of the brain, and these are reflected in approach/avoidance motivations such that the left hemisphere is biased toward approach (positive) emotions and the right toward avoidance (negative) emotions (Canli, Desmond, Zhao, Glover & Gabrieli, 1998; Davidson 1992; Paradiso et al., 1999). It is possible to conceive of behaviour as an outcome based on the summation of approach/avoid calculations in our conscious and unconscious mind. This is an important concept to come to grips with.

Basic needs have a neural foundation from birth that initiates behaviour like crying, sucking, and wiggling the body to meet those needs (Panksepp & Biven, 2012). These genetically governed behaviours are the beginning of what will develop into much more personal and sophisticated motivational goals. The first need that develops into an "approach" goal is the need for proximity of the primary attachment figure. As the infant experiences encounters with its mother, it starts to develop a repertoire of behaviours to influence the mother to meet her needs. Neural activation patterns emerge that represent this and other goals, and these are strengthened with the help of oxytocin and dopamine. Both baby and mother are rewarded by oxytocin and dopamine release when in loving, mutually satisfying connectedness. The increasing strength and complexity of these neural patterns continues to form circuits, which are readily activated, leading eventually to very sophisticated and spontaneously activated schemas. The specific groups of motivational schemas that develop to satisfy the basic needs of an individual are infinitely richer and more multifaceted than what might be suggested by the classification of just a few attachment styles. As the individual grows, motivational goals are shaped by his or her wider environment along with social expectations, limitations, and other cultural forces, shaping the neural architecture of personal motivational schemas.

On a physiological level, approach goals are associated with the left dorsolateral prefrontal cortex (PFC), while avoidance is more closely aligned with the right. For the processing of emotions, the left ventromedial PFC is associated with positive emotions and the right for negative emotions. These motivations and evaluations of approach/positive and avoidance/negative are thus physiologically lateralized across the brain. There are correlations to this same lateralization in the deeper limbic system, giving credence to the theory that approach and avoidance are indeed neurally independent systems.

As they relate to pleasure maximization (approach) and pain minimization (avoidance), approach and avoidance schemas may seem to be opposites, like a positive and negative charge. But they are just different goals with different modes of operation. The approach schema is about closing the gap between a desired goal and perceived reality to attain that goal which satisfies a need. There is often progress toward a goal, with rewards along the way, culminating in attainment (or otherwise) of that goal. However, the avoidance schema is about increasing the distance between something undesirable and perceived reality, often to preserve or protect a basic need—a goal frequently not achieved, but nonetheless necessitating a state of continuous surveillance. When pursuing a positive goal, like completing a university course, it is relatively easy to determine whether one has come closer to the goal: there are sub-goals and markers (such as completing a semester) along the way to the final destination of the goal. However, avoidance goals require constant control, as well as distributed, rather than focused, attention. For example, a husband may be anxious to avoid an argument with his wife: he has to keep vigilant, watch what he says, be careful to read the signs of a possible argument, and he can never reach the goal of avoidance because there is always the possibility that conflict may come in the future. This sort of avoidance is more a matter of continuous attention, and often anxious tension, than simply apprehending a concrete goal. Individuals with strongly formed avoidance goals (or with a dominance of avoidance over approach goals) experience fewer positive emotions and less satisfaction of need because of the disproportionate amount of energy and focus invested in avoidance. In fact, strongly developed avoidance tendencies, both implicit and explicit, have many unfavourable effects on mental health, self-esteem and general well-being (Grawe, 2007).

How does this translate into the classroom setting? In a nutshell, teachers should aim to reduce the inclination toward avoidance goals and promote more positive approach goals to satisfy a child's basic needs. Approach goals would include having a classroom that is stimulating and interesting, where curiosity is encouraged and learning is more an exciting daily journey or discovery, rather than a tedious requirement that all children have

to do! But more than a classroom of excitement and interest, it is a classroom of inclusivity, where attachments are secure between the teacher and the student, and self-esteem is enhanced due to the value and respect.

In the previous section on Memory we learnt that dopamine is a critical factor in establishing new learning and reinforcing neural change. Dopamine is the reinforcing agent and represents neural motivation, or motivational salience, in establishing behaviour. Any behaviour that is reinforced involves the release of dopamine. Because dopamine is essential for motivation and learning (establishing and reinforcing synaptic connections), in therapy, learning must have high motivational salience to be effective. In real terms, without the activation of the dopamine system, substantial, positive long-term learning will not take place. Dopamine is the intrinsic motivator and energizer of approach/avoidance schemas and is therefore of central importance to a classroom environment.

The Consistency Principle

Consistency is the overarching concept of systemic agreement that can be considered a "core principle of mental functioning" (Grawe, 2007, p. 168). The myriad of simultaneously occurring processes in the nervous system function optimally only to the extent that the various elements of the system remain in harmony and are not conflicted.

The now famous Stroop test (Stroop, 1935) is a classic example of activating conflicting mental processes and thus compromising performance speed as the anterior cingulate cortex and the dorsolateral PFC work through inconsistent patterns to arrive at a resolution (Milham, 2003). On a more complex level, an individual's experience of the world, internal model of the world, and meeting of needs can be in conflict—a state of internal inconsistency from which dissatisfaction and stress arise. An effective classroom induces a state of controlled incongruence within a system striving for consistency.

The consistency theory (Grawe, 2004, 2007) view of mental functioning is derived both from broadly accepted findings that goals and schemas govern mental activity and from Grawe's own argument that goal formation is developed to satisfy four basic psychological needs: attachment, orientation & control, avoidance of pain/maximization of pleasure, and self-esteem enhancement. The core constructs of consistency and congruence are the keys to understanding the development and maintenance of both normal and pathological mental processes.

Consistency is described as the "compatibility of many simultaneously transpiring mental processes" (Grawe, 2007, p. 170), and is a systemic demand, on a neural level, for harmonious neural flow. When the relationship between intrapsychic processes and states is harmonious, there exists a state of consistency. The human nervous system strives to avoid inconsistency and develops various mechanisms to move from a dissonant, inconsistent state to a more harmonious state. Consistency regulation is predominantly unconscious and only rises to conscious awareness under exceptional circumstances. The mechanisms an individual uses to avoid or correct significant inconsistencies have been termed defence mechanisms, coping strategies, or affect regulation.

Congruence, a construct that comes under the umbrella of consistency, is the harmony or compatibility between motivational goals and current perceptions of reality. According to Powers (1973), incongruence signals are generated from the feedback mechanism that contrasts our perceptions with our goals. Grawe argues that "an elevated incongruence level can be regarded . . . as a highly complex stress state" (Grawe, 2007, p. 172).

Change

Let's look at an example from a typical educational situation. A student has completed primary school and is moving into high school at a new campus. The student has an element of doubt about how he will fit in, which causes mild stress, but the student has had friends in primary school and generally believes he can cope with the new school environment. The nervousness and anxiety the student feels trigger some arousal in the associative cortex and the limbic system. Adrenalin is released and permeates the entire brain, which leads to a chain reaction in the glia cells. This stimulation increases readiness to learn, motivates and increases ener-

gy, which leads to increased neural connections which prompts a desire to 'give it a go'. The student goes to school the first day, reaches out to others to make new friends and they respond back. Even though the situation is uncomfortable for him with an element of anxiety and nervousness, due to his shyness, the repeated confrontation with the same type of incongruence leads to a strong facilitation of a new behaviour. We find that the student is able to adapt to new environments and make friends even easier next time he is in an unfamiliar situation with people he doesn't know. The stress has been controllable and new pathways and activation patterns are formed. The more a person is repeatedly exposed to challenging incongruent situations that require effort, but can be mastered, their ability to cope with similar future incongruent situations become more efficient. Incongruent situations are motivating, with positive learning, as long as they remain controllable.

To recap, incongruence is the discrepancy between an individual's perception of reality (his or her actual experience) and beliefs, expectations, and goals. Such incongruence will cause inconsistency within the mental system. Controllable incongruence describes a situation of incongruence that the individual believes he or she can cope with—it may be a challenge, but not an overwhelming one. Uncontrollable incongruence, on the other hand, is a circumstance that exceeds one's ability to cope, or at least one's belief in that ability, with the mismatch between what is experienced and one's goals.

However, if the student is in a challenging or threatening incongruence situation and does not find the means to reduce the incongruence then there is increased arousal which remains in place and continues to escalate until eventually the HPA is activated and glucocorticoids are released. Let's take the situation of the same student as in our previous example. The boy arrives at the new school, but instead of being welcomed and included in the school environment, no-body talks to him, in fact they turn away and shun him. The student is not sure of the school layout and finds himself frequently lost and unable to locate the correct classrooms. He is reprimand by the teacher when he is late to class, whereby he feels a keen embarrassment causing his fellow classmates to giggle and whisper. The boy does not find the means to reduce incongruence through his own activities, therefore the situation has become one of uncontrollable incongruence.

Uncontrollable incongruence, then is a stressful state that heightens arousal, potentially beyond one's window of tolerance and, if not resolved, as in, if the student receives the same negative treatment and experiences isolation day after day, the result is a hyper activated HPA-axis cascade, releasing damaging amounts of glucocorticoids into the system. In a regulated stress response, a feedback loop will down-regulate the HPA-axis activation and attenuate the release of stress hormones (Kandel, Schwartz, Jessell, Siegelbaum, & Hudspeth, 2012). In a state of continued stress—as with unresolved uncontrollable incongruence—this feedback mechanism is overridden, and a continued flow of glucocorticoids can inhibit the formation of new synapses (new learning) while degenerating existing glutamate synapses, especially in the hippocampus, destabilizing previously formed neural connections (established learning) and even inducing complex negative structural changes in various brain regions (Lupien, McEwen, Gunnar, & Heim, 2009; Popoli, Yan, McEwen, & Sanacora, 2012). To limit such a destructive cascade of events, a teacher should aim to introduce a sense of control in order to reduce arousal and in turn restore HPA-axis regulation.

A sense of control can be as simple as a teacher smiling and saying 'hi' to a new student, asking him if he knows where his next class is and providing him with guidance so that he doesn't feel trapped and unsure of what to do next. Controllable incongruence is a state in which a stressor (the incongruence) is raising arousal levels through sympathetic excitation and noradrenergic activation and may exceed a certain threshold to activate the HPA-axis, but the situation is perceived as manageable, and feedback loops are intact to down-regulate the stress response in a timely manner. Such a controlled stress reaction causes a moderate amount of adrenalin to permeate the nervous system, including the neurons, glia, and endothelial cells, which can facilitate a constructive response to the incongruence in the form of learning. As adrenergic receptors are stimulated at blood vessels and astrocytes, glucose release is increased, with a corresponding increase in metabolism. This metabolic increase, in conjunction with the release of neurotrophic factors from astrocytes (Verkhratsky & Butt, 2007) and the stimulation of adrenergic receptors, will help stabilize neural connections activated when coping with the incongruence (in a process representing existing coping strategies) and also improve the facilitation of new neural connections (new coping strategies)—the opposite to what occurs in the case of uncontrollable incongruence. In fact, rising to the challenge of controlling incongruence is essential to "the formation of ever more complex and differentiated neu-

ral circuits to an optimal expression of [one's] genetic potential" (Grawe, 2007, p. 222).

As the individual continues to deal with a controllable incongruent situation, coping behaviour is established. Eventually such situations will no longer elicit a stress response, because the neural networks required to effectively assess and cope with the situation are now firmly in place. Within the safety of a stress free classroom, with positive and caring student–teacher relationships, stress responses can be down-regulated to a state of optimal learning, and incongruence can be broken down into controllable, manageable parts to which new strategies can be applied.

Only from a place of trust and security can an individual actively engage within his or her window of tolerance and take advantage of the brain's natural neuroplasticity. Research has shown that "a safe, enriched environment actually facilitates the development of new neural patterns, which, in turn, leads to enhanced attachment and control, and stress reduction. Approaches that provide safe environments will thus enhance the positive social interaction that is an essential element of healthy neural proliferation" (Allison & Rossouw, 2013, p. 23). To establish such a safe environment requires a down-regulation of avoidance motivational schemas that may be activated.

Applying what is essentially a bottom-up approach in a classroom setting to deal with students who may be experiencing physiological stress before any active cognitive learning takes place now appears logical. A bottom up approach affectively focusses on right-brain to right-brain relationships. Engaging with students, smiling, communicating in an empathetic manner, showing care and genuine interest can establish safety for students and down-regulate heightened limbic reactivity.

Once a student feels safe, the teacher has created the ideal environment for facilitating neural proliferation in an integrative manner, because the nervous system is essentially socially oriented: it thrives on interpersonal love, acceptance, and security (Cozolino, 2014; Schore,

2012, Siegel, 2012).

Having discussed fear and anxiety in some detail, it is important to reiterate the practical implications of what happens to a student when anxiety increases—a decrease in cortical blood flow in the left PFC and an increase in the right PFC and limbic system, inhibiting the ability of the left PFC to modulate emotional arousal. When the left PFC is engaged and activated and the limbic system is down-regulated, as is our goal in a safe classroom environment, more cortical blood flows to the left PFC, and the student can manage his or her emotions more easily. This works in much the same way that a sympathetic response can cause peripheral shutdown to shunt more blood to essential organs like the heart when there is an immediate threat. When a system like the left PFC is required to down-regulate an overreaction elicited by an overactive amygdala, for example, yet is robbed of the resources needed to do that job (blood flow and the precious oxygen it supplies), then we have a problem: the student is in the grip of a feeling of uncontrollable incongruence.

One of the ways to mitigate the problem of an essential control system like the PFC going "offline" in times of stress is to increase its integrative connectivity to those areas that need higher-order control, such as the amygdala. Mindfulness is one practice that can achieve this. Described as focused attention in the present without judgment (Kabat-Zinn, 1994, 2013), mindfulness can increase mid-PFC and right anterior insula activity and thickening, and increase activity in the superior temporal gyrus and anterior cingulate (Badenoch, 2008). The result is an enhanced integration of these systems with the limbic system, providing better modulatory control over amygdala overreactions and fostering a propensity to approach rather than avoid challenging situations (Siegel, 2012). Such an increase in control brings previously overwhelming situations back into the realm of controllable incongruence. Research sug-

gests that meditative practices like mindfulness not only increase the integration and plasticity of neural networks, but can also offset ageing processes and increase our ability to be present, attuned and compassionate with others (Badenoch, 2008).

Siegel (2007) suggests another "mindful" strategy to gain greater prefrontal management of limbic responsiveness that involves a change in language. Rather than saying, "I'm sad," an example of self-talk that would facilitate a greater sense of separation for the client between the self and the emotion is, "There's a feeling of sadness right now." Positioning the emotion as an objectively observable phenomenon apart from the "observing self" elicits a greater sense of control over what would otherwise be an immersive emotional experience.

Whatever mindful strategy is utilized, there are some common outcomes to such practices: less dysregulation and reactivity to emotional experiences; remaining present with feelings, thoughts, or actions without being distracted; the ability to label beliefs, opinions, emotions, and expectations; and having a nonjudgmental stance toward our experiences (Badenoch, 2008; Baer, Smith, Hopkins, Krietemeyer, & Toney, 2006).

Motivational priming, resource activation, the creation of safety, and techniques like mindfulness are all designed to bring the client into a place of optimal learning where incongruence is perceived to be within the client's window of tolerance, controllable, and therefore an opportunity for new learning and positive change. The teacher armed with an understanding of how the brain works and influences the mind can proceed with more awareness and skill than ever before. It is our hope that this book has inspired you to learn more about the human neurobiology for your students, your classroom methodologies, and for yourself.

REFERENCES

Aben, B., Stapert, S., & Blokland, A. (2012). About the distinction between working memory and short-term memory. *Frontiers in Psychology, 3*, 301. doi:10.3389/fpsyg.2012.00301

Agerberth, B., & Gudmundsson, G. H. (2006). Host antimicrobial defence peptides in human disease. *Current Topics in Microbiology and Immunology, 306*, 67–90.

Ainsworth, M. D., Blehar, M. C., Waters, E., & Wall, S. (1978). Patterns of attachment: A psychological study of the strange situation. Hillsdale, NJ: Lawrence Erlbaum Associates.

Alexander, G. E., DeLong, M. R., & Strick, P. L. (1986). Parallel organization of functionally segregated circuits linking basal ganglia and cortex. *Annual Review of Neuroscience, 9*, 357–381.

Alexander, S. (2009). Stephanie Alexander's kitchen garden companion: Dig, plant, water, grow, harvest, chop, cook. Melbourne, Australia: Lantern.

Allen, K. A., & Bowles, T. (2012). Belonging as a guiding principle in the education of adolescents. Australian Journal of Educational & Developmental Psychology, 12, 108–119.

Allison, K. L., & Rossouw, P. J. (2013). The therapeutic alliance: Exploring the concept of "safety" from a neuropsychotherapeutic perspective. *International Journal of Neuropsychotherapy, 1*, 21–29. doi:10.12744/ijnpt.2013.0021-0029

American Psychiatric Association. (2013). Depressive disorders. In *Diagnostic and statistical manual of mental disorders* (5th ed.). Washington, DC: American Psychiatric Publishing. doi:10.1176/appi.books.9780890425596.dsm04

Andrade, C., & Rao, N. S. K. (2010). How antidepressant drugs act: A primer on neuroplasticity as the eventual mediator of antidepressant efficacy. *Indian Journal of Psychiatry, 52*, 378–386. doi:10.4103/0019-5545.74318

Andrews, P. W., Bharwani, A., Lee, L. R., Fox, M., & Thomson, J. A., Jr. (2015). Is serotonin an upper or a downer? The evolution of the serotonergic system and its role in depression and the antidepressant response. *Neuroscience & Biobehavioral Reviews, 51*, 164–188. doi:10.1016/j.neubiorev.2015.01.018

Anonymous. (1996). Moving forward on brain-based learning. Vocational Education Journal, 71, 21.

Aoun, C. (2013). Strengthening attachment: A multifamily group for mother child dyads following domestic violence (Doctoral dissertation). Available from ProQuest Dissertations & Theses Global database. (Dissertation No. 3557486)

Atkinson, R. C., & Shiffrin, R. M. (1968). Human memory: A proposed system and its control processes. In K. Spence & J. T. Spence (Eds.), *The psychology of learning and motivation* (Vol. 2, pp. 89–195). Oxford, United Kingdom: Academic Press. doi:10.1016/S0079-7421(08)60422-3

Arden, J. B., & Linford, L. (2009). *Brain-based therapy with children and adolescents: Evidence-based treatment for everyday practice.* Hoboken, NJ: John Wiley & Sons.

Austin, M. A., Riniolo, T. C., & Porges, S. W. (2007). Borderline personality disorder and emotion regulation: Insights from the Polyvagal Theory. *Brain and Cognition, 65*, 69–76. 10.1016/j.bandc.2006.05.007

Australian Law Reform Commission. (2013). *Children in Education: Truancy* (ALRC Report No. 84–10.49). Retrieved from http://www.alrc.gov.au/publications/10-children-education/truancy

Baddeley, A., Eysenck, M. W., & Anderson, M. C. (2009). *Memory*. Oxford, United Kingdom: Psychology Press.

Badenoch, B. (2008). *Being a brain-wise therapist: A practical guide to interpersonal neurobiology.* New York, NY: W. W. Norton.

Baer, R. A., Smith, G. T., Hopkins, J., Krietemeyer, J., & Toney, L. (2006). Using self-report assessment methods to explore facets of mindfulness. *Assessment, 13*, 27–45. doi:10.1177/1073191105283504

Ball, C. R., Finch, W. H., Gettinger, M., & K–3 Reading and Behavior Intervention Project. (2014). Classroom-level effects on the reading and behavior of at-risk kindergarteners. *Preventing School Failure: Alternative Education for Children and Youth, 58*(2), 80-89.

Baldoni, J. (2005). Effective leadership communications. In The results-driven manager series: Getting people on board (pp. 103–114). Boston, MA: Harvard Business School Press.

Bancroft, L., Silverman, J. G., & Ritchie, D. (2012). Shock waves: The batterer's impact on the home. In Sage series on violence against women: Vol. 2. The batterer as parent: Addressing the impact of domestic violence on family dynamics (2nd ed., pp. 69–107). Thousand Oaks, CA: Sage. doi:10.4135/9781452240480.n3

Baratta, M. V., Kodandaramaiah, S. B., Monahan, P. E., Yao, J., Weber, M. D., Lin, P.-A., . . . Goosens, K. A. (2016). Stress enables reinforcement-elicited serotonergic consolidation of fear memory. *Biological Psychiatry, 79*, 814–822. doi:10.1016/j.biopsych.2015.06.025

Baumeister, R. F., & Leary, M. R. (1995). The need to belong: Desire for interpersonal attachments as a fundamental human motivation. Psychological Bulletin, 117, 497–529. doi:10.1037/0033-2909.117.3.497

Baylin, J. (2013, October). Behavioral epigenetics and attachment: The new science of trust and mistrust. *The Neuropsychotherapist, 3*, 68–79.

Becker, E. (1971). *The birth and death of meaning: An interdisciplinary perspective on the problem of man* (2nd ed.). Florence, MA: Free Press.

Benarroch, E. E. (2009). The locus ceruleus norepinephrine system: Functional organization and potential clinical significance. *Neurology, 73*, 1699–1704. doi:10.1212/WNL.0b013e3181c2937c

Bender, K. J., & Trussell, L. O. (2012). The physiology of the axon initial segment. *Annual Review of Neuroscience, 35*, 249–265. doi:10.1146/annurev-neuro-062111-150339

Bennett, B. T., Abee, C. R., & Henrickson, R. (Eds.). (1998). *Nonhuman primates in biomedical research: Diseases* (American College of Laboratory Animal Medicine; 1st ed.). Cambridge, MA: Academic Press.

Benson, P. L., Leffert, N., Scales, P. C., & Blyth, D. A. (2012). Beyond the "village" rhetoric: Creating healthy communities for children and adolescents. Applied Developmental Science, 16, 3–23.

Betts, Rotenberg, & Trueman. (2013). Young children's interpersonal trust consistency as a predictor of future school adjustment. Journal of Applied Developmental Psychology, 34(6), 310-318.

Bewernick, B. H., Hurlemann, R., Matusch, A., Kayser, S., Grubert, C., Hadrysiewicz, B., . . . Schlaepfer, T. E. (2010). Nucleus accumbens deep brain stimulation decreases ratings of depression and anxiety in treatment-resistant depression. *Biological Psychiatry, 67*, 110–116. doi:10.1016/j.biopsych.2009.09.013

Blair, D. (2009). The child in the garden: An evaluative review of the benefits of school gardening. The Journal of Environmental Education, 40, 15–38. doi:10.3200/JOEE.40.2.15-38

Block, K., Gibbs, L., Staiger, P. K., Gold, L., Johnson, B., Macfarlane, S., . . . Townsend, M. (2012). Growing community: The impact of the Stephanie Alexander Kitchen Garden Program on the social and learning environment in primary schools. Health Education & Behavior, 39, 419–432. doi:10.1177/1090198111422937

Bilton, H. (2014). Playing outside: Activities, ideas and inspiration for the early years (2nd ed.). Abingdon, United Kingdom: Routledge.

Boden, J. M., Fergusson, D. M., & Horwood, L. J. (2008). Does adolescent self-esteem predict later life outcomes? A test of the causal role of self-esteem. *Development and Psychopathology, 20*, 319–339.

Bora, E., Fornito, A., Panetlis, C., & Yücel, M. (2011). Gray matter abnormalities in Major Depressive Disorder: A meta-analysis of voxel based morphometry studies. *Journal of Affective Disorders, 138*, 1–2, 9–18. doi:10.1016/j.jad.2011.03.049

Bowlby, J. (1973). *Attachment and loss* (Vol. 1): *Attachment*. New York, NY: Basic Books.

Bowlby, J. (1988). *A secure base: Parent–child attachment and healthy human development*. New York, NY: Basic Books.

Brackenreed, D. (2010). Resilience and risk. International Education Studies, 3(3), 111–121.

Bravo, J. A., Forsythe, P., Chew, M. V., Escaravage, E., Savignac, H. M., Dinan, T. G., . . . Cryan, J. F.

(2011). Ingestion of Lactobacillus strain regulates emotional behavior and central GABA receptor expression in a mouse via the vagus nerve. *Proceedings of the National Academy of Sciences, 108,* 16050–16055. doi:10.1073/pnas.1102999108

Bremner, J. D., Randall, P., Vermetten, E., Staib, L., Bronen, R. A., Mazure, C., … Charney, D. S. (1997). Magnetic resonance imaging-based measurement of hippocampal volume in posttraumatic stress disorder related to childhood physical and sexual abuse: A preliminary report. *Biological Psychiatry, 41,* 23–32.

Brien, J. (2014). Childhood nutrition and the Stephanie Alexander Kitchen Garden Program. Every Child, 20, No. 3.

Bromberg-Martin, E. S., & Hikosaka, O. (2011). Lateral habenula neurons signal errors in the prediction of reward information. *Nature Neuroscience, 14,* 1209–1216. doi:10.1038/nn.2902

Buehlmann, E., Berger, G. E., Aston, J., Gschwandtner, U., Pflueger, M. O., Borgwardt, S. J., Radue, E. W., & Riecher-Rössler, A. (2010). Hippocampus abnormalities in at risk mental states for psychosis? A cross-sectional high resolution region of interest magnetic resonance imaging study. Journal of Psychiatric Research, 44, 447–453 doi:10.1016/j.jpsychires.2009.10.008

Busch, A. J., Barber, K. A. R., Overend, T. J., Peloso, P. M. J., & Schachter, C. L. (2007). Exercise for treating fibromyalgia syndrome. *Cochrane Database of Systematic Reviews*, Issue 4, Art. No. CD003786. doi:10.1002/14651858.CD003786.pub2

Buskila, D., & Cohen, H. (2007). Comorbidity of fibromyalgia and psychiatric disorders. *Current Pain and Headache Reports, 11,* 333–338. doi:10.1007/s11916-007-0214-4

Cameron, D. L. (2013). An examination of teacher–student interactions in inclusive classrooms: Teacher interviews and classroom observations. Journal of Research in Special Educational Needs, 14, pp. 264–273. doi:10.1111/1471-3802.12021

Canli, T., Desmond, J. E., Zhao, Z., Glover, G., & Gabrieli, J. D. E. (1998). Hemispheric asymmetry for emotional stimuli detected with fMRI. *NeuroReport, 9,* 3233–3239.

Capaldi, C., Passmore, H-A., Nisbet, E. K., Zelenski, J. M., & Dopko, R. L. (2015). Flourishing in nature: A review of the benefits of connecting with nature and its application as a well-being intervention. International Journal of Wellbeing, 5, 1–16. doi:10.5502/ijw.v5i4.1

Carr, L., Iacoboni, M., Dubeau, M. C., Maziotta, J. C., & Lenzi, L. G. (2003). Neural mechanisms of empathy in humans: A relay from neural systems for imitation to limbic areas. *Proceedings of the National Academy of Sciences, 100,* 5497–5502. doi:10.1073/pnas.0935845100

Caspi, A., Sugden, K., Moffitt, T. E., Taylor, A., Craig, I. W., Harrington, H., … Poulton, R. (2003). Influence of life stress on depression: Moderation by a polymorphism in the 5-HTT gene. *Science, 301*(5631), 386–389. doi:10.1126/science.1083968

Castrén, E., & Hen, R. (2013). Neuronal plasticity and antidepressant actions. *Trends in Neurosciences, 36,* 259–267. doi:10.1016/j.tins.2012.12.010

Castrén, E., Võikar, V., & Rantamäki, T. (2007). Role of neurotrophic factors in depression. *Current Opinion in Pharmacology, 7,* 18–21. doi:10.1016/j.coph.2006.08.009

Caviness, L. B. (2001). Educational brain research as compared with E. G. White's counsels to educators (Unpublished dissertation). Andrews University, Michigan.

Chaffin, M., & Friedrich, B. (2004). Evidence-based treatments in child abuse and neglect. Children and Youth Services Review, 26(11), 1097–1113. doi:10.1016/j.childyouth.2004.08.008

Chakrabarty S, & Zoorob, R. (2007). Fibromyalgia. *American Family Physician, 76,* 247–254. Retrieved from http://www.aafp.org/afp/2007/0715/p247.html

Chang, Y.-S., Gratiot, M., Owen, J. P., Brandes-Aitken, A., Desai, S. S., Hill, S. S., … Mukherjee, P. (2016). White matter microstructure is associated with auditory and tactile processing in children with and without sensory processing disorder. *Frontiers in Neuroanatomy, 9:*169. doi:10.3389/fnana.2015.00169

Cheetham, S. C., Katona, C. L. E., & Horton, R. W. (1991). Post-mortem studies of neurotransmitter biochemistry in depression and suicide. In R. W. Horton & C. L. E. Katona (Eds.), *Biological aspects of affective disorders* (pp. 192–221). London, United Kingdom: Academic Press.

Cherney, K., & Holland, K. (2016, December 1). Everything you need to know about fibromyalgia [Web log post]. Retrieved from http://www.healthline.com/health/fibromyalgia

Clauw, D. J., Arnold, L. M., & McCarberg, B. H. (2011). The science of fibromyalgia. *Mayo Clinic Proceedings, 86*, 907–911. doi:10.4065/mcp.2011.0206

Clauw, D. J. (2014). Fibromyalgia: A clinical review. *JAMA, 311*, 1547–1555. doi:10.1001/jama.2014.3266

Coleman, J. C., & Hagell, A. (2007). The nature of risk and resilience in adolescence. In J. C. Coleman & A Hagell (Eds.), Adolescence, risk and resilience: Against the odds (pp. 1–17). Hoboken, NJ: John Wiley & Sons.

Comb, M., & Goodman, H. M. (1990). CpG methylation inhibits proenkephalin gene expression and binding of the transcription factor AP-2. *Nucleic Acids Research, 18*, 3975–3982.

Cook, F., Ciorciari, J., Varker, T., & Devilly, G. J. (2009). Changes in long term neural connectivity following psychological trauma. Clinical Neurophysiology, 120, 309–314. doi:10.1016/j.clinph.2008.11.021

Cook, P. (2014, December 1). This Will Revolutionize Education [YouTube video]. Retrieved from https://www.youtube.com/watch?v=GEmuEW-jHr5c&feature=youtube_gdata_player

Cooper, P. (2011). Teacher strategies for effective intervention with students presenting social, emotional and behavioural difficulties: An international review, *European Journal of Special Needs Education, 26* (1), 71-86, DOI: 10.1080/08856257.2011.543547

Coulter, M. L., & Mercado-Crespo, M. C. (2015). Co-occurrence of intimate partner violence and child maltreatment: Service providers' perceptions. Journal of Family Violence, 30, 255–262. doi:10.1007/s10896-014-9667-5

Cozolino, L. (2013). The social neuroscience of education: Optimizing attachment and learning in the classroom. New York, NY: W. W. Norton & Company

Cozolino, L. (2014). *The neuroscience of human relationships: Attachment and the developing social brain* (2nd ed.). New York, NY: W. W. Norton.

Craig, J. B., & Lindsay, N. J. (2001). Quantifying "gut feeling" in the opportunity recognition process. In W. Bygrave, E. Autio, C. G. Brush, P. Davidsson, P. G. Green, P. D. Reynolds, & H. J. Sapienza (Eds.), *Frontiers of entrepreneurship research: Proceedings of the twenty-first annual Entrepreneurship Research Conference* (pp. 124–137). Wellesley, MA: Babson College.

Craik, F. I. M., & Lockhart, R. S. (1972). Levels of processing: A framework for memory research. *Journal of Verbal Learning and Verbal Behavior, 11*, 671–684.

Cryan, J. F., & O'Mahony, S. M. (2011). The microbiome–gut–brain axis: From bowel to behavior. *Neurogastroenterology & Motility, 23*, 187–192.

Csikszentmihalyi, M. (1991). *Flow: The psychology of optimal experience.* New York, NY: Harper Perennial.

Dahlitz, M. J., & Rossouw, P. J. (2014). The consistency-theoretical model of mental functioning: Towards a refined perspective. In P. J. Rossouw (Ed.), *Neuropsychotherapy: Theoretical underpinnings and clinical applications.* Brisbane, Australia: Mediros.

Damir, J. (Ed.). (2009). Mammalian brain development. New York, NY: Humana Press.

Dane, E., & Pratt, M. G. (2007). Exploring intuition and its role in managerial decision making. *Academy of Management Review, 32*, 33–54. doi:10.5465/AMR.2007.23463682

Danese, A., & Baldwin, J. R. (2017). Hidden wounds? Inflammatory links between childhood trauma and psychopathology. *Annual Review of Psychology, 68*, 517–544. doi:10.1146/annurev-psych-010416-044208

Dapretto, M., Davies, M. S., Pfeifer, J. H., Scott, A. A., Sigman, M., Bookheimer, S. Y., & Iacoboni, M. (2006). Understanding emotions in others: Mirror neuron dysfunction in children with autism spectrum disorders. *Nature Neuroscience, 9*, 28–30.

Davidson, R. J. (1992). Emotion and affective style: Hemispheric substrates. *Psychological Science, 3*, 39–43.

Davidson, R. J. (2000). Affective style, psychopathology, and resilience: Brain mechanisms and plasticity. *American Psychologist, 55*, 1196–1214.

Davidson, R. J., & Henriques, J. B. (2000). Regional brain function in sadness and depression. In J. C. Borod (Ed.), *The neuropsychology of emotion* (pp. 269–297). New York, NY: Oxford University Press.

Davidson, R. J., & McEwan, B. S. (2012). Social influences on neuroplasticity: Stress and interventions to promote well-being. Nature Neuroscience, 15,

689–695. doi:10.1038/nn.3093

Davidson, R. J., Pizzagalli, D., Nitschke, J. B., & Putnam, K. (2002). Depression: Perspectives from affective neuroscience. *Annual Review of Psychology, 53*, 545–574.

Davis, R. L. (2008). Domestic violence: Intervention, prevention, policies, and solutions. Boca Raton, FL: CRC Press. E-book available from http://www.eblib.com

Desbonnet, L., Garrett, L., Clarke, G., Bienenstock, J., & Dinan, T. G. (2008). The probiotic Bifidobacteria infantis: An assessment of potential antidepressant properties in the rat. *Journal of Psychiatric Research, 43*, 164–174.

DeWall, C. N., MacDonald, G., Webster, G. D., Masten, C. L., Baumeister, R. F., Powell, C., . . . Eisenberger, N. I. (2010). Acetaminophen reduces social pain: Behavioral and neural evidence. *Psychological Science, 21*, 931–937. doi:10.1177/0956797610374741

Diamond, A. (2013). Executive functions. *Annual Review of Psychology, 64*, 135–168. doi:10.1146/annurev-psych-113011-143750

DiGangi, J. A., Tadayyon, A., Fitzgerald, D. A., Rabinak, C. A., Kennedy, A., Klumpp, H., . . . Phan, K. L. (2016). Reduced default mode network connectivity following combat trauma. *Neuroscience Letters, 615*, 37–43. doi:10.1016/j.neulet.2016.01.010

Dinan, T. G., & Cryan, J. F. (2013). Melancholic microbes: A link between gut microbiota and depression? *Neurogastroenterology & Motility, 25*, 713–719. doi:10.1111/nmo.12198

Doidge, N. (2010). The brain that changes itself: Stories of personal triumph from the frontiers of brain science (Rev. ed.). Melbourne, Australia: Scribe.

Doidge, N. (2015). The brain's way of healing: Remarkable discoveries and recoveries from the frontiers of neuroplasticity. New York, NY: Penguin.

Donnelly, M. and Wilson, R. (1994), The dimensions of depression in early adolescence. *Personality and Individual Differences 15* (7), 25-430

Dolby, R. (2007). The circle of security: Roadmap to building supportive relationships. In J. Fleetwood (Series Ed.), Research in Practice Series: Vol. 14. Early Childhood Australia. Available as e-book from http://www.earlychildhoodaustralia.org.au/shop/product/the-circle-of-security-road-map-to-building-supportive-relationships/

Drachman, D. A. (2005). Do we have brain to spare? *Neurology, 64*, 2004–2005. doi:10.1212/01.WNL.0000166914.38327.BB

Drewes, A. A., Bratton, S. C., & Schaefer C. E. (Eds.). (2011). Integrative play therapy. New York, NY: Wiley.

Duman, R. S., & Aghajanian, G. K. (2012). Synaptic dysfunction in depression: Potential therapeutic targets. *Science, 338*(6103), 68–72. doi:10.1126/science.1222939

Duman, R. S., & Voleti, B. (2012). Signaling pathways underlying the pathophysiology and treatment of depression: Novel mechanisms for rapid-acting agents. *Trends in Neurosciences, 35*, 47–56. doi:10.1016/j.tins.2011.11.004

Dutton, D. G. (2007). Violence and control in intimate relationships (2nd ed.). New York, NY: Guilford Press.

Ecker, B. (2015). Memory reconsolidation understood and misunderstood. *International Journal of Neuropsychotherapy, 3*, 2–46. doi:10.12744/ijnpt.2015.0002-0046

Ecker, B., Ticic, R., & Hulley, L. (2012). *Unlocking the emotional brain: Eliminating symptoms at their roots using memory reconsolidation.* New York, NY: Routledge.

Eisch, A. J., & Petrik, D. (2012). Depression and hippocampal neurogenesis: A road to remission? *Science, 338*(6103), 72–75. doi:10.1126/science.1222941

Eisenberger, N. I. (2012). The neural bases of social pain: Evidence for shared representations with physical pain. *Psychosomatic Medicine, 74*, 126–135. doi:10.1097/PSY.0b013e3182464dd1

Eisenberger, N. I., Lieberman, M. D., & Williams, K. D. (2003). Does rejection hurt? An fMRI study of social exclusion. *Science, 302*(5643), 290–292. doi:10.1126/science.1089134

Elliot, A. J. (2006). The hierarchical model of approach–avoidance motivation. *Motivation and Emotion, 30*, 111–116.

Elliot, A. J. (2008). *Handbook of approach and avoidance motivation.* New York, NY: Psychology Press.

Epstein, S. (1973). The self-concept revisited, or a theory of a theory. *American Psychologist, 28*, 404–416

Epstein, S. (1980). The self-concept: A review and the proposal of an integrated theory of personality. In E. Staub (Ed.), *Personality: Basic issues and current research* (pp. 82–132). Englewood Cliffs, NJ: Prentice Hall.

Epstein, S. (1990). Cognitive-experiential self-theory. In L. A. Pervin (Ed.), *Handbook of personality: Theory and research* (pp. 165–192). New York, NY: Guilford Press.

Epstein, S. (1991). Cognitive–experiential self-theory: An integrative theory of personality. In R. Curtis (Ed.), *The relational self: Convergences in psychoanalysis and social psychology* (pp. 111–137). New York, NY: Guilford Press.

Epstein, S. (1993). Implications of cognitive–experiential self-theory for personality and developmental psychology. In D. Funder, R. Parke, C. Tomlinson-Keasey, & K. Widamen (Eds.), *Studying lives through time: Personality and development* (pp. 399–438). Washington, DC: American Psychological Association.

Epstein, S. (1994). Integration of the cognitive and the psychodynamic unconscious. *American Psychologist, 49*, 709–724.

Epstein, S. (1998). Cognitive–experiential self-theory. In D. F. Barone, M. Hersen, & V. B. Van Hasselt (Eds.), *Advanced personality* (pp. 212–238). New York, NY: Springer.

Etherington, N. (2012). Gardening for children with autism spectrum disorders and special educational needs: Engaging with nature to combat anxiety, promote sensory integration and build social skills. London, United Kingdom: Jessica Kingsley Publishers.

Evans, S. E., Davies, C., & DiLillo, D. (2008). Exposure to domestic violence: A meta-analysis of child and adolescent outcomes. Aggression and Violent Behavior, 13, 131–140. doi:10.1016/j.avb.2008.02.005

Evrensel, A., & Ceylan, M. E. (2015). The gut–brain axis: The missing link in depression. *Clinical Psychopharmacology and Neuroscience, 13*, 239–244. doi:10.9758/cpn.2015.13.3.239

Fales, C. L., Barch, D. M., Rundle, M. M., Mintun, M. A., Mathews, J., Snyder, A. Z., & Sheline, Y. I. (2009). Antidepressant treatment normalizes hypoactivity in dorsolateral prefrontal cortex during emotional interference processing in major depression. *Journal of Affective Disorders, 112*, 206–211. doi:10.1016/j.jad.2008.04.027

Fang, J., Rong, P., Hong, Y., Fan, Y., Liu, J., Wang, H., . . . Kong, J. (2016). Transcutaneous vagus nerve stimulation modulates default mode network in major depressive disorder. *Biological Psychiatry, 79*, 266–273. doi:10.1016/j.biopsych.2015.03.025

Fenwick, C. (2012). Get outside and smell the roses: The benefits of contact with nature during designated work breaks (Honours Dissertation). The University of Queensland, Brisbane, Australia.

Fisher, P. A., Kim, H. K., & Pears, K. C. (2009). Effects of multidimensional treatment foster care for preschoolers (MTFC-P) on reducing permanent placement failures among children with placement instability. Children and Youth Services Review, 31, 541–546. doi.org/10.1016/j.childyouth.2008.10.012

Flückiger, C., & Grosse Holtforth, M. (2008). Focusing the therapist's attention on the patient's strengths: A preliminary study to foster a mechanism of change in outpatient psychotherapy. *Journal of Clinical Psychology, 64*, 876–890.

Flückiger, C., Caspar, F., Grosse Holtforth, M., & Willutzki, U. (2009). Working with patients' strengths: A microprocess approach. *Psychotherapy Research, 19*, 213–223.

Flückiger, C., Wüsten, G., Zinbarg, R. E., & Wampold, B. E. (2009). *Resource activation: Using clients' own strengths in psychotherapy and counseling.* Cambridge, MA: Hogrefe & Huber.

Fox, M. D., Snyder, A. Z., Vincent, J. L., Corbetta, M., van Essen, D. C., & Raichle, M. E. (2005). The human brain is intrinsically organised into dynamic, anticorrelated functional networks. *Proceedings of the National Academy of Sciences, 102*, 9673–9678. doi:10.1073/pnas.0504136102

Freud, S. (1959). Beyond the pleasure principle. New York, NY: W. W. Norton. (Original work published 1920)

Frodl, T., Möller, H.-J., & Meisenzahl, E. (2008). Neuroimaging genetics: New perspectives in research on major depression? *Acta Psychiatrica Scandinavica, 118*, 363–372. doi:10.1111/j.1600-0447.2008.01225.x

Fusar-Poli, P., Perez, J., Broome, M., Borgwardt, S., Placentino, A., Caverzasi, E., . . . McGuire, P. (2007). Neurofunctional correlates of vulnerability to psychosis: A systematic review and meta-analysis. *Neuroscience & Biobehavioral Reviews, 31*, 465–484. doi:10.1016/j.neubiorev.2006.11.006

Gallese, V., Fadiga, L., Fogassi, L., & Rizzolati, G. (1996). Action recognition in the premotor cortex.

Brain, 119, 593–609.

Gassmann, D., & Grawe, K. (2006). General change mechanisms: The relation between problem activation and resource activation in successful and unsuccessful therapeutic interactions. *Clinical Psychology and Psychotherapy, 13*, 1–11. doi:10.1002/cpp.442

Gatt, J. M., Williams, L. M., Schofield, P. R., Dobson-Stone, C., Paul, R. H., Grieve, S. M., . . . Nemeroff, C. B. (2010). Impact of the HTR3A gene with early life trauma on emotional brain networks and depressed mood. *Depression and Anxiety, 27*, 752–759. doi:10.1002/da.20726

Geldard, K., & Geldard, D. (2009). *Counselling adolescents: The proactive approach for young people*. Sage

Geldard, K., & Geldard, D. (2010). Counselling adolescents: The proactive approach for young people (3rd ed.). Los Angeles, CA: Sage.

Geldard, K., Geldard, D., & Foo, R. Y. (2013). Counselling children: A practical introduction (4th ed.). London, United Kingdom: SAGE.

Geuze, E., Vermetten, E., & Bremner, J. D. (2005). MR-based in vivo hippocampal volumetrics: 2. Findings in neuropsychiatric disorders. *Molecular Psychiatry, 10*, 160–184. doi:10.1038/sj.mp.4001579

Gill, S. R., Pop, M., Deboy, R. T., Eckburg, P. B., Turnbaugh, P. J., Samuel, B. S., . . . Nelson, K. E. (2006). Metagenomic analysis of the human distal gut microbiome. *Science, 312*(5778), 1355–1359. doi:10.1126/science.1124234

Gjerris, A. (1988). Baseline studies on transmitter substances in cerebrospinal fluid in depression. *Acta Psychiatrica Scandinavica, 78*, 1–35. doi:10.1111/j.1600-0447.1988.tb10571.x

Glass, J. M. (2006). Cognitive dysfunction in fibromyalgia and chronic fatigue syndrome: New trends and future directions. *Current Rheumatology Reports, 8*, 425–429. doi:10.1007/s11926-006-0036-0

Goff, B., Gee, D. G., Telzer, E. H., Humphreys, K. L., Gabard-Durnam, L., Flannery, J., & Tottenham, N. (2013). Reduced nucleus accumbens reactivity and adolescent depression following early-life stress. *Neuroscience, 249*, 129–138.

Gowans, S. E., & deHueck, A. (2004). Effectiveness of exercise in management of fibromyalgia. *Current Opinion in Rheumatology, 16*, 138–142. doi:10.1097/00002281-200403000-00012

Grawe, K. (2004). *Psychological therapy*. Toronto, Canada: Hogrefe & Huber.

Grawe, K. (2007). Neuropsychotherapy: How the neurosciences inform effective psychotherapy. Mahwah, NJ: Lawrence Erlbaum.

Grenham, S., Clarke, G., Cryan, J. F., & Dinan, T. G. (2011). Brain–gut–microbe communication in health and disease. *Frontiers in Physiology, 2*, 94. doi:10.3389/fphys.2011.00094

Grieve, S. M., Korgaonkar, M. S., Koslow, S. H., Gordon, E., & Williams, L. M. (2013). Widespread reductions in gray matter volume in depression. *NeuroImage: Clinical, 3*, 332–339. doi:10.1016/j.nicl.2013.08.016

Groves, J. O. (2007). Is it time to reassess the BDNF hypothesis of depression? *Molecular Psychiatry, 12*, 1079–1088. doi:10.1038/sj.mp.4002075

Grunstein, M. (1997). Histone acetylation in chromatin structure and transcription. *Nature, 389*, 349–352. doi:10.1038/38664

Guillemin, G. J. (2012). Quinolinic acid, the inescapable neurotoxin. *The FEBS Journal, 279*, 1356–1365. doi:10.1111/j.1742-4658.2012.08485.x

Haapakoski, R., Mathieu, J., Ebmeier, K. P., Alenius, H., & Kivimäki, M. (2015). Cumulative meta-analysis of interleukins 6 and 1β, tumour necrosis factor α and C-reactive protein in patients with major depressive disorder. *Brain, Behavior, and Immunity, 49*, 206–215. doi:10.1016/j.bbi.2015.06.001

Habib, M. (2004). Athymhormia and disorders of motivation in basal ganglia disease. *The Journal of Neuropsychiatry and Clinical Neurosciences, 16*, 509–524. doi:10.1176/jnp.16.4.509

Hajcak, G., Moser, J. S., Holroyd, C. B., & Simons R. F. (2006). The feedback-related negativity reflects the binary evaluation of good versus bad outcomes. *Biological Psychology, 71*, 148–154. doi:10.1016/j.biopsycho.2005.04.001

Hallam, Dorothy E. (2003). *The Aetiology of Childhood Depression*. (Unpublished Doctoral dissertation.) Queensland University, Brisbane, Queensland, Australia

Hamilton, J. P., Farmer, M., Fogelman, P., & Gotlib, I. H. (2015). Depressive rumination, the default-mode network, and the dark matter of clinical neuroscience. *Biological Psychiatry, 78*, 224–230. doi:10.1016/j.biopsych.2015.02.020

Hamilton, J. P., Siemer, M., & Gotlib, I. H. (2008). Amygdala volume in Major Depressive Disorder: A meta-analysis of magnetic resonance imaging studies. *Molecular Psychiatry, 13*, 993–1000. doi:10.1038/mp.2008.57

Hariri, A. R., Goldberg, T. E., Mattay, V. S., Kolachana, B. S., Callicott, J. H., Egan, M. F., & Weinberger, D. R. (2003). Brain-derived neurotrophic factor Val66Met polymorphism affects human memory-related hippocampal activity and predicts memory performance. *Journal of Neuroscience, 23*, 6690–6694.

Häuser, W., Bernardy, K., Uçeyler, N., & Sommer, C. (2009). Treatment of fibromyalgia syndrome with antidepressants: A meta-analysis. *JAMA, 301*, 198–209. doi:10.1001/jama.2008.944

Hawkins, J., & Blakeslee, S. (2004). *On intelligence: How a new understanding of the brain will lead to the creation of truly intelligent machines.* New York, NY: Times Books.

Hawkins, R. A. (2013). Fibromyalgia: A clinical update. *The Journal of the American Osteopathic Association, 113*, 680–689. doi:10.7556/jaoa.2013.034

Healy, D., & Leonard, B. E. (1987). Monoamine transport in depression: Kinetics and dynamics. *Journal of Affective Disorders, 12*, 91–103.

Henriques, J. B., & Davidson, R. J. (2000). Decreased responsiveness to reward in depression. *Cognition and Emotion, 14*, 711–724. doi:10.1080/02699930050117684

Henson, C., & Rossouw, P. J. (2013). *BrainWise leadership.* Sydney, Australia: Learning Quest.

Heshmati, M., & Russo, S. J. (2015). Anhedonia and the brain reward circuitry in depression. *Current Behavioral Neuroscience Reports, 2*, 146–153. doi:10.1007/s40473-015-0044-3

Hester, M., Pearson, C., & Harwin, N. (2006). Making an impact: Children and domestic violence: A reader (2nd ed.). London, England: Jessica Kingsley. E-book available from http://www.eblib.com

Higuera, V. (2016, August 17). Fibromyalgia: Real or imagined? [Web log post]. Retrieved from http://www.healthline.com/health/fibromyalgia-real-or-imagined

Hill, R. (2013, April). Malleable genetics. *The Neuropsychotherapist, 1*, 102–103.

Ho, T. C., Connolly, C. G., Blom, E. H., LeWinn, K. Z., Strigo, I. A., Paulus, M. P., . . . Yang, T. T. (2015). Emotion-dependent functional connectivity of the default mode network in adolescent depression. *Biological Psychiatry, 78*, 635–646. doi:10.1016/j.biopsych.2014.09.002

Holden, S. (2008). From little things, big things grow: Why not start your own kitchen garden? Teacher, 196, 42–45.

Holt, S., Buckley, H., & Whelan, S., (2008). The Impact of exposure to domestic violence on children and young people: A review of the literature. Child Abuse & Neglect, 32, 797–810. doi:10.1016/j.chiabu.2008.02.004

Holtzheimer, P. E., Kelley, M. E., Gross, R. E., Filkowski, M. M., Garlow, S. J., Barrocas, A., . . . Mayberg, H. S. (2012). Subcallosal cingulate deep brain stimulation for treatment-resistant unipolar and bipolar depression. *Archives of General Psychiatry, 69*, 150–158. doi:10.1001/archgenpsychiatry.2011.1456

Hornor, G. (2005). Domestic violence and children. Journal of Pediatric Health Care, 19, 206–212. doi:10.1016/j.pedhc.2005.02.002

Howard, J. A. (2013). Distressed or deliberately defiant: Managing challenging student behaviour due to trauma and disorganised attachment. Brisbane, Australia: Australian Academic Press Group.

Hsu, D. T., Sanford, B. J., Meyers, K. K., Love, T. M., Hazlett, K. E., Wang, H., . . . Zubieta, J.-K. (2013). Response of the μ-opioid system to social rejection and acceptance. *Molecular Psychiatry, 18*, 1211–1217. doi:10.1038/mp.2013.96

Iacoboni, M., Koski, L. M., Brass, M., Bekkering, H., Woods, R. P., Dubeau, M., . . . Rizzolati, G. (2001). Reafferent copies of imitated actions in the right superior temporal cortex. *Proceedings of the National Academy of Sciences, 98*, 13995–13999. doi:10.1073/pnas.241474598

Iannetti, G. D., Salomons, T. V., Moayedi, M., Mouraux, A., & Davis, K. D. (2013). Beyond metaphor: Contrasting mechanisms of social and physical pain. *Trends in Cognitive Sciences, 17*, 371–378. doi:10.1016/j.tics.2013.06.002

Immordino-Yang, M. H. & Damasio, A. (2007). We feel, therefore we learn: The relevance of affective and social neuroscience to education. Mind, Brain, and Education 1, 3–10. doi:10.1111/j.1751-228X.2007.00004.x

Jaycox, L. H., Reivich, K. J., Gillham, J., & Seligman,

M. E. (1994). Prevention of depressive symptoms in school children. *Behaviour research and therapy, 32*(8), 801-816.

Jeffries, S., Field, R., & Bond, C. E. W. (2015). Protecting Australia's Children: A Cross-Jurisdictional Review of Domestic Violence Protection Order Legislation. Psychiatry, Psychology and Law, 22, 800–813. doi:10.1080/13218719.2015.1015204

Jensen, F. E., & Nutt, A. E. (2015). The teenage brain: A neuroscientist's survival guide to raising adolescents and young adults. New York, NY: Harper Collins.

Kabat-Zinn, J. (1994). *Wherever you go there you are: Mindfulness meditation in everyday life* (10th anniversary ed.). New York, NY: Hyperion.

Kabat-Zinn, J. (2013). *Full catastrophe living: Using the wisdom of your body and mind to face stress, pain, and illness* (Rev. ed.). New York, NY: Bantam Books.

Kaminsky, Z. A., Tang, T., Wang, S., Ptak, C., Oh, G. H., Wong, A. H., . . . Petronis, A. (2009). DNA methylation profiles in monozygotic and dizygotic twins. *Nature Genetics, 41*, 240–245. doi:10.1038/ng.286

Kandel, E. R. (2006). *In search of memory: The emergence of a new science of mind*. New York, NY: W. W. Norton.

Kandel, E. R. (2013, December 10). We are what we remember: Memory and the biological basis of individuality [Video file]. Retrieved from https://youtu.be/skyvzMxtLu8

Kandel, E. R., Schwartz, J. H., Jessell, T. M., Siegelbaum, S. A., & Hudspeth, A. J. (Eds.). (2012). *Principles of neural science* (5th ed.). New York, NY: McGraw-Hill.

Karg, K., Burmeister, M., Shedden, K., & Sen, S. (2011). The serotonin transporter promoter variant (5-HTTLPR), stress, and depression meta-analysis revisited: Evidence of genetic moderation. *Archives of General Psychiatry, 68*, 444–454. doi:10.1001/archgenpsychiatry.2010.189

Kauffman, A., & Meaney, M. J. (2007). Neurodevelopmental sequelae of postnatal maternal care in rodents: Clinical and research implications of molecular insights. *Journal of Child Psychology and Psychiatry, 48*, 224–244.

Keeley, M. L., & Storch, E. A. (2009). Anxiety disorders in youth. Journal of Pediatric Nursing, 24, 26–40.

Keleman, S. (2013, January 6). Slow attending: The art of forming intimacy [Web log post]. Retrieved from http://www.neuropsychotherapist.com/slow-attending-article

Kempton, M. J., Salvador, Z., Munafò, M. R., Geddes, J. R., Simmons, A., Frangou, S., & Williams, S. C. R. (2011). Structural neuroimaging studies in major depressive disorder: Meta-analysis and comparison with bipolar disorder. *Archives of General Psychiatry, 68*, 675–690. doi:10.1001/archgenpsychiatry.2011.60

Kendler, B. S. (1996). [Review of the book Melatonin: Your body's natural wonder drug, by R. J. Reiter & J. Robinson]. Nutrition, 12, 735–736. doi:10.1016/S0899-9007(96)00276-6

Keysers, C. (2011). *The empathic brain: How the discovery of mirror neurons changes our understanding of human nature* [Kindle reader version]. Retrieved from https://www.amazon.com/Empathic-Brain-Christian-Keysers-ebook/dp/B0054S7DOO

Kiliaan, A. J., Saunders, P. R., Bijlsma, P. B., Berin, M. C., Taminiau, J. A., Groot, J. A., & Perdue, M. H. (1998). Stress stimulates transepithelial macromolecular uptake in rat jejunum. *American Journal of Physiology, 275*, G1037–G1044.

Kitamura, T., Ogawa, S. K., Roy, D. S., Okuyama, T., Morrissey, M. D., Smith, L. M., . . . Tonegawa, S. (2017). Engrams and circuits crucial for systems consolidation of a memory. *Science, 356*(6333), 73–78. doi:10.1126/science.aam6808

Kitzmann, K. M., Gaylord, N. K., Holt, A. R., & Kenny, E. D. (2003). Child witnesses to domestic violence: A meta-analytic review. Journal of Consulting and Clinical Psychology, 71, 339–352.

Kohn, A. (1993). Choices for children: Why and how to let students decide. The Phi Delta Kappan, 75, 8–16, 18–21.

Kohn, A. (1999). Punished by rewards: The trouble with gold stars incentive plans, A's, praise, and other bribes (2nd ed.). Boston, MA: Mariner Books.

Konishi, M., McLaren, D. G., Engen, H., & Smallwood, J. (2015). Shaped by the past: The default mode network supports cognition that is independent of immediate perceptual input. *PLoS One, 10*: e0132209. doi:10.1371/journal.pone.0132209

Kottman, T. (2014). Play therapy: Basics and beyond. Alexandria, VA: American Counselling Association.

Kovacs, M. (1981), Rating scales to assess depression in school-age children. *Acta Paedopsychiatrica 46*, 305-315.

Krueger, S. J. (2013). Cognitive behavioral and integrative treatment of abused children: Examining cognitive and emotional processes and developmental considerations (Doctoral dissertation). Retrieved from The Catholic University of America, Digital Collections. (Accession No. 2013-02-08T16:06:02Z)

Kruger, J., Nelson, K., Klein, P., McCurdy, L. E., Pride, P., & Carrier, A. J. (2010). Building on partnerships: Reconnecting kids with nature for health benefits. Health Promotion Practice, 11, 340–346. doi:10.1177/1524839909348734

Lacey, B. C., & Lacey J. I. (1974). Studies of heart rate and other bodily processes in sensorimotor behavior. In P. A. Obrist, A. H. Black, J. Brener, & L. V. DiCara (Eds.), *Cardiovascular psychophysiology* (pp. 538–564). Chicago, IL: Aldine.

Laakso, M., Porkka-Heiskanen, T., Alila, A., Peder, M., & Johansson, G. (1988). Twenty-four-hour patterns of pineal melatonin and pituitary and plasma prolactin in male rats under "natural" and artificial lighting conditions. Neuroendocrinology, 48, 308–313.

Lambert, K. G., & Kinsley, C. H. (2004). *Clinical neuroscience: The neurobiological foundations of mental health*. New York, NY: Worth.

Lambert, K. G., & Kinsley, C. H. (2010). *Clinical neuroscience: Psychopathology and the brain* (2nd ed.). Melbourne, Australia: Oxford University Press.

Langer, E. J., & Rodin, J. (1976). The effects of choice and enhanced personal responsibility for the aged: A field experiment in an institutional setting. *Journal of Personality and Social Psychology, 34*, 191–198.

Lawson, R. P., Nord, C. L., Seymour, B., Thomas, D. L., Dayan, P., Pilling, S., & Roiser, J. P. (2017). Disrupted habenula function in major depression. *Molecular Psychiatry, 22*, 202–208. doi:10.1038/mp.2016.81

Leavitt, F., Katz, R. S., Mills, M., & Heard, A. R. (2002). Cognitive and dissociative manifestations in fibromyalgia. *Journal of Clinical Rheumatology, 8*, 77–84. doi:10.1097/00124743-200204000-00003

Lee, R.M., Draper, M., & Lee, S. (2001). Social connectedness, dysfunctional interpersonal behaviors, and psychological distress: Testing a mediator model. *Journal of Counseling Psychology, 48*, 310-318

Leotti, L. A., & Delgado, M. (2011). The inherent reward of choice. *Psychological Science, 22*, 1310–1318. doi:10.1177/0956797611417005

Leotti, L. A., Iyengar, S. S., & Ochsner, K., N. (2010). Born to choose: The origins and value of the need for control. *Trends in Cognitive Sciences, 14*, 457–463. doi:10.1016/j.tics.2010.08.001

Lesch, K.-P., Bengel, D., Heils, A., Sabol, S. Z., Greenberg, B. D., Petri, S., . . . Murphy, D. L. (1996). Association of anxiety-related traits with a polymorphism in the serotonin transporter gene regulatory region. *Science, 274*(5292), 1527–1531. doi:10.1126/science.274.5292.1527

Levenson, J. M., & Sweatt, J. D. (2005). Epigenetic mechanisms in memory formation. *Nature Reviews Neuroscience, 6*, 108–118. doi:10.1038/nrn1604

Ley, R. E., Peterson, D. A., & Gordon, J. I. (2006). Ecological and evolutionary forces shaping microbial diversity in the human intestine. *Cell, 124*, 837–848. doi:10.1016/j.cell.2006.02.017

Lieberman, M. D. (2013). *Social: Why our brains are wired to connect*. New York, NY: Crown.

Lindauer, R. J., Vlieger, E. J., Jalink, M., Olff, M., Carlier, I. V., Majoie, C. B., . . . Gersons, B. P. (2005). Effects of psychotherapy on hippocampal volume in out-patients with post-traumatic stress disorder: An MRI investigation. *Psychological Medicine, 10*, 1421–1431. doi:10.1017/S0033291705005246

Linden, D. E. J. (2006). How psychotherapy changes the brain: The contribution of functional neuroimaging. *Molecular Psychiatry, 11*, 528–538. doi:10.1038/sj.mp.4001816

Lopez, D., & Alipoon, L. (2001). Experience is the network to mind: Brain-based learning applications in higher education. Journal of Adventist Education, 63, 29–34.

Lozano, A. M., Giacobbe, P., Hamani, C., Rizvi, S. J., Kennedy, S. H., Kolivakis, T. T., . . . Mayberg, H. S. (2012). A multicenter pilot study of subcallosal cingulate area deep brain stimulation for treatment-resistant depression. *Journal of Neurosurgery, 116*, 315–322. doi:10.3171/2011.10.JNS102122

Lozano, A. M., Mayberg, H. S., Giacobbe, P., Hamani, C., Craddock, R. C., & Kennedy, S. H. (2008). Subcallosal cingulate gyrus deep brain stimulation for treatment-resistant depression. *Biological Psychiatry, 64*, 461–467. doi:10.1016/j.biopsych.2008.05.034

Luby, J. L., Belden, A. C., Jackson. J. J., Lessov-Schlaggar, C. N., Harms, M. P., Tillman, R., . . . Barch, D. M. (2016). Early childhood depression and alterations in the trajectory of gray matter maturation in middle childhood and early adolescence. *JAMA Psychiatry, 73*, 31–38. doi:10.1001/jamapsychiatry.2015.2356

Lumpkin, A. (2008). Teachers as role models teaching character and moral virtues. Journal of Physical Education, Recreation & Dance, 79(2), 45–49.

Lundqvist, L., & Dimberg, U. (1995). Facial expressions are contagious. *Journal of Psycophysiology, 9*, 203–211.

Lupien, S. J., McEwen, B. S., Gunnar, M. R., & Heim, C. (2009). Effects of stress throughout the lifespan on the brain, behaviour and cognition. *Nature Reviews Neuroscience, 10*, 434–445. doi:10.1038/nrn2639

MacLean, P. D. (1990). *The triune brain in evolution: Role in paleocerebral functions*. New York, NY: Plenum Press.

Macmillan, H. L., Wathen, C. N., Barlow, J., Fergusson, D. M., Leventhal, J. M., & Taussig, H. N. (2009). Interventions to prevent child maltreatment and associated impairment. The Lancet, 373, 250–266. doi:10.1016/S0140-6736(08)61708-0

Maguire, E. A. (2008, November 25). Mapping memory: The brains behind remembering [Video file]. Retrieved from https://youtu.be/JW23BPngkQ8

Maher, E. J., Jackson, L. J., Pecora, P. J., Schultz, D. J., Chandra, A., & Barnes–Probye, D. S. (2009). Overcoming challenges to implementing and evaluating evidence-based interventions in child welfare: A matter of necessity. Children and Youth Services Review, 31, 555–562. doi.org/10.1016/j.childyouth.2008.10.013

Main, M., & Solomon, J. (1986). Discovery of an insecure-disorganized/disoriented attachment pattern. In T. B. Brazelton & M. Yogaman (Eds.), *Affective development in infancy* (pp. 95–124). Norwood, NJ: Ablex.

Malenka, R. C., Nestler, E. J., & Hyman, S.E. (2009). Widely projecting systems: Monoamines, acetylcholine, and orexin. In A. Sydor & R. Y. Brown (Eds.), *Molecular neuropharmacology: A foundation for clinical neuroscience* (2nd ed., pp. 145–180). New York, NY: McGraw-Hill.

Maletic, V., & Raison, C. L. (2009). Neurobiology of depression, fibromyalgia and neuropathic pain [Special issue]. *Frontiers in Bioscience, 14*, 5291–5338. doi:10.2741/3598

Matsumoto, M., & Hikosaka, O. (2007). Lateral habenula as a source of negative reward signals in dopamine neurons. *Nature, 447*(7148), 1111–1115. doi:10.1038/nature05860

Matthews, P. R., & Harrison, P. J. (2012). A morphometric, immunohistochemical, and in situ hybridization study of the dorsal raphe nucleus in major depression, bipolar disorder, schizophrenia, and suicide. *Journal of Affective Disorders, 137*, 125–134. doi:10.1016/j.jad.2011.10.043

Maughan, A., & Cicchetti, D. (2002). Impact of child maltreatment and interadult violence on children's emotion regulation abilities and socioemotional adjustment. Child Development, 73, 1525-1542. doi:10.1111/1467-8624.00488

Maulana, R., Opdenakker, M.-C., den Brok, P., & Bosker, R. (2011). Teacher–student interpersonal relationships in Indonesia: Profiles and importance to student motivation. Asia Pacific Journal of Education, 31, 33–49.

Mawe, G. M., & Hoffman, J. M. (2013). Serotonin signalling in the gut: Functions, dysfunctions and therapeutic targets. *Nature Reviews Gastroenterology & Hepatology, 10*, 473–486. doi:10.1038/nrgastro.2013.105

Mayer, E. A. (2011). Gut feelings: The emerging biology of gut–brain communication. *Nature Reviews Neuroscience, 12*, 453–466. doi:10.1038/nrn3071

Mayer, E. A., Knight, R., Mazmanian, S. K., Cryan, J. F., & Tillisch, K. (2014). Gut microbes and the brain: Paradigm shift in neuroscience. *Journal of Neuroscience, 34*, 15490–15496. doi:10.1523/JNEUROSCI.3299-14.2014

McCraty, R. (2015a). Heart–brain neurodynamics: The making of emotions. In M. Dahlitz & G. Hall (Eds.), *An issue of the heart* [Special issue of *The Neuropsychotherapist*] (pp. 76–110). Brisbane, Australia: Dahlitz Media.

McCraty, R. (2015b). *Science of the heart: Exploring the role of the heart in human performance* (Vol. 2). Boulder Creek, CA: HeartMath Institute. Retrieved from https://www.heartmath.org/research/science-of-the-heart/

McDermot K (2015) 17 Quotes That Prove OCD Is So Much More Than Being Neat. Retrieved from URL https://themighty.com/2015/10/what-ocd-feels-like/

McDougall, W. (1936). *An introduction to social psychology* (Rev. ed.). London, United Kingdom: Methuen.

McGilchrist, I. (2009). The master and his emissary: The divided brain and the making of the Western world. New Haven, CT: Yale University Press.

McKim, D. B., Patterson, J. M., Wohleb, E. S., Jarrett, B. L., Reader, B. F., Godbout, J. P., & Sheridan, J. F. (2016). Sympathetic release of splenic monocytes promotes recurring anxiety following repeated social defeat. *Biological Psychiatry, 79*, 803–813. doi:10.1016/j.biopsych.2015.07.010

McNeil, F. (2009). Learning with the brain in mind. London, England: Sage.

McWhirter, J. J., McWhirter, B.T., McWhirter, E.H., McWhirter, R.J. (2013). *At Risk Youth: A Comprehensive Response for Counselors, Teachers, Psychologists, and Human Service Professionals*, 5th Edition. Brooks/Cole Cengage Learning

Medina, J. (2011). Brain rules for baby: How to raise a smart and happy child from zero to five. Melbourne, Australia: Scribe.

Meltzoff, A. N., Kuhl, P. K., Movellan, J., & Sejnowski, T. J. (2009). Foundations for a new science of learning. *Science, 325*(5938), 284–288. doi:10.1126/science.1175626

Meyer, P. W., Müller, L. E., Zastrow, A., Schmidinger, I., Bohus, M., Herpertz, S. C., & Bertsch, K. (2016). Heart rate variability in patients with post-traumatic stress disorder or borderline personality disorder: Relationship to early life maltreatment. *Journal of Neural Transmission,123*, 1107–1118. doi:10.1007/s00702-016-1584-8

Milham, M (2003). Practice-related effects demonstrate complementary roles of anterior cingulate and prefrontal cortices in attentional control. *NeuroImage, 18*, 483–493. doi:10.1016/s1053-8119(02)00050-2.

Miller, G. A. (1956). The magical number seven, plus or minus two: Some limits on our capacity for processing information. *Psychological Review, 63*, 81–97.

Modell, J. G., Mountz, J. M., Curtis, G. C., & Greden, J. F. (1989). Neurophysiologic dysfunction in basal ganglia/limbic striatal and thalamocortical circuits as a pathogenetic mechanism of obsessive–compulsive disorder. *Journal of Neuropsychiatry & Clinical Neuroscience, 1*, 27–36. doi:10.1176/jnp.1.1.27

Monahan, K. C., & Steinberg, L. (2011). Accentuation of individual differences in social competence during the transition to adolescence. Journal of Research on Adolescence, 21,576–585. doi:10.1111/j.1532-7795.2010.00705.x

Morelan, B. (2002). The fun factor: How active enjoyment impacts learning. Journal of Adventist Education, 64, 37–40. Retrieved from http://circle.adventist.org/files/jae/en/jae200164023704.pdf

Moss, R. A. (2006). Of bits and logic: Cortical columns in learning and memory. *The Journal of Mind and Behavior, 27*, 215–246.

Moss, R. A. (2007). Negative emotional memories in clinical practice: Theoretical considerations. *Journal of Psychotherapy Integration, 17*, 209–224.

Moss, R. A. (2014). Brain-based views on psychotherapy integration: Clinical biopsychology. *New Therapist, 89*, 6–15.

Moss, R. A. (2016, February). The hippocampus and memory: The binding of parallel cortical circuits. *The Neuropsychotherapist, 4*(2), 16–19.

Moss, R. A., & Mahan, M. C. (2014). Emotional restructuring: Clinical biopsychological perspective on brain involvement. *The Neuropsychotherapist, 5*, 54–65. doi:10.12744/tnpt(5)054-065

Moss, R. A., & Moss, J. (2014a). The role of cortical columns in explaining gamma-band synchronization and NMDA receptors in cognitive functions. *AIMS Neuroscience, 1*, 65–88. doi:10.3934/Neuroscience2014.1.65

Moss, R. A., & Moss, J. (2014b). Commentary on the Pinotsis and Friston neural fields DCM and the Cadonic and Albensi oscillations and NMDA receptors articles. *AIMS Neuroscience, 1*, 158–162. doi:10.3934/Neuroscience.2014.2.158

Murray, C. E., Horton, G. E., Johnson, C. H., Notestine, L., Garr, B., Pow, A. M. . . . Doom, E. (2015).

Domestic violence service providers' perceptions of safety planning: A focus group study. Journal of Family Violence, 30, 381–392. doi:10.1007/s10896-015-9674-1

Must, A., & Tybor, D. J. (2005). Physical activity and sedentary behavior: A review of longitudinal studies of weight and adiposity in youth [Supplemental material]. International Journal of Obesity, 29, S84–96.

Nader, K., & Hardt, O. (2009). A single standard for memory: The case for reconsolidation. *Nature Reviews Neuroscience, 10*, 224–234. doi:10.1038/nrn2590

Naranjo, C. A., Tremblay, L. K., & Busto, U. E. (2001). The role of the brain reward system in depression. *Progress in Neuro-Psychopharmacology & Biological Psychiatry, 25*, 781–823.

Nedley, N. (2009). Depression the Way Out. Nedley Publishing. Ardmore.

Nemeroff, C. B. (1998, June). The neurobiology of depression. *Scientific American, 278*(6), 42–49. doi:10.1038/scientificamerican0698-42

Ngian, G.-S., Guymer, E. K., & Littlejohn, G. O. (2011). The use of opioids in fibromyalgia. *International Journal of Rheumatic Diseases, 14*, 6–11. doi:10.1111/j.1756-185X.2010.01567.x

Nicklas, E. (2010). Family violence in a community sample: Incidence and effects on child development (Doctoral dissertation). Available from ProQuest Dissertations & Theses Global database. (Dissertation No. 3400593)

Nieuwenhuis, S., Slagter, H. A., Von Geusau, N. J. A., Heslenfeld, D. J., & Holroyd, C. B. (2005), Knowing good from bad: Differential activation of human cortical areas by positive and negative outcomes. *European Journal of Neuroscience, 21*, 3161–3168. doi:10.1111/j.1460-9568.2005.04152.x

O'Keefe, J., & Dostrovsky, J. (1971). The hippocampus as a spatial map: Preliminary evidence from unit activity in the freely moving rat. *Brain Research, 34*, 171–175. doi:10.1016/0006-8993(71)90358-1

Okifuji, A., & Hare, B. D. (2013). Management of fibromyalgia syndrome: Review of evidence. *Pain and Therapy, 2*, 87–104. doi:10.1007/s40122-013-0016-9

Orth, U., Robins, R. W., & Roberts, B. W. (2008). Low self-esteem prospectively predicts depression in adolescence and young adulthood. *Journal of Personality and Social Psychology, 95*, 695–708.

Osofsky, J. D. (2003). Prevalence of children's exposure to domestic violence and child maltreatment: Implications for prevention and intervention. Clinical Child and Family Psychology Review, 6, 161–170. doi:10.1023/A:1024958332093

Paddock, C. (2007, April 2). Soil bacteria work in similar way to antidepressants. Retrieved from www.medicalnewstoday.com/articles/66840.php

Palazidou, E. (2012). The neurobiology of depression. *British Medical Bulletin, 101*, 127–145. doi:10.1093/bmb/lds004

Panksepp, J., & Biven, L. (2012). *The archaeology of mind: Neuroevolutionary origins of human emotions*. New York, NY: W. W. Norton.

Paradiso, S., Johnson, D. L., Andreasen, N. C., O'Leary, D. S., Watkins, G. L., Ponto, L. L. B., & Hichwa, R. D. (1999). Cerebral blood flow changes associated with attribution of emotional valence to pleasant, unpleasant, and neural visual stimuli in a PET study of normal subjects. *American Journal of Psychiatry, 156*, 1618–1629. doi:10.1176/ajp.156.10.1618

Park, L. E., & Crocker, J. (2013). Pursuing self-esteem: Implications for self-regulation and relationships. In V. Zeigler-Hill (Ed.), *Self-esteem* (pp. 43–59). Florence, KY: Psychology Press.

Partanen, E., Kujala, T., Näätänen, R., Liitola, A., Sambeth, A., & Huotilainen, M. (2013). Learning-induced neural plasticity of speech processing before birth. Proceedings of the National Academy of Sciences, 110, 15145–15150. doi:10.1073/pnas.1302159110

Pawluk, S. (1998). Layers of significance: Influencing students' moral default settings. Journal of Adventist Education, 61, 24–27. Retrieved from http://circle.adventist.org/files/jae/en/jae199861012404.pdf

Payne-Bryson T., Siegal, D. (2011). *The Whole-Brain Child: 12 Revolutionary Strategies to Nurture Your Child's Developing Mind*. Bantom Books Trade Paperbacks USA

Peckham, H. (2013). Epigenetics: The dogma-defying discovery that genes learn from experience. *International Journal of Neuropsychotherapy, 1*, 9–20. doi:10.12744/ijnpt.2013.0009-0020

Peckham, H. (2015). The unexpected interdependence

of heart and mind. In M. Dahlitz & G. Hall (Eds.), *An issue of the heart* [Special issue of *The Neuropsychotherapist*] (pp. 111–118). Brisbane, Australia: Dahlitz Media.

Peddie, C. (2015, June 16). Gardens help sprout brains. The Advertiser, p. 3.

Perkins, T., Stokes, M., McGillivray, J., & Bittar, R. (2010). Mirror neuron dysfunction in autism spectrum disorders. *Journal of Clinical Neuroscience, 17,* 1239–1243. doi:10.1016/j.jocn.2010.01.026

Perry, B. D. (2000). Traumatized children: How childhood trauma influences brain development. The Journal of the California Alliance for the Mentally Ill. Retrieved from http://www.aaets.org/article196.htm

Piccinni, A., Del Debbio, A., Medda, P., Bianchi, C., Roncaglia, I., Veltri, A., . . . Dell'Osso, L. (2009). Plasma brain-derived neurotrophic factor in treatment-resistant depressed patients receiving electroconvulsive therapy. *European Neuropsychopharmacology, 19,* 349–355. doi:10.1016/j.euroneuro.2009.01.002

Pinel, P. J., & Barnes, S. J. (2012). *Introduction to biopsychology* (9th ed.). Essex, United Kingdom: Pearson Education.

Pittenger, C., & Duman, R. S. (2008). Stress, depression and neuroplasticity: A convergence of mechanisms. Neuropsychopharmacology, 33, 88–109.

Plummer, D. (2012). Focusing and calming games for children: Mindfulness strategies and activities to help children to relax, concentrate and take control. London, England: Jessica Kingsley. Available as e-book from http://www.eblib.com

Popoli, M., Yan, Z., McEwen, B. S., & Sanacora, G. (2012). The stressed synapse: The impact of stress and glucocorticoids on glutamate transmission. *Nature Reviews Neuroscience, 13,* 22–37. doi:10.1038/nrn3138

Porges, S. (2011). *The polyvagal theory: Neurophysiological foundations of emotions, attachment, communication, and self-regulation.* New York, NY: W. W. Norton.

Porter, L. (2007). Student behaviour: Theory and practice for teachers (3rd ed.). Crows Nest, Australia: Allen & Unwin.

Posner, J., Cha, J., Wang, Z., Talati, A., Warner, V., Gerber A., . . . Weissman, M. (2016). Increased default mode network connectivity in individuals at high familial risk for depression. *Neuropsychopharmacology, 41,* 1759–1767. doi:10.1038/npp.2015.342

Powers, W. T. (1973). *Behavior and the control of perception.* New York, NY: Aldine.

Prochaska, J. O., & Norcross, J. C. (2010). Systems of psychotherapy: A transtheoretical analysis (7th ed.). Belmont, CA: Brooks/Cole.

Qin, J., Li, R., Raes, J., Arumugam, M., Burgdorf, K. S., Manichanh, C., . . . Wang, J. (2010). A human gut microbial gene catalogue established by metagenomic sequencing. *Nature, 464,* 59–65. doi:10.1038/nature08821

Quiroga, R. Q., Reddy, L., Kreiman, G., Koch, C., & Fried, I. (2005). Invariant visual representation by single neurons in the human brain. *Nature, 435,* 1102–1107. doi:10.1038/nature03687

Ramachandran, V. S. (2011). *The tell-tale brain: Unlocking the mystery of human nature.* London, United Kingdom: Windmill Books.

Ressler, K. J., & Nemeroff, C. B. (2000). Role of serotonergic and noradrenergic systems in the pathophysiology of depression and anxiety disorders. *Depression and Anxiety, 12*(S1), 2–19.

Revlin, R. (2012). *Cognition: Theory and practice.* New York, NY: Worth.

Reynolds, J., Houlston, C., Coleman, L. (2014). Parental conflict: Outcomes and interventions for children and families. Bristol, England: Policy Press. Available as e-book from http://www.eblib.com

Rhee, S. H., Pothoulakis, C., & Mayer, E. A. (2009). Principles and clinical implications of the brain–gut–enteric microbiota axis. *Nature Reviews Gastroenterology & Hepatology, 6,* 306–314. doi:10.1038/nrgastro.2009.35

Rietz, T. A. (2001). Students' Perceptions of Motivation: The Importance of the Student–Teacher Relationship (Doctoral dissertation). Available from ProQuest Dissertations & Theses Global database. (Dissertation No. 3025009)

Riggs, L. (2013, October 18). Why do teachers quit? And why do they stay? The Atlantic. Retrieved from http://www.theatlantic.com/education/archive/2013/10/Why-Do-Teachers-Quit/280699/

Rizzolatti, G., & Arbib, M. A. (1998). Language within our grasp. *Trends in Neurosciences, 21,* 188–194.

Rosch, P. J. (2015). Why the heart is much more than

a pump. In M. Dahlitz & G. Hall (Eds.), *An issue of the heart* [Special issue of *The Neuropsychotherapist*] (pp. 1–13). Brisbane, Australia: Dahlitz Media.

Rosenberg, D. R., & Keshavan, M. S. (1998). Toward a neurodevelopmental model of obsessive–compulsive disorder. *Biological Psychiatry 43*, 623–640. doi:10.1016/S0006-3223(97)00443-5

Rossouw, P. J. (2011, July). The triune brain: Implications for neuropsychotherapy. *Neuropsychotherapy News, 5*, 2–4. Retrieved from mediros.com.au/wp-content/uploads/2012/11/NPTIG-Newsletter-5.pdf

Rossouw, P. J. (2012, November). Childhood trauma and neural development: Indicators for interventions with special reference to rural and remote environments. Neuropsychotherapy in Australia, 18, 3–8. Retrieved from http://mediros.com.au/wp-content/uploads/2012/11/NPTIG-e-journal-18.pdf

Rossouw, P. J. (2012a). Bullying: A neurobiological perspective [Monograph]. Retrieved from http://www.neuropsychotherapist.com/bullying-rossouw/

Rossouw, P. J. (2012b, January). Effective client focused interventions: The top-down and bottom-up discourse. Neuropsychotherapy News, 11, 2–4. Retrieved from http://mediros.com.au/wp-content/uploads/2012/11/NPTIG-Newsletter-11.pdf

Rossouw, P. J. (2013, April 30). Introduction to neuropsychotherapy. Theories of Counselling. Lecture conducted from the University of Queensland, Brisbane, Australia.

Rossouw, P. J. (Ed.). (2014). *Neuropsychotherapy: Theoretical underpinnings and clinical applications.* Brisbane, Australia: Mediros.

Rothschild, B. (2000). *The body remembers: The psychophysiology of trauma and trauma treatment.* New York, NY: W. W. Norton.

Rowe, F., & Stewart, D. (2011). Promoting connectedness through whole school approaches: Key elements and pathways of influence. Health Education, 111, 49–65.

Savitz, J. B., Nugent, A. C., Bogers, W., Roiser, J. P., Bain, E. E., Neumeister, A., . . . Drevets, W. C. (2011). Habenula volume in bipolar disorder and major depressive disorder: A high-resolution magnetic resonance imaging study. *Biological Psychiatry, 69*, 336–343. doi:10.1016/j.biopsych.2010.09.027

Saxena, S., & Rauch, S. L. (2000). Functional neuroimaging and the neuroanatomy of obsessive–compulsive disorder. *Psychiatric Clinics of North America, 23*, 563–586.

Saxena, S., Gorbis, E., O'Neil, J., Baker, S. K., Mandelkern, M. A., Maidment, K. M., . . . London, E. D. (2009). Rapid effects of brief intensive cognitive-behavioral therapy on brain glucose metabolism in obsessive–compulsive disorder. *Molecular Psychiatry, 14*, 197–205. doi:10.1038/sj.mp.4002134

Schacter, D. L. (1987). Implicit memory: History and current status. *Journal of Experimental Psychology: Learning, Memory, and Cognition, 13*, 501–518. doi:10.1037/0278-7393.13.3.501

Schenck, J. (2011). *Teaching and the Adolescent Brain: An Educator's Guide.* New York, NY: W. W. Norton.

Schenck, J. (2011). Teaching and the adolescent brain. New York, NY: W.W. Norton.

Schildkraut, J. J. (1965). The catecholamine hypothesis of affective disorders: A review of supporting evidence. *American Journal of Psychiatry, 122*, 509–522. doi:10.1176/ajp.122.5.509

Shipp J. (2018). The power of one caring adult. Retrieved from https://joshshipp.com/one-caring-adult/

Schmaal, L., Veltman, D. J., van Erp, T. G. M., Samann, P. G., Frodl, T., Jahanshad, N., . . . Hibar, D. P. (2016). Subcortical brain alterations in major depressive disorder: Findings from the ENIGMA Major Depressive Disorder working group. *Molecular Psychiatry, 21*, 806–812. doi:10.1038/mp.2015.69

Schore, A. N. (2012). *The science of the art of psychotherapy.* New York, NY: W. W. Norton.

Schore, J. R., & Schore, A. N. (2007). Modern attachment theory: The central role of affect regulation in development and treatment. Clinical Social Work Journal, 11, 9–20. doi:10.1007/s10615-007-0111-7

Shulman, G. L., Corbetta, M., Buckner, R. L., Fiez, J. A., Miezin, F. M., Raichle, M. E., & Petersen, S. E. (1997). Common blood flow changes across visual tasks: I. Increases in subcortical structures and cerebellum but not in nonvisual cortex. *Journal of Cognitive Neuroscience, 9*, 624–647. doi:10.1162/jocn.1997.9.5.624

Shulman, G. L., Fiez, J. A., Corbetta, M., Buckner, R. L., Miezin, F. M., Raichle, M. E., & Petersen, S. E.

(1997). Common blood flow changes across visual tasks: II. Decreases in cerebral cortex. *Journal of Cognitive Neuroscience, 9*, 648–663. doi:10.1162/jocn.1997.9.5.648

Shelton, R. C., & Miller, A. H. (2010). Eating ourselves to death (and despair): The contribution of adiposity and inflammation to depression. *Progress in Neurobiology, 91*, 275–299. doi:10.1016/j.pneurobio.2010.04.004

Shepherd, A. M., Laurens, K. R., Matheson, S. L., Carr, V. J., & Green M. J. (2012). Systematic meta-review and quality assessment of the structural brain alterations in schizophrenia. *Neuroscience & Biobehavioral Reviews, 36*, 1342–1356. doi:10.1016/j.neubiorev.2011.12.015

Shimizu, E., Hashimoto, K., Okamura, N., Koike, K., Komatsu, N., Kumakiri, C., . . . Iyo, M. (2003). Alterations of serum levels of brain-derived neurotrophic factor (BDNF) in depressed patients with or without antidepressants. *Biological Psychiatry, 54*, 70–75. doi:10.1016/S0006-3223(03)00181-1

Siegel, D. J. (2006). An interpersonal neurobiology approach to psychotherapy. Psychiatric Annals, 36, 248–256.

Siegel, D. J. (2007). *The mindful brain: Reflections and attunement in the cultivation of well-being.* New York, NY: W. W. Norton.

Siegel, D. J. (2012). *The developing mind: How relationships and the brain interact to shape who we are* (2nd ed.). New York, NY: Guilford Press.

Siegel, D., & Bryson, T. P. (2012). The whole-brain child: 12 revolutionary strategies to nurture your child's developing mind. New York, NY: Scribe.

Siegel, D., & Hartzell, M. (2004). Parenting from the inside out: How a deeper self-understanding can help you raise children who thrive. New York, NY: J. P. Tarcher/Penguin.

Smith, E. C., & Grawe, K. (2003). What makes psychotherapy sessions productive? A new approach to bridging the gap between process research and practice. *Clinical Psychology & Psychotherapy, 10*, 275–285. doi:10.1002/cpp.377

Smith S.M., & Moynan S.C. (2008). Forgetting and Recovering the Unforgettable. *Psychological Science* 19 (5), pp. 462 - 468 https://doi.org/10.1111/j.1467-9280.2008.02110

Smith, S. M., Nichols, T. E., Vidaurre, D., Winkler, A.

M., Behrens, T. E. J., Glasser, M. F., . . . Miller, K. L. (2015). A positive-negative mode of population covariation links brain connectivity, demographics and behavior. *Nature Neuroscience, 18*, 1565–1567. doi:10.1038/nn.4125

Sousa, C., Herrenkohl, T. I., Moylan, C. A., Tajima, E. A., Klika, J. B., Herrenkohl, R. C., & Russo, M. J. (2011). Longitudinal study on the effects of child abuse and children's exposure to domestic violence, parent–child attachments, and antisocial behavior in adolescence. Journal of Interpersonal Violence, 26, 111–136. doi:10.1177/0886260510362883

Sousa, D.A. (2011). *How the Brain Learns.* 4th Edition. Corwin A Sage Company USA

Sousa, D. A. (Ed.). (2010). Mind, brain, and education: Neuroscience implications for the classroom, Leading Edge Series: Vol. 6. Bloomington, IN: Solution Tree Press.

Sousa, D. A. (2015). How the brain influences behaviour: Strategies for managing K–12 classrooms. New York, NY: Skyhorse.

Squire, L. R. (2004). Memory systems of the brain: A brief history and current perspective. *Neurobiology of Learning and Memory, 82*, 171–177. doi:10.1016/j.nlm.2004.06.005

Stamatakis, A. M., & Stuber, G. D. (2012). Activation of lateral habenula inputs to the ventral midbrain promotes behavioral avoidance. *Nature Neuroscience, 15*, 1105–1107. doi:10.1038/nn.3145

Sternberg, K. J., Lamb, M. E., Guterman, E., & Abbott, C. B. (2006). Effects of early and later family violence on children's behavior problems and depression: A longitudinal, multi-informant perspective. Child Abuse & Neglect, 30, 283–306. doi:10.1016/j.chiabu.2005.10.008

Sterne, A., & Poole, L. (2009). Domestic violence and children: A handbook for schools and early years settings. London, England: Routledge. Available as e-book from http://www.eblib.com

Stroop, J. R. (1935). Studies of interference in serial verbal reactions. *Journal of Experimental Psychology, 18*, 643–662. doi:10.1037/h0054651.

Sudo, N., Chida, Y., Aiba, Y., Sonoda, J., Oyama, N., Yu, . . . Koga, Y. (2004). Postnatal microbial colonization programs the hypothalamic–pituitary–adrenal system for stress response in mice. *The Journal of Physiology, 558*, 263–275. doi:10.1113/jphysiol.2004.063388

Sukoff Rizzo, S. J., Neal, S. J., Hughes, Z. A., Beyna, M., Rosenzweig-Lipson, S., Moss, S. J., & Brandon, N. J. (2012). Evidence for sustained elevation of IL-6 in the CNS as a key contributor of depressive-like phenotypes. *Translational Psychiatry, 2*, e199. doi:10.1038/tp.2012.120

Sullivan, P. F., Neale, M. C., & Kendler, K. S. (2000). Genetic epidemiology of major depression: Review and meta-analysis. *The American Journal of Psychiatry, 157*, 1552–1562. doi:10.1176/appi.ajp.157.10.1552

Suomi, S. J. (1999). Attachment in rhesus monkeys. In J. Cassidy & P. R. Shaver (Eds.), *Handbook of attachment: Theory, research, and clinical applications* (pp. 181–197). New York, NY: Guilford Press.

Svob, C., Wang, Z., Weissman, M. M., Wickramaratne, P., & Posner, J. (2016). Religious and spiritual importance moderate relation between default mode network connectivity and familial risk for depression. *Neuroscience Letters, 634*, 94–97. doi:10.1016/j.neulet.2016.10.009

Tarlacı, S., & Pregnolato, M. (2016). Quantum neurophysics: From non-living matter to quantum neurobiology and psychopathology. *International Journal of Psychophysiology, 103*, 161–173. doi:10.1016/j.ijpsycho.2015.02.016

Teglasi, H., & Epstein, S. (1998). Temperament and personality theory: The perspective of cognitive-experiential self-theory. *School Psychology Review, 27*, 534–550.

Teicher, M. H., Andersen, S. L., Polcari, A., Anderson, C. M., Navalta, C. P., & Kim, D. M. (2003). The neurobiological consequences of early stress and childhood maltreatment. Neuroscience & Biobehavioral Reviews, 27, 33–44. doi:10.1016/S0149-7634(03)00007-1

Thayer, J. F., & Lane, R. D. (2000). A model of neurovisceral integration in emotion regulation and dysregulation. *Journal of Affective Disorders, 61*, 201–216. doi:10.1016/S0165-0327(00)00338-4

The Neuropsychotherapy Institute (Producer). (2014a). Genes, neurons & glia: The wonder of the social brain [Video file]. Retrieved from http://neuropsychotherapyinstitute.com/genes-neurons-glia/

The Neuropsychotherapy Institute (Producer). (2014b). Key neurochemicals [Video file]. Retrieved from http://neuropsychotherapyinstitute.com/c07-key-neurochemicals/

Thomas, B. (2014). How to get kids offline, outdoors, and connecting with nature: 200+ Creative activities to encourage self-esteem, mindfulness, and wellbeing. London, United Kingdom: Jessica Kingsley Publishers.

Thomason, M. E., Chang, C. E., Glover, G. H., Gabrieli, J. D. E., Greicius, M. D., & Gotlib, I. H. (2008). Default-mode function and task-induced deactivation have overlapping brain substrates in children. *NeuroImage, 41*, 1493–1503. doi:10.1016/j.neuroimage.2008.03.029c

Tokuhama–Espinosa, T. (2011). Mind, brain, and education science: A comprehensive guide to the new brain-based teaching. New York, NY: W.W. Norton.

Tokuhama-Espinosa, T. (2014). Making classrooms better: 50 practical applications of mind, brain, and education science. New York, NY: W. W. Norton & Company New York/London

Tokuhama-Espinosa, T. (2014b). *Mind, Brain, and Education Science: A Comprehensive Guide to The New Brain-Based Teaching.* New York, NY: W. W. Norton.

Townsend, K.C., & McWhirter, B.T. (2005). Connectedness: A review of current literature, with implications for counseling, assessment, and research. *Journal of Counseling, & Development, 83*(2), 191-201.

Townsend, M., & Weerasuriya, R. (2010). Beyond blue to green: The benefits of contact with nature for mental health and well-being. Melbourne, Australia: Beyond Blue Limited. Retrieved from https://das.bluestaronline.com.au/api/prism/document?token=BL/0817

Trafton, A. (2015, August 31). Possible new weapon against PTSD: Blocking a newly identified memory pathway could prevent the disorder [Web log post]. Retrieved from http://news.mit.edu/2015/blocking-memory-pathway-prevent-ptsd-0831

Trafton, A. (2017, April 6). Neuroscientists identify brain circuit necessary for memory formation [Web log post]. Retrieved from http://news.mit.edu/2017/neuroscientists-identify-brain-circuit-necessary-memory-formation-0406

Treadway, M. T., & Zald, D. H. (2011). Reconsidering anhedonia in depression: Lessons from translational neuroscience. *Neuroscience & Biobehavioral Reviews, 35*, 537–555. doi:10.1016/j.neubiorev.2010.06.006

Trzesniewski, K. H., Donnellan, M. B., & Robins, R. W. (2013). Development of self-esteem. In V. Zeigler-Hill (Ed.), *Self-esteem* (pp. 60–79). Florence, KY: Psychology Press.

Van Praag, H., Fleshner, M., Schwartz, M. W., & Mattson, M. P. (2014). Exercise, energy intake, glucose homeostasis, and the brain. The Journal of Neuroscience: 34, 15139–15149. doi:10.1523/JNEUROSCI.2814-14.2014

Velden, M., & Wölk, C. (1987). Depicting cardiac activity over real time: A proposal for standardization. *Journal of Psychophysiology, 1*, 173–175.

Verkhratsky, A., & Butt, A. (2007). *Glial neurobiology: A textbook.* Chichester, United Kingdom: John Wiley & Sons.

Villanueva, R. (2013). Neurobiology of major depressive disorder. *Neural Plasticity, 2013*, e873278. doi:10.1155/2013/873278

Vollenweider, F. X., & Kometer, M. (2010). The neurobiology of psychedelic drugs: Implications for the treatment of mood disorders. *Nature Reviews Neuroscience, 11*, 642–651. doi:10.1038/nrn2884

Wagatsuma, A., Azami, S., Sakura, M., Hatakeyama, D., Aonuma, H., & Ito, E. (2006). De Novo synthesis of CREB in a presynaptic neuron is required for synaptic enhancement involved in memory consolidation. *Journal of Neuroscience Research, 84*, 954–960. doi:10.1002/jnr.21012

Wallace, D. J., & Hallegua, D. S. (2002). Fibromyalgia: The gastrointestinal link. *Current Pain and Headache Reports, 8*, 364–368. doi:10.1007/s11916-996-0009-z

Wallin, D. J. (2007). *Attachment in psychotherapy.* New York, NY: Guilford Press.

Washington, S. D., Gordon, E. M., Brar, J., Warburton, S., Sawyer, A. T., Wolfe, A., . . . VanMeter, J. W. (2013). Dysmaturation of the default mode network in autism. *Human Brain Mapping, 35*, 1284–1296. doi:10.1002/hbm.22252

Weinberg, I. (2013). Accessing the chemistry of consciousness and emotion. New Therapist, 84. Retrieved from http://www.newtherapist.com/back-82to84.html

WHO. (2016). Depression fact sheet. Retrieved from http://www.who.int/mediacentre/factsheets/fs369/en/

Williams, K. C. (2012). Creating physical & emotional security in schools (2nd ed.). Bloomington, IN: Solution Tree Press.

Williams, K. C. (2012). Essentials for principals creating physical & emotional security in schools (2nd ed.). Bloomington, IN: Solution Tree Press.

Wilson, E. O. (1984). *Biophilia.* Cambridge, MA: Harvard University Press.

Wilson, R. Z. (2014). *Neuroscience for counsellors: Practical applications for counsellors, therapists and mental health practitioners.* London, United Kingdom: Jessica Kingsley Publishers.

Withers, G., & Russell, J. (2001). Educating for resilience: Prevention and intervention strategies for young people at risk. Melbourne, Australia: ACER Press.

Wölk C., & Velden, M. (1989). Revision of the baroreceptor hypothesis on the basis of the new cardiac cycle effect. In N. W. Bond & D. A. T. Siddle (Eds.), *Psychobiology: Issues and applications* (pp. 371–379). Amsterdam, Netherlands: Elsevier.

Woo, C.-W., Koban, L., Kross, E., Lindquist, M. A., Banich, M. T., Ruzic, L., . . . Wager, T. D. (2014). Separate neural representations for physical pain and social rejection. *Nature Communications, 5*, e5380. doi:10.1038/ncomms6380

Yerys, B. E., Gordon, E. M., Abrams, D. N., Satterthwaite, T. D., Weinblatt, R., Jankowski, K. F., . . . Vaidya, C. J. (2015). Default mode network segregation and social deficits in autism spectrum disorder: Evidence from non-medicated children. *NeuroImage: Clinical, 9*, 223–232. doi:10.1016/j.nicl.2015.07.018

Zavala, E., Melander, L. A., & Kurtz, D. L. (2015). The importance of social learning and critical incident stressors on police officers' perpetration of intimate partner violence. Victims & Offenders, 10, 51–73. doi:10.1080/15564886.2014.890688

Zeigler-Hill, V. (Ed.). (2013). *Self-esteem.* Florence, KY: Psychology Press.

INDEX

IMAGES

Bigstockphoto.com image credits:

Cover: dolgachov
IX: monkeybusinessimages
1: oksun70
3: Inked Pixels
5-6: guniita
7: Cyborgwitch
11: ktsdesign
12: guniita
13: guniita
14: designua
15: designua
16: guniita
17: Wordley Calvo Stock
18: VH-studio
19-20: guniita, Eraxion
22: guniita, Eraxion
23: Eraxion
24: guniita, Eraxion
26: Eraxion
27: szefei
30: decade3d
31: decade3d, Nerthuz
33: guniita
34: Expensive
35: ktsdesign
36-37: udaix
39: zurijeta
40: logoboom
42: pressmaster
43: Anna Kucherova
45: mlorenz
46: guniita

50: obey leesin
51: subodhsathe
52: leeser
53: Tom Wang
54: Kasia Bialasiewicz
55: zurijeta
56: wiseangel
57: Dakota
58: tloventures
59: Eraxion, alptraum
60: AntonioGuillem
61: smaglov
62: CebotariN
63: gemenacom
65: jorgenmac
66: mandygodbehear
67: Yastremska
68: monkeybusinessimages
69: Rawpixel.com
71: guniita
74: vcoscaron
75: guniita
76: oolulu
78: sanchairat
80: CHOReograPH
81: Eraxion
82: Croisy
84: Eraxion
85: Eraxion, Kateryna Kon
86: Eraxion
87-88: dolgachov
89: TitovStudio
91: ktsdesign
92: wrangler

93: Oleg Golovnev
95: Yastremska
97: Yastremska
98: Wavebreak Media Ltd
99: zurijeta
100: monkeybusinessimages
101: zurijeta
103: pressmaster
106: 26666054
107: romrodinka
109: lightkeeper
110: djedzura
111: CHOReograPH
112: Ilike
113: Goodmoments
114-115: Rawpixel.com
117: zurijeta
120: DMPhoto
121: NinaMalyna
122: marty
124: dolgachov
125: EpicStockMedia
127: alenkasm
128: AntonioGuillem
130: dolgachov
131: Tatyana_Tomsickova
132: auremar
133: dolgachov
134: Rawpixel.com
135: Chinnapong
136: monkeybusinessimages
138: monkeybusinessimages
139-140: dolgachov
141-142: vectorfusionart

www.ingramcontent.com/pod-product-compliance
Lightning Source LLC
Chambersburg PA
CBHW060800270326
41926CB00002B/35